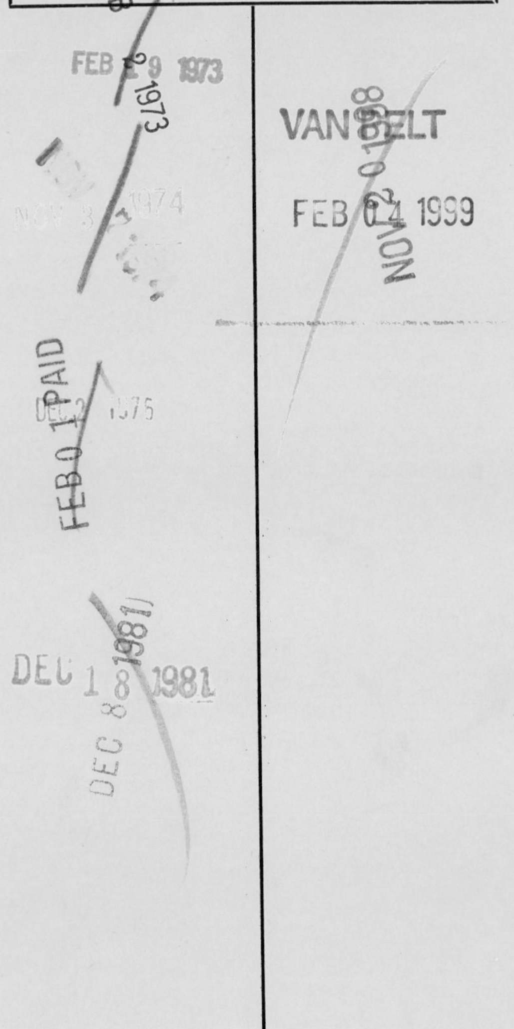

THE ENGLISH AND IMMIGRATION
1880–1910

The Institute of Race Relations is an unofficial and non-political body, founded in England in 1958 to encourage and facilitate the study of relations between races everywhere. The Institute is precluded by the Memorandum and Articles of its incorporation from expressing a corporate view. The opinions in this work are those of the author.

THE ENGLISH AND IMMIGRATION 1880–1910

John A. Garrard

Published for the Institute of Race Relations
by
OXFORD UNIVERSITY PRESS
LONDON NEW YORK TORONTO
1971

Oxford University Press, Ely House, London W.1

GLASGOW NEW YORK TORONTO MELBOURNE WELLINGTON
CAPE TOWN SALISBURY IBADAN NAIROBI LUSAKA ADDIS ABABA
BOMBAY CALCUTTA MADRAS KARACHI LAHORE DACCA
KUALA LUMPUR SINGAPORE HONG KONG TOKYO

SBN 19 218195 5

Printed in Great Britain by The Camelot Press Ltd.,
London and Southampton

TO MY PARENTS

Preface

This is a study of English reactions to immigration, particularly as they affect the political left wing. Taking as its starting-point the parallels that are observable in reactions to the present Commonwealth immigration and to Jewish immigration at the turn of the century, this book goes on to analyse the latter in detail and finally attempts to draw generalizations from the two cases about the politics of immigration in England. It may be seen as a case study in political science: it also stands by itself as a purely historical study.

Since most of my sources are documentary rather than oral and, for the most part, readily available, the acknowledgements that I have to make are comparatively few. They are none the less important. I would like to acknowledge, in the first place, the excellent resources of the Manchester Central Reference Library, and to thank particularly the staff of the Jewish Library, whose help I greatly appreciated and whose patience with the person who, for weeks on end, spoke no words to them other than '*Jewish Chronicle*, please', was quite remarkable. I would like to thank Mrs. Margaret Stott who typed the manuscript for me and greatly assisted in the tedious process of proof-reading. I would like also to express my appreciation to Dr. Archie Syngham for his comments on the first few chapters, and for the good-natured brutality that he exerted to make me write them. Above all, I would like to thank Professor W. J. M. Mackenzie, my supervisor, for his general encouragement, for his patience in reading through an M.A. thesis of record-shattering length, and for the comments that were often some three months ahead of my own train of thought. Any sins of omission or commission are, of course, entirely my own.

J. A. G.

Contents

Contents

PART I

THE IMMIGRATION

I

Introduction: Parallels between Two Immigrations[1]

These poor people seem the butt, at which all sections and persuasions level their contempt. They are the sojourners and aliens in every kingdom on earth, and yet few have the hospitality to give them welcome. I do not know any good reason why these poor people should be so treated. . . .

'ABRAHAM ABRAHAMS'[2]

Over the past three-quarters of a century, England has on two occasions acted as 'a major land of settlement':[3] for Jews fleeing from East European persecution and poverty between 1870 and 1914 on the one hand, and on the other, since 1948 for Commonwealth immigrants coming to seek employment and better living conditions. There are many similarities in the interactions between immigrant and host in the two cases, and the opening quotation serves to highlight the common factor in situations half a century apart. For whether or not one equates all interracial criticism with prejudice, it seems to be undeniable that Jews and coloured people share a unique sociological position in that each group is, or is believed to be, physically distinguishable, and the object of some special hostility quantitatively and qualitatively different from that experienced by, say, Scandinavians or Italians.

This chapter will focus mainly on the present situation. An attempt will be made to identify, in the light of the underlying factor just mentioned, a number of themes which, as will become evident in the course of this book, are also characteristic of the pattern of reactions three-quarters of a century ago.

[1] For a more detailed study of the similarities between Jewish and Commonwealth immigrants, see John A. Garrard, 'Parallels of Protest: English Reactions to Jewish and Commonwealth Immigration', *Race* (Vol. IX, No. 1, July 1967).

[2] Letter to the *Observer*, 1798, quoted in H. F. Modder, *The Jew in the Literature of England* (Philadelphia, Jewish Publication Society of America, 1944), p. 44.

[3] Ibid.

In the first place, partly as a result of discrimination emanating from their sociological position, both Jewish and coloured immigrants have tended to congregate into areas of urban decay, and to produce what is loosely termed 'a ghetto',[1] an area also normally distinguished by overcrowding and multi-occupation, dirt and dilapidation, high rents, and 'key-money'. The present areas of immigrant concentration—in South and West London, Bradford, the West Midlands, and so on—find their turn-of-the-century counterparts particularly in the East End, but also in parts of Manchester, Salford, and Leeds.

In a sense, the alien Jews would have had more in common with present immigrants from the Indian subcontinent than with those from the Caribbean since they possessed, on arrival, a high degree of communal consciousness, and thus their concentration was, and is, at least as much a matter of choice as of necessity.[2] This is scarcely important to our central point, however, since the appearance of a ghetto necessarily seems to reinforce the sociological position of Jew and Negro: it intensifies their strangeness and conspicuousness; and it gives rise to legends of clannishness and, paradoxically, of mongrelization, and to fears of 'invasion' and 'flood'. Complaints of dirt, dilapidation, immorality, and disease were as commonplace in 1905 as they are now:

> But these people are ruining our town . . . the houses are falling apart, and they have a very high rate of T.B.
>
> Their habits are pretty terrible. They use the front garden as a rubbish dump, and heaven knows what they do in the toilets.[3]

In the chapter on the anti-alien agitation, we shall also discover the forerunners for the familiar fears of mongrelization and invasion:

[1] As Gartner points out in regard to Jewish immigrants: 'The term "ghetto", although widely used, is a misnomer. Historically, the word signifies compulsory residence in a segregated locality. The immigrant's domicile was, in the last resort, a matter of choice.' See Lloyd P. Gartner, *The Jewish Immigrant in England 1870–1914* (London, Allen & Unwin, 1960), p. 40.

[2] 'Such people are their own Ghetto gates; when they migrate they carry them across the seas to lands where they are not.' See Israel Zangwill, *Children of the Ghetto* (London, Heinemann, 1909).

[3] Mrs. Mansell, Secretary of the Smethwick Branch, Birmingham Immigration Control Association, quoted in Paul Foot, *Immigration and Race in British Politics* (Harmondsworth, Penguin, 1965), p. 36.

It is tragic, indeed, to see a fine race destroyed by blood poisoning.[1]

West Indians could in less than half a century outnumber us English, and with one man, one vote, they could do something Hitler couldn't do—take over this country.[2]

. . . if they once get any power, then they will multiply, and we will be snowed under by them.[3]

We shall see how the equally familiar, if less overtly racialist, idea that the immigrants have somehow interrupted and destroyed an earlier golden age, can be startlingly paralleled at the turn of the century:

Edgbaston Road used to be a lovely road . . . you used to have nannies up that way you know. Really good class people used to live there, and it was a pleasure to walk in that area. Now they've taken over, and the place is a slum. It's horrible.[4]

These quotations show how the immigrant becomes the scapegoat for a number of social problems which existed before he came, and whose intensity is not decreased by preventing his entry.[5] However, the similarities between the two periods go beyond the violence and exaggeration contained in the language of scapegoat denunciation. They extend more significantly to the social niceties that are apparently felt to be demanded before one can indulge in denunciation at all. In both situations, overt racial prejudice and its direct or indirect result, discrimination, are never respectable. 'We are all against discrimination just as, theoretically, we are all against sin.'[6]

At least in this respect, therefore, the present age can scarcely

[1] Letter to *Smethwick Telephone*, quoted in Foot, p. 33.

[2] Councillor Finney in letter to *Smethwick Telephone*, quoted in N. Deakin (ed.), *Colour and the British Electorate 1964* (London, Pall Mall Press, 1965), p. 91.

[3] Bradford resident quoted ibid., p. 153.

[4] Mrs. Mansell, quoted in Foot, p. 36. Enoch Powell's evocation of England's 'green and pleasant land' in the middle of Wolverhampton presumably relies on the same sort of emotion.

[5] In a sense the presence of the immigrant both obscures and highlights existing social problems: i.e. these problems are obscured by the fact that the immigrant becomes the focus for grievance in anti-immigrant propaganda, and highlighted by the need to answer that propaganda. Thus in the case of anti-sweating legislation it is doubtful whether the Liberals would have noticed the problem of sweating—at least to the extent of legislating against it—if they had not been forced to focus on such legislation as an alternative to the Aliens Bill.

[6] Lord Silkin, quoted in Ruth Glass, *The Newcomers: The West Indian in London* (London, Allen & Unwin, for Centre for Urban Studies, 1960), p. 158.

be accused of betraying what, as we shall see later, was a part of its Victorian inheritance. This seems to be characteristic not only of the Parliamentary agitators, but also of those leaders and followers of the agitation outside Parliament. Alderman Griffith's claim never to have used the term 'coloured people', but only the word 'immigrant',[1] his assurance that 'none of us has ever played on prejudice',[2] and his anxiety to 'make it clear that there is no resentment at all in Smethwick on the grounds of race or colour',[3] would, in all respects, have received the frenzied acclamation of the Parliamentary anti-aliens. Similarly John Bean, leader of the British National Party, a man 'anxious to dissociate himself from the rash of sticker bills which had recently appeared in the constituency with the message "Stop Southall becoming a Black Slum and Vote Bean" ',[4] would have been recognized as a kindred soul by the founder of the British Brothers League who made it a first principle 'that the word Jew should never be mentioned'.[5]

Finally, in both cases these denials of sin extend into the areas directly or indirectly affected by the immigrations. Ruth Glass has drawn attention to 'an all-pervasive ambivalence towards colour . . . concealed behind a parade of polite phrases and manners',[6] reflected, for example, in the preference for the label 'Europeans only', rather than 'no coloureds', on discriminatory housing advertisements, or in the embarrassed reactions of discriminating employers to inquiries by coloured people:

> Occasionally, the answer is offensive; more often it is quite blunt, 'we don't take coloured people; it is one of the rules of the firm'. But usually, the refusal is stated with embarrassment, and the responsibility for it is shifted to someone else—to a nameless group, or a particular person.[7]

All of these are paralleled half a century earlier. Indeed A. G. Bennett's coloured immigrant in *Because They Know Not* might

[1] Interview with writer, 5 October 1964.

[2] Foot, p. 52.

[3] Ibid., p. 67.

[4] Deakin (ed.), p. 42.

[5] William Stanley Shaw in letter to *East London Advertiser* (5 July 1902); see also p. 64 for full quotation.

[6] Glass, p. 112. See also Griffith, Henderson, Usborne, and Wood, *Coloured Immigrants in Britain* (London, Oxford University Press, 1960), p. 125.

[7] Glass, p. 112.

well have been walking down the Whitechapel Road, when he commented wryly:

> Since I came 'ere, I never met a single English person who 'ad any colour prejudice. Once I walked the whole length of a street looking for a room and everyone told me he or she 'ad no prejudice. It was the neighbour who was stupid. . . . Neighbours are the worst people to live beside in this country.[1]

There is, in other words, an underlying ambiguity in British attitudes towards immigrants,[2] extending even to the juxtaposition of sentiments of tolerance and intolerance in the same statements.[3] It seems to confirm Paul Foot's analysis that 'the working-class are balanced on a knife-edge',[4] and to underlie the other parallels which we can draw between the two situations and the conclusions which then suggest themselves.

Thus, in a situation where 'we are all a little scared of being thought to be illiberal',[5] and where none want to appear prejudiced, the accusation of racial prejudice becomes as potentially powerful a weapon as the exploitation of prejudice itself. This explains why the attitudes towards immigration control of Conservative Governments led respectively by Salisbury and Balfour should have had an ambiguous undertone, so similar to that of a Conservative Government led by Harold Macmillan. It perhaps explains why an administration which 'most reluctantly'[6] announced an Immigration Bill on

[1] Quoted in Glass, p. 108.

[2] There is some evidence, however, that, at the time of writing, social niceties are breaking down. All observers felt that there was a definite hardening of British attitudes towards coloured immigrants after the 1964 election—perhaps due in part to the use made of the issue by some Conservative party candidates, and the failure of their party leaders to repudiate such exploitation. The reactions to Enoch Powell's speech in April 1968—particularly the dockers' march—suggest that, for some groups at least, the fear that protest will be given a racialist label is less daunting than it used to be. Both examples are indicative of the way in which hostility can be legitimized by sources that are regarded as respectable.

[3] Mrs. Mansell (already quoted above) is a case in point, especially since her husband is, at the time of writing, also a member of the Immigration Control Association: 'I've nothing whatever against black people. My husband once objected in one of the pubs when they refused to serve a coloured man. I work in the schools and I know how well most of the children are looked after.' Quoted in Foot, p. 36.

[4] Ibid., p. 165.

[5] Martin Lindsay, Conservative M.P., quoted in Glass, p. 157.

[6] Cyril Osborne, quoted in Foot, p. 137.

31 October 1961, and which, according to some sources, had more or less decided in favour of control in February[1] of that year, should still have been officially opposed to such legislation in April[2] and in no decided hurry as late as 11 October 1961.[3] Insufficient preparation prompted by the fear of accusation, and the subsequent levelling of accusations of prejudice, probably also explain why the same Government should then have proceeded to get itself into such a muddle over the exclusion of immigrants from the Irish Republic.[4]

As we shall see, this tendency to walk backwards to immigration control was paralleled almost to the letter by a Conservative front bench which resisted legislation until 1892, which ignored its promises until 1903, and which, in 1904, introduced an Aliens Bill, shown to be so inadequately prepared as to be sentenced to death by Grand Committee. Indeed it will be suggested that control would have been both easier and more difficult if only the two sets of immigrants had not had the gross inconsideration to be Jews[5] or coloured people: easier since the danger of accusation of prejudice would have been absent; more difficult because had they been merely, say, Frenchmen or Poles,[6] few would have noticed them.

However, if the possibility of being accused of racial prejudice is embarrassing to the political right, we may expect it positively to paralyse the political left—given its opposing ideology, together with its commitment to those most closely affected by immigration. Certainly, there is evidence that at least one left-

[1] *Birmingham Evening Mail* (9 February 1961), cited in Foot, p. 134.

[2] Ibid., p. 135.

[3] See Butler's speech to the Conservative Conference: 'This is obviously a matter in which we have to have the fullest consultation with the Commonwealth and overseas Governments. This must be carried through. Also, the Conference will know that the final decision must be that of Her Majesty's Government and must be taken at the time of year when decisions are taken about the forward legislative programme. That is the constitutional position and we cannot go behind it.' Quoted ibid., p. 138.

[4] Ibid., pp. 139–40.

[5] And even worse, Jews fleeing from persecution.

[6] The latter part of this thesis seems to be confirmed by J. A. Tannahill's post-Second World War study of *European Volunteer Workers in Britain* (Manchester, Manchester University Press, 1958), p. 74. For example: 'If allowance be made . . . for the British suspicion of the foreigner and the tendency of the E.V.W. to over-sensitivity to suspected slights and discrimination, the settling-in process does not seem to have been unduly prolonged.'

wing newspaper in each period changed its line on the issue for this reason alone.[1]

We can, and shall, see a similar situation in the case of the trade unions. At present, discriminatory or restrictive resolutions passed by union branches are rarely allowed up to the level of union conference, and the issue has never been debated by the Trades Union Congress, although the General Council has, from time to time, made a few vague and ambiguous references to the issue in its Annual Reports.[2] Moreover, when motions do get to the union conference level, they seem to receive the sort of treatment meted out at the A.S.L.E.F. Conference of 1957. Here the delegate from Stratford moved a resolution that the recruitment of British colonial and foreign labour for footplate grades on British Railways should cease forthwith and that 'those not already working in footplate grades be not considered in the line of promotion'. The delegate was at pains to point out that this was not a colour-bar resolution; rather, it was merely that coloured workers were slow, virtually unintelligible, and found it difficult to understand instructions. They were, therefore, a danger to public safety. The motion was lost 49 to 6 after a speech by the General Secretary, A. Hallworth, which said, in part:

> No matter which way you look at this question, it is a colour bar. Stratford can put all the trimmings round it that he likes, but it makes not the slightest difference. It is a fine thing to stand anywhere and say that you are a socialist . . . and then when it comes to applying the principles of socialism on your own door-step, to deny them. . . . I would say that elementary socialism is uplifting, not just the men in the line of promotion in the ASLEF, but uplifting the workers of the world without regard to race, colour or creed. . . . Regardless of the colour of the skin, the heart is not black.[3]

[1] See the *Reynolds News* editorial quoted in *Jewish Chronicle* (26 July 1895), p. 12, and *Reynolds News* (23 April 1905), p. 1. See also the behaviour of the *News Chronicle* during and after the Notting Hill and Notting Dale riots of 1958. Immediately after the first outbreak, the paper editorialized on the theme 'Too Many Immigrants' (7 August 1958), saying that 'some form of immigration control—distasteful though that is' seemed to be necessary. But by 4 September, 'Remain on Guard' (cited in Glass, p. 157) was less certain: 'The Government is right to consider immigration control with great caution.' By 11 September, it was quite certain that while it had once advocated immigration control 'applied without discrimination of colour or race . . . a restrictive policy must be abandoned'.

[2] See Trades Union Congress Reports for the years 1955, 1958, 1962, and 1965.

[3] Quoted in Sheila Patterson, *Dark Strangers* (London, Tavistock Publications, 1963), p. 161.

Finally, there is the series of embarrassed and partly unpremeditated somersaults which the Labour party has performed in recent years. These have resulted in a change of line from outright opposition to the Immigration Bill to something beyond 'me-too-ism', and they seem to be the most obvious example of the sort of problems that the spectre of racial prejudice produces for the political left. When taken together with the vacillations of the Conservative front bench, it is this which makes the similarities between the two immigrations so ironic and intriguing a starting-point for an investigation of the behaviour of the political left wing in regard to alien Jews. For, like the Labour party in 1951, the Liberals in 1886 and 1895, left power before the issue really began to assume major proportions. In both cases, a long period in opposition was occupied by an equally long process of factionalization, reassessment, and self-analysis. The main pressure for immigration control centred around the Conservative party. Thus, when the Liberals and the Labour party returned to power in 1905 and 1964, respectively, each found itself having to administer control legislation whose passing it had only recently opposed vigorously.

Although the Liberals and socialists behaved with considerably more consistency before and after the Aliens Act than has the Labour party in regard to the Immigration Act, it will be shown that there were potentialities within the former liable to make their action identical to that of the latter. Basically, what a cursory study of the present situation seems to suggest, a detailed analysis of the aliens question seems to confirm: namely, that in a situation where 'the working class are balanced on a knife-edge', a left-wing party finds the interpretation of public opinion peculiarly difficult. When all are afraid of appearing prejudiced, the party cannot know what its grass-roots are thinking for its grass-roots will not tell—and some may not know.

II

The Historical Context

> Anti-Semitism is a unique phenomenon, qualitatively different from other forms of prejudice, only in so far as historical and other forces have combined to produce a unique social situation, for example the widespread distribution of the Jewish people and their frequent availability in the past for use as scapegoats. W. H. ROBB[1]

Having examined the similarities between the two immigrations, it is worth balancing the picture by emphasizing those factors peculiar to the turn of the century that seem likely to make English reactions then significantly different from those witnessed since about 1950. How different those reactions were will emerge in the chapters that follow.

One of the more relevant arguments levelled against the present anti-immigrant agitation and against the Labour party's apparent surrender to the pressures created by it, has been that the problem could have been more efficiently solved by special Government aid to local authorities, more public housing, an anti-discrimination bill, and increased overseas development aid. This argument, however, would have had considerably less force had it been put forward as a remedy for the problems created or highlighted by Jewish immigration. Even by the end of the nineteenth century the areas of state action were still closely circumscribed. As much as the Liberals might press for a 'Newcastle Programme' that recognized the State as an instrument for the easing of social problems, it is arguable that, even in 1906, they 'advanced on social reform with noisy mouths and mouselike feet';[2] that 'Cobden and Bright were still abroad. . . . New causes were always related directly to old ones';[3] that consequently, as we shall see

[1] W. H. Robb, *Working Class Anti-Semite* (London, Tavistock Publications, 1954), p. 173.

[2] G. Dangerfield, *The Strange Death of Liberal England* (New York, Capricorn Books, 1961), p. 10.

[3] Asa Briggs, 'The Political Scene', in Simon Nowell Smith (ed.), *Edwardian England 1901–14* (London, Oxford University Press, 1964), p. 57.

later, the Liberals semi-consciously continued to see temperance reform as the universal panacea and the alien Jew as the living and socially mobile proof that this was so.

The continuing strength of notions about the beneficence of the free market had an important effect on the way contemporaries reacted to the problems associated with Jewish immigration. From the point of view of host reactions perhaps the most important of these was overcrowding. In 1893, Samuel Montagu, the Jewish Liberal M.P. for Whitechapel, offered to donate to the London County Council twenty-five acres of land owned by him in Edmonton on which to build dwellings for the relief of East London's housing problem. In the light of what we have been saying, this was an act significant in itself; the reply was even more so. His offer was regretfully declined on the grounds that the Council had no powers to operate outside its immediate administrative area.[1]

Another problem exacerbated by Jewish immigration was that of sweating, a 'system' whereby the component parts of an article were handed out by factories to subcontractors or 'small masters' who 'made them up' into the finished product on their own premises, usually a basement or attic of the master's house, with the assistance of a small group of operatives working long hours for little pay, even by East End standards. Various solutions to the problem of sweating were attempted. The Conservative Factory Act of 1901 expanded and clarified the powers of factory inspectors to take in small workshops. A House of Lords Commission of Inquiry had reported in favour of anti-sweating legislation in 1890, a recommendation that, as a result of the work of Charles Dilke, had been incorporated in the official Liberal party programme. But it was at least still possible to argue, as did Sir John Gorst, M.P., a Conservative pro-alien, that there was no remedy for sweating 'so long as there is a demand for cheap things. . . . The real sweater . . . is the buyer of cheap articles, but then that demand is itself occasioned by conditions beyond legislation.'[2]

Even so, the Liberals eventually attempted to deal with the problems of sweated labour via the Trades Boards Act of 1909, the first Act of Parliament in modern history to intervene in the

[1] *Jewish Chronicle* (3 November 1893), p. 18.
[2] *Jewish Chronicle* (1 June 1894), p. 10.

determination of wages. As far as the other problems were concerned, however, apart from a few election cries in the wilderness from East End M.P.s, there appears to have been little serious demand, within the conventional two-party nexus, for state-initiated solutions. Against this background, the prohibited areas clause of the 1904 Aliens Bill[1] appears remarkably anomalous. For the most part, overcrowding, high rents, and insecurity of tenure were regarded as 'a vast field for silent and unobtrusive philanthropy'.[2]

Let us turn now to those factors tending to produce a greater degree of host tolerance for the immigrant and begin with a statement of the obvious. However much the anti-aliens might complain of the Jew's exclusiveness and clannishness, and of his refusal to intermarry, however much the more neurotic of them might believe that you could tell a man by the shape of his nose, and however much the aliens might seem strange in complexion, language, and dress, the alien Jew was potentially more assimilable than the coloured immigrant is ever likely to be.

The alien was aided in this process by a number of factors. One of these was that very adaptability which so appalled those trade unionists who saw him as raw material for the sweater's den. Over and above this, he wanted to become 'English' and, in doing so, became at times more like the stereotype of his hosts than they were themselves. We can see these twin processes at work in 1910 in Louis Golding's novel *Magnolia Street*, a street which lay at the frontier of the 'Doomington' ghetto, with Jews on one side, Gentiles on the other. The observer, Mr. Emmanuel, is an Anglo-Jew:

> As for the Jews, every element in their confusion thrilled him. The elder ones did not feel themselves to be in their own land. They looked back to Poland and Russia, they looked forward to America. But he saw the hearts of the younger Jews divided in another way. Not all of them wanted to 'get on'. In these few years of their boyhood and girlhood, they had become more impregnated with England than other foreigners might in two generations. He saw the small boys conforming to the type of small boys opposite. They played football and cricket, and studied the team scores with, if

[1] See p. 42. This was a clause, moreover, which played a major part in the eventual withdrawal of the first Bill.

[2] 'Notes of the Week', *Jewish Chronicle* (1 April 1898), p. 20.

anything, more passion. They became, or yearned to be, 'sports' and 'decent chaps'. Just as successfully, the little Jewish girls were becoming English 'misses'.[1]

Walter Besant discovered the same processes to be at work with, if anything, even more success two hundred miles to the south-east, in the East End of London:

As for their children, you may look for them in the Board-schools; they have become English—both boys and girls; except for their names, they are English through and through; they accept our institutions, laws and customs; they rejoice with our successes, they grieve with our misfortunes; never yet has it been known that the second generation of the alien has failed to become English through and through. I believe that our power of absorbing alien immigrants is even greater than that of the United States.[2]

Besant's final prognostications were, perhaps, a little optimistic, but that they were not without foundation is revealed when we look at Louis Golding's picture of Magnolia Street's celebrations of an English and local boxing triumph in 1930:

The people gathered that night in the private bar were Gentiles. The people opposite were Jews. They lived their own lives, for the most part, though the distance between the pavements was now felt to be a matter of thirty feet or so. It was not now, as it had been in the pre-War years, as if a sea, a prairie separated them. But 'the Kid' was neither Jew nor Gentile. He was an Englishman, lightweight champion of the world. If you had mentioned casually that Mick Shulman was, as a mere matter of fact, a Jew, they would have looked up rather startled, as some Christians do when it is stated that the first Christian was a Jew.[3]

This passage also reveals that there was, and is, something more to assimilation than the mere desire to assimilate. After all, Pakistanis in the Bradford of 1966 are as capable of coming out on strike, less to air a grievance than to reveal an English style of industrial militancy,[4] as were the Jews of forming a Judaeo-Irish Home Rule Association in the Dublin of 1908.[5]

[1] Louis Golding, *Magnolia Street* (London, Gollancz, 1932), pp. 191–2. 'Doomington', presumably Salford, is reviewed over a twenty-year period, 1910–30.

[2] Walter Besant, *East London* (London, Chatto & Windus, 1899), p. 191.

[3] Golding, p. 499.

[4] *Guardian* (10 January 1966), p. 10.

[5] The objects of this Association are outlandishly indicative of its purposes: 'in order to dispel the delusion and darkness which surrounded them . . . to support and assist . . . the Home Rule policy of the Irish people, and to promote a better feeling of good fellowship and comradeship between them and their fellow

Louis Golding's final sentence reveals that, in extreme cases, a sense of strangeness might appear only upon verbal reminder. In a sense, to become an Anglo-Jew, an alien had only to learn the English language, change his clothes, and submit his complexion to a few years in the sunless streets of Salford or Whitechapel. An Anglo-Jew was commonly distinguishable from other Englishmen only by his religion. However much the anti-aliens might complain of the Jew's clannishness, by linking that complaint with his refusal to marry outside his religion, they paradoxically admitted his ultimate acceptability, an admission which, at least at present, is rarely made in regard to the coloured immigrant.

Reference to the Anglo-Jew brings out a further factor likely on the whole to produce a greater degree of tolerance towards the Jewish newcomer: for, unlike West Indians, Indians, and Pakistanis, the Jewish aliens at the turn of the century were entering an England where their co-religionists had long since established a large, wealthy, and powerful community. This was useful to the aliens in a number of ways. In the first place, it provided them with a working example showing that assimilation was not only possible, but positively desirable. Secondly, the presence in this period of between seven and sixteen practising Jewish M.P.s in Parliament meant that the aliens had at least a few official spokesmen in both parties,[1] plus a source of continual embarrassment to the Parliamentary anti-aliens. Thirdly, the presence of a pre-existing Jewish community in England meant that the 'vast field for silent and unobtrusive philanthropy' was filled by an equally vast network of Jewish charitable organizations, which, if only occasionally 'silent and unobtrusive', was at least extremely efficient. Together with the almost notorious independence of the Jewish immigrants, it gave the lie to the charge that 'they came on the rates'. The existence and activities of such institutions as the Poor Jews Temporary Shelter and the more important Jewish Board of Guardians admittedly laid the Jewish community open to the charge of attracting 'the alien swarm'. However,

Christian countrymen.' An address to the Association's inaugural meeting, quoted in *Jewish Chronicle* (18 September 1908), p. 7.

[1] Several of these—among them H. S. Samuel, Conservative M.P. for Limehouse, 1892–1906—were, in fact, staunch anti-aliens.

the Jewish Board of Guardians was at least as much concerned with preventing the immigrant from coming at all, or with sending him on to America should he have the temerity to arrive, as it was with maintaining him while he was here. So there was at least an alternative argument, one that could be supplemented by the justifiable claim that these and other institutions also provided a means of making the alien into an Englishman.

Finally, and more generally, a pre-existing Jewish community meant, if we are to believe H. F. Modder, the presence of a Hebrew aristocracy:[1]

> . . . in whose princely homes brilliant society assembled and invitations to whose parties were regarded as a social distinction. . . . The advantages reaped by England . . . were not only material, but intellectual and artistic. Consequently, the presence of this class did much to prevent the outbreak of any anti-Semitic demonstration in English society during the latter part of the century.[2]

Modder's analysis is, in fact, only partly true, and provides us with a starting-point for the examination of another factor. Although this aristocracy did in some ways symbolize the social and political arrival of Anglo-Jewry, it was, by its very conspicuousness, the potential focusing point for any English version of that anti-Semitism which characterized Europe at the turn of the century, and found expression in the Russian and Rumanian pogroms, the entrance of anti-Semitic Ministers into the governments of Germany and Austria-Hungary, and the furious division of French opinion which followed the two Dreyfus trials. Although England seems, for the most part, to have retained her 'splendid isolation' in this as in other matters, she was not completely unaffected by the general European movement.

Because of the disreputability of anti-Semitism, this could, in fact, cut both ways. Thus the Russian pogroms gave rise to large protest meetings in London, Manchester, and

[1] A Hebrew aristocracy, moreover, whose nobility was honoured by English peerages. Thus, Sir Nathan Meyer Rothschild became Lord Rothschild in 1885, and within the twenty-five years that followed, Henry de Worms became Lord Purbright; Sir Samuel Montagu became Lord Swaythling; Sir Rufus Isaacs became Lord Reading.

[2] Modder, p. 237.

other urban centres. The second Dreyfus trial in 1899 gave rise to a demonstration by 15,000 people in Hyde Park and to movements to boycott French trade; and according to the *Westminster Gazette* of 20 September 1899: 'For the future every Jew will be treated a little better because of Dreyfus.'[1]

On the other hand, the ascription of British involvement in two South African wars to the supposed machinations of international Jewish finance could lead some English socialists, as we shall see, into a curious form of rich Jew anti-Semitism; or could cause Hilaire Belloc (from 1906 Liberal M.P. for Salford North) to embark upon a poetic flight of Jew hatred:[2]

We also know the sacred height
Up on Tuegla side
Where those three hundred fought with Beit
And fair young Wernher died

The daybreak where Eckstein stood
The final sabres drawn
Tall Goltman, silent on his horse
Superb against the dawn

The little mound where Eckstein stood
And gallant Albu fell
And Oppenheim, half-blind with blood
Went fording through the rising flood
My Lord, we know them well.

In addition, and partly as a consequence, there were complaints of Jewish control of the Press; the predilections of both A. J. Balfour and the Prince of Wales for long week-ends with Lord Rothschild produced sneers about their 'Jewish friends' and hints about the nature of the power behind the throne.

Partly underlying, mainly reinforcing, but also weakening these manifestations of anti-Semitism was the prevalence of that bastardized extension of 'the survival of the fittest' known as Social Darwinism. In one way or another, this doctrine seems to have permeated English opinion right across the political spectrum, although not all accepted the policy implication that ruthlessly competitive self-help was the agent of social progress, whereas mutual aid was its enemy.

[1] Quoted in *Jewish Chronicle* (22 September 1899), p. 13.
[2] Quoted in Roy Jenkins, *Asquith* (London, Collins, 1964), p. 162.

As far as the aliens were concerned, the Social Darwinist theory provided a major part of the intellectual framework within which the argument about them was conducted. The idea that only the racially fit could or should survive might be used either to attack or to defend the immigrant. From one point of view, one could see his dirty and dishevelled appearance as a permanent source of racial degradation. Thus Harry Lawson, Conservative M.P. for Mile End, could talk of 'a backward march to physical deterioration'.[1] Likewise, Arnold White, one of the most rabid of anti-aliens, and a believer in the sterilization of the racially unfit, could describe the immigrant as 'the lowest type' and define his position in the following terms:

> I mean persons who . . . have no regard to any provision for sanitation, and scanty regard for cleanliness and for whom the conditions of life are very low; those who are comparatively indifferent to anything outside the mere sensual indulgence of eating, drinking and sleeping, and those who have no hope or ideal in life, no pleasure in the past and no amusements, and who nearly approach the condition of animal life.[2]

Moreover, when the immigration of foreigners was seen in conjunction with the emigration of Englishmen, Social Darwinism could produce a very powerful emotional jumping-off point for anti-alien hostility. It seems to have been used not merely by Conservatives, but to have affected the left wing as well. Howard Vincent's claim that 'while over 260,000 people emigrated from the United Kingdom last year, their places were taken by no less than 82,000 of the scum of Europe',[3] found its counterpart on the opposite benches in the dire warnings of Henry Norman, M.P. for Northampton:

> Whole shiploads of our skilled mechanics emigrated to Canada, and if we continued to export our best, and to receive the worst of other countries, it would not be long before the quality of our own people would be seriously impaired and deteriorated.[4]

[1] Hansard 4S H(145)740, 2 May 1905.

[2] House of Commons Select Committee on Alien Immigration (hereafter, R.S.C.), *Report and Minutes of Evidence*, Vol. I, S.P. 1888, IX, p. 92. White could also talk of even more mysterious beings like 'the type of pauper, and the type of man with heart disease'.

[3] Conservative M.P. for Sheffield Central, in Hansard 4S H(129)157, 2 February 1904.

[4] Hansard 4S H(133)1112–3, 25 April 1904.

On grounds such as these, even a socialist could bring himself to join in the general chorus of discontent:

> Thus is the Old World depleting itself of its best and most adventurous blood . . . while we accept with open arms all the broken-spirited physical wrecks which Northern Europe cares to dump down.[1]

Yet if one adopted the alternative stereotype of the Jew and focused on his competitive nature, his social mobility, and his industry, one could defend him, with equal fervour, within the intellectual confines of Social Darwinism. Thus, the attacks which we have already quoted had to be met not by trying to destroy the terms of reference, but by arguing within them. Charles Rolleston, a fervent Liberal, could therefore maintain in *The New Liberal Review* of March 1904:

> Even if we view the question from the most material standpoint, the British race must gain by this assimilation . . . as it stands to reason that the wealth and stability of a country must exist in relation to the moral and physical qualities of its inhabitants, the Israelite is proving himself to be a regenerating force, and a most useful acquisition to our citizenship.[2]

Even Charles Dilke felt himself bound to point out at the end of a speech that the Russian Jews 'are not a stock inferior to our own. They are a stock which, when it mixes with our own in [the] course of years, goes rather to improve than to deteriorate the British race.'[3]

However, if the doctrine provided a part of the framework within which the debate took place, only rarely does it seem to have dictated one's position within the debate. Even if J. Bruce Glazier, a prominent member of the Independent Labour party, might find his internationalism somewhat curbed by the realization that 'we do not know to what extent, and under what conditions, the intermixing, or even the co-operation of different races is good or bad for the physical health and social progress of nations',[4] on the whole his stance remained that of a staunch pro-alien. In this regard

[1] J. A. Dixon, 'On Emigrants', in *Labour Leader* (9 June 1894), p. 7.

[2] Quoted in *Jewish Chronicle* (11 March 1904), p. 15.

[3] Hansard 4S H(132)995, 29 March 1904.

[4] 'Socialism and the Anti Alien Sentiment', *Labour Leader* (30 April 1904), p. 40.

it seems that its only real effect was to lend a limited amount of respectability to anti-Semitism,[1] or, to judge by the savagery of some of the comments already quoted, to narrow the definition of what was popularly regarded as anti-Semitism.

Let us turn now to our last factor, the one most likely to produce hostility towards the immigrants, and which, moreover, brings us back to our starting-point. Although the annual rate of unemployment during this period, ranging as it did, between 7·5 per cent and 2·1 per cent,[2] was not nearly as high as it was to become in the inter-war period—a rate of between 10 per cent and 21 per cent—it was still considerably higher than it is at present.

There was also a much greater degree of employment insecurity. While skilled trade unions had been firmly established since about the middle of the nineteenth century, the unionization of unskilled workers, under the leadership of such people as John Burns and Ben Tillett, was still in its infancy, and was a sufficiently novel idea to be called the 'new unionism'. This was, moreover, a period when the whole basis of unionism was being questioned under the influence of the Taff Vale and Osbourne judgements.

Worse still, this was the age of the deliberate importation of foreigners (and rural workers) by employers for the purpose of strike-breaking, a practice which gave rise to a Labour Aliens Bill in 1906; and which ingrained in the English working class that mistrust of all foreign labour which has contributed to hostility not only towards the alien Jews, but also towards the present coloured immigrants. The real effect of this will be examined in detail in the section of this study dealing with the new left. Suffice it to say here that in this situation any influx of labour, particularly labour that was unskilled and foreign, was likely to be regarded with an alarm out of proportion to the number of immigrants actually involved.

[1] Thus, 'Mary Boole' could write, without apology, to the *Jewish Chronicle* (31 July 1885), p. 10: 'But the true *fons et orige* of anti-Semitism, its backbone, its source of true power, is the horror which all those who study heredity conceive for renegade Jews.' Similarly, J. Bruce Glazier announced his ignorance of whether anti-alienism, like racial prejudice, was 'a still useful social instinct' or, alternatively, 'a no longer beneficial prejudice'.

[2] Royal Commission on Alien Immigration (hereafter, R.C.), Vol. III, Appendix, Cd. 1741, 1903, pp. 18–19.

PART II

THE AGITATION

III

How the Act was Passed

> ... let us earn some credit for originating and passing useful measures such as appeal to the working classes.
>
> SIR A. B. FORWOOD, CONSERVATIVE M.P. FOR ORMSKIRK[1]

This chapter will attempt to trace the broad outlines and events of the agitation inside and outside of Parliament which led to the passing of the Aliens Bill in 1905 and to relate them, so far as is possible,[2] to changes in the volume of immigration. There will be little attempt at causal analysis beyond identifying the main actors, but the story will provide a narrative framework for later analysis.

The Issue Emerges: 1870–1885

During the course of 1871, the first large group of immigrants from Eastern Europe arrived in England, driven to flee by the expulsion of Jews from the Russian border regions in [illegible] and the beginning of the systematic persecution in Roumania in the same year. Further impetus was given in 1875–6 by the Russo-Turkish War and the resultant calling up of reservists into an army where anti-Semitism was one of the orders of [illegible]. The first peak, however, was not reached until [illegible] widespread pogroms in Southern Russia caused [illegible] Jews pent up in the towns and villages of the Pale [illegible] [to contrast] emigration [illegible].[3]

Viewing the progress of the issue of aliens [illegible] the entire period from the arrival of the first immigrants [illegible] passing of the Aliens Bill in 1905, one is immediately [illegible] the length of time it took for the aliens to become a political issue at all. In fact, only [illegible] Anglo-Jews who [illegible] and were [illegible]

[1] Letter to [illegible] [illegible]

[2] Exact statistical analysis was not [illegible]; see Appendix [illegible].

[3] Gartner, p. [illegible]

III

How the Act was Passed

. . . let us earn some credit for originating and passing useful measures such as appeal to the working classes.

SIR A. B. FORWOOD, CONSERVATIVE M.P. FOR ORMSKIRK[1]

This chapter will attempt to trace the broad outlines and events of the agitation inside and outside of Parliament which led to the passing of the Aliens Bill in 1905 and to relate them, so far as is possible,[2] to changes in the volume of immigration.

There will be little attempt at causal analysis, beyond identifying the main actors, but the story will provide a narrative framework for later analysis.

The Issue Emerges: 1880–1888

During the course of 1871, the first large group of immigrants from Eastern Europe arrived in England, driven to flee by the expulsion of Jews from the Russian border regions in 1870, and the beginning of the systematic persecution in Rumania in the same year. Further impetus was given in 1875–6 by the Russo-Turkish War and the resultant calling of reservists into an army where anti-Semitism was one of the orders of the day. The first peak, however, was not reached until 1881–2 when widespread pogroms in Southern Russia caused 'the millions of Jews pent up in the towns and villages of the Pale of Settlement [to contract] emigration fever'.[3]

Viewing the progress of the issue of alien immigration over the entire period from the arrival of the first immigrants to the passing of the Aliens Bill in 1905, one is immediately struck by the length of time it took for the aliens to become a political issue at all. In fact, over the first decade and a half, it was the Anglo-Jews who noticed and worried over the arrival of the

[1] Letter to Akers Douglas (15 July 1886), quoted in Viscount Chilston, *Chief Whip* (London, Routledge & Kegan Paul, 1963), p. 82.

[2] Exact statistical analysis was, and is, impossible. See Appendix I.

[3] Gartner, p. 41.

immigrants; it was they who were concerned to keep them out rather than Parliament, which contented itself with expressing its sense of outrage at the pogroms that produced the exodus.[1]

Up to 1880, the relevant Jewish organizations made rather vague efforts to prevent the emigrants from coming to England. Not until the emergency of 1881–2 did they fully realize the malevolence of the Russian régime towards its Jewish subjects and dilute their sympathy with more systematic efforts to keep the refugees out. In this period, for instance, the Jewish Board of Guardians attempted energetically to help those who arrived, but, at the same time, never abated its attempts to avert the 'great danger of the emigrants coming over to England in still larger numbers'.[2] It was at this time also that Samuel Montagu visited Poland for the sole purpose of averting emigration to England.[3]

In the same year, the United States reacted to the influx by passing an Aliens Act which imposed a poll-tax of fifty cents and banned idiots, criminals, and others likely to become a public charge. Together with its extension in 1891, this legislation later came to assume the importance of a blue-print for anti-alien agitators in England.

Immigration proceeded at such a heightened pace throughout the 1880s that as early as 1883 the *Jewish Chronicle* could claim that of an estimated 44,000 Jews in London, 'nearly half... have been in London, or indeed England, for an average of ten years or so'.[4] Gartner asserts, moreover, that 'the increase in Leeds and Manchester was in an even higher proportion'.[5]

Yet, in spite of all these factors, the influx of population does not seem to have been noticed by English spokesmen until February 1886 (at least, this is the first occasion on which the ultra-sensitive *Jewish Chronicle* makes reference to such an English reaction). In that month, the *Pall Mall Gazette* suddenly discovered 'A *Judenhetz* Brewing in East London', as evidenced by a letter which began: 'The foreign Jews of no nationality whatever are becoming a pest and a menace to the poor native-

[1] See, for instance, the questions of Seargent Simon, Hansard 3S H(250)794, 17 February 1880, and Lord Randolph Churchill, 3S H(261)825, 19 May 1881.

[2] *Jewish Chronicle* (3 March 1882).

[3] Gartner, p. 42.

[4] *Jewish Chronicle* (3 March 1882), p. 12.

[5] Gartner, p. 43.

born East Ender'; and which alleged that 'fifteen or twenty thousand Jewish refugees of the lowest type . . . have a greater responsibility for the distress which prevails [in the East End] than probably all other causes put together'.[1]

Immigration reached a second peak in the same year with Bismarck's expulsion of alien Poles from Prussia. Even so, in a letter published in the *Jewish Chronicle* of 26 February 1880, N. S. Joseph of the Jewish Board of Guardians seems to have preceded English spokesmen in advocating restriction, on the grounds that since America had closed her doors, 'What can happen, but an inundation?'

Even then, over three months were to elapse before the idea reached Parliament. The issue does not appear to have been used in the election of 1886. However, in March 1887, Captain Colomb, Conservative M.P. for Tower Hamlets, Bow, and Bromley, proclaimed its inauguration with an inquiry about the number of immigrants coming in during the previous five years and followed it up with a piece of rhetoric presented in a style that was to become typical in the years that followed:

> What great states of the world other than Great Britain permit the immigration of destitute aliens without restriction; and whether Her Majesty's Government is prevented by any Treaty obligations from making such regulations as shall put a stop to the free importation of destitute aliens into the United Kingdom.[2]

A negative answer to the second of Colomb's questions seems to have cleared the way for the beginning of the agitation. A further piece was added to the pattern of agitation on All Fools' Day when an outraged *Jewish Chronicle* reported:

> . . . a virulent attack on Jewish immigration, filled with the grossest mis-statement of facts . . . last Wednesday in the *St. James's Gazette*. The writer refers to the figures of the Board of Guardians as those of only one body and calmly proceeds to multiply the whole number of applicants by five to get at the number of immigrants for the year. . . .[3]

The *St. James's Gazette* followed this up with a long series of articles by the same writer, who completed the pattern by charging that the immigrants were immoral, replete with vice,

[1] *Jewish Chronicle* (26 February 1880), p. 4.
[2] Hansard 3S H(311)1724, 10 March 1887.
[3] *Jewish Chronicle* (1 April 1887), p. 5.

'a heavy charge upon the rates', a 'colony of 30,000 or 40,000 steeped to the lips in every form of moral and physical degradation'; and that 'the vast majority of these foreign Jews are nihilists and anarchists of the very worst type'.[1] By May, the series had received the title 'Jewish Pauperism' and other papers such as the *Spectator* and the *Observer* had begun to identify their positions.

In this first period, however, much of the anti-alien agitation outside Parliament seems to have been both tentative and, in spite of the passage quoted above, fairly moderate. Thus, the first recorded public meeting (held before 'the ratepayers of Mile End') to petition for the exclusion of destitute aliens, took the form of a debate (chaired by Arnold White) with Conservative M.P.s Captain Colomb, Howard Vincent, and Lord Charles Beresford together with Lord Brabazon on the one side, and Samuel Montagu, M.P., and other leaders of the Jewish community on the other. The meeting, held on 19 April 1887, concluded mildly by unanimously passing a motion for an inquiry.[2] Similarly, early in 1888, a deputation to Lord Salisbury from Lord Campion's Committee on the Condition of the Working Classes put forward a number of resolutions including one for the prohibition of foreign immigration. Several of its members, however, stressed that they were not in agreement with this resolution.[3]

Much of the pressure, at this stage, was probably being exerted behind the scenes. Otherwise, it becomes difficult to explain the ease with which the Government was persuaded, after only a few Parliamentary questions and a relatively unorganized agitation outside Parliament, first to announce that legislation was 'under consideration',[4] and then, on 10 February 1888, to agree to the appointment of a Select Committee of Inquiry.[5] Certainly, apart from Captain Colomb and, perhaps, Sir Henry Howorth of Salford South, most of the

[1] Quoted in *Jewish Chronicle* (8 April 1887) in a letter from an Arnold White at this stage concerned to refute all but one of the allegations.

[2] *Jewish Chronicle* (22 April 1887), p. 5.

[3] *Jewish Chronicle* (3 February 1888), p. 3.

[4] W. H. Smith, First Lord of the Treasury, Hansard 3S H(520)490, 12 July 1887, and possibly earlier than this. See Sir James Ferguson, Hansard 3S H(315), 514, 19 May 1887.

[5] Ritchie, President of Local Government Board to Howorth, Hansard 4S H(322)149, 10 February 1888.

leaders of the anti-aliens do not identify themselves by overt action in Parliament until during the Inquiry, or after the Select Committee had reported.

For whatever reason, however—and others will be suggested in the next chapter—on 13 February 1888, a Select Committee was appointed:

to inquire into the laws existing in the United States and elsewhere on the subject of the Immigration of destitute aliens, and as to the extent and effect of such Immigration into the United Kingdom and to report whether it is desirable to impose any, and if so, what restrictions, on such Immigration with power to send for persons, papers and records.[1]

Alien immigration as a political, if not as a partisan, issue had arrived.

Organization: 1888–1895

In this period, we find the aliens becoming an important political and partisan problem, via the organization of agitation, via electoral exploitation, via private members' Bills, Government pledges, and Liberal opposition, and via trade union and Trades Union Congress resolutions. This first period of prominence coincides, moreover, and is connected with a situation in which, as Gartner points out, 'the position of the lower classes penetrated the public consciousness more than at any time after Chartist days forty years earlier.'[2]

But this time, it was 'the outcast classes' who were provoking attention rather than merely the working class, and thus it was the East End which became the focus of that attention. The 1890s was the decade of Charles Booth's voluminous study of *Life and Labour of the People of London*, and of the efforts of the Salvation Army and university settlements, among others, to elevate the condition of this English version of 'skid-row'. In other words, 'the aliens became an issue when social reform became a dominant concern in English politics'.[3]

The Select Committee sat for approximately fifteen months.

[1] *Commons Journals* (143)32, 13 February 1888. Of those appointed to the Committee, only Captain Colomb and William Marriot, on one side, and Baron de Rothschild and Samuel Montagu, on the other, were later to become prominent on the issue.

[2] Gartner, p. 276.

[3] Ibid., p. 275.

Its sources of evidence ranged from parsons to trade unionists, from employers to employees in the bootmaking and tailoring trades, from doctors to sanitary inspectors, and from prominent Anglo-Jews to a rather picturesque group of fifty aliens, selected for their peculiarly depraved and destitute appearance by Arnold White and paid by him to attend at five shillings a time '. . . in order to produce the effect they previously had on me'. He also paid £10 to a Jewish agent to collect the aliens from the docks, and admitted to a desire to bring more Chinese and alien Jewish labour into England 'to bring the matter to a head'.[1]

The Committee reported in August 1889.[2] Its main conclusions were that 'though the number is not sufficiently large to create alarm, the proportion of aliens to native population has been for many years, and is, on the increase'; that 'the better class of immigrants only arrive in transit to other countries but the poorest and worst remain here'; that although the immigrants were independent, industrious, and frugal and rarely came upon the rates, they were 'very dirty and uncleanly in their habits', tended to work for long hours at low wages, and probably crowded many Englishmen into pauperism.

There were two main recommendations. Following their own continued emphasis upon the extreme unreliability of the statistics available, the Committee recommended, in the first place, that more accurate, frequent, and detailed data be collected about the aliens who remained in England, and resurrected for the purpose some defunct clauses of an act of William IV.[3]

The second major recommendation concluded the report:

> That while your Committee see great difficulties in the way of enforcing laws similar to those of the United States and certain other countries against the importation of pauper and destitute aliens, and while they are not prepared to recommend such legislation at present, they contemplate the possibility of such legislation becoming necessary in the future, in view of the crowded conditions of our great towns, the extreme pressure for existence among the poorer part of the population, and the tendency of destitute foreigners to reduce still lower the social and material condition of our own poor.

[1] R.S.C., Vol. I, pp. 61 ff. and 95.

[2] R.S.C., Vol. II, *Report and Minutes of Evidence,* S.P. 1889, X, pp. 265 ff.

[3] 6 Will. IV., cxl, s.2.

The report was both a blow and an encouragement for the nascent agitation. While the Committee foresaw no immediate need for legislation, its recommendations as to the collection of statistics merely required every master of a ship to report the number of aliens on board and the number landed at any port, with their names, trade, occupation, and general description. It made no attempt to remedy the inadequate distinction in Board of Trade Returns of Emigration and Immigration between immigrants '*en route*' and those 'not stated to be *en route*'. Thus, the reformed figures were of no more value than were previous statistics, except that they now had additional official approval and provided vast scope for inaccuracy and alarmism.

A further blow, however, was delivered to the anti-aliens by the House of Lords Sweating Committee. After an inquiry which had run concurrently with, overlapped, and handicapped that of the Commons, this Committee reported in the same year that 'undue stress had been laid on the injurious effect caused by foreign immigration, inasmuch as we find the evils complained of obtain in trades which do not appear to be affected by foreign immigration'.[1]

It is important to remember that these committees were conducting their inquiries and producing reports at a time when both the rate of unemployment and the flow of immigration were relatively low, and when the latter had temporarily stabilized itself—factors that were to be transformed fairly radically within a year of the reports' appearance.

In the first place, the year 1890 brought a further shock to East European Jewry with the expulsion of Jews from major Russian cities like Moscow and Kiev, together with the rigorous enforcement of earlier decrees. Thus, the Board of Trade Report of 1894 estimated the number of immigrants who actually settled in England as over 7,000 in 1891. By 1892, it had slipped back to about 3,000, and was less than 3,000 by 1893. Assuming similar proportions of transmigrants to immigrants as that worked out in this report, Gartner estimates that immigration remained relatively stationary after 1893, at

[1] V. D. Lipman, *Social History of the Jews in England, 1850–1950* (London, Watts & Co., 1954), p. 136.

about 2,500, until the close of the 1890s—in his words, 'an unfailing and substantial stream'.[1]

That the agitation maintained a high level of intensity until 1895 and did not follow the relative volume of immigration (that is, did not subside in 1893) is, perhaps, attributable in part to the exaggeration that the Board of Trade Annual Returns made possible and, even more, to a rate of unemployment which had risen from a low point of 2·5 per cent in 1889 and 1890, to 3·5 per cent in 1891, 6·3 per cent in 1892, and 7·5 per cent in 1893, and which did not slip below 5 per cent until 1896 when it became 3·4 per cent. The figures did not begin to rise again until 1901.[2]

The reports of the two select committees seem at first, however, to have quietened the agitation. During the course of 1890, those M.P.s who were gradually becoming identifiable for their hostility to the immigrants, contented themselves with pressing an already eager Government to adopt the statistical recommendations of the Commons Committee. The Lords signified their recognition of the issue in a four-man debate which took up no more than ten columns of Hansard, and whose most extreme speakers went no further than pleading for accurate statistics and hoping 'sincerely . . . that something will be done to stop this immigration'.[3]

In September of 1890, however, a Mr. Wilkins, writing in the *National Review*, greeted the arrival of increased numbers of refugees (or 'hordes of destitute Jews', as he preferred to call them) by advocating the establishment of 'a society for the protection of British workmen against the unlimited influx of destitute foreign labour'.[4] By April 1891, the *Jewish Chronicle* was referring to an Association for Preventing the Immigration of Destitute Aliens, whose secretary was Mr. Wilkins and which was being run by Arnold White and the Earl of Dunraven. On 24 July, this organization held its first public meeting, which was addressed by 'several representative gentlemen and

[1] Gartner, pp. 45, 286. Gartner attests to the accuracy of this report. Unlike the annual returns, it is, he claims, 'of the highest accuracy'.

[2] These figures are taken from the table entitled 'Prosperity of the Working Classes 1888–1902', in R.C., Vol. III, Appendix IX, pp. 18–19.

[3] Hansard 3S H(346)632–42, 3 July 1890.

[4] Quoted in *Jewish Chronicle* (5 September 1890), p. 4.

several gentlemen who represented only themselves'.[1] These significantly included Liberal M.P.s and prominent trade unionists.

The intensification of agitation which the appearance of this organization represented was paralleled by increasing pressure within Parliament from a, by now, identifiable group of Conservative back-benchers;[2] so much so, in fact, that in May 1892, with an election in the offing, a Conservative Government was reluctantly persuaded to announce the preparation of an Aliens Bill,[3] although ultimately it was saved from having to carry out a promise that it never intended to keep[4] by the return of the Liberal Government in July 1892. In spite of both the widespread use of the issue in the East End during the general election, and the first of three Trades Union Congress resolutions supporting immigration control in September, the Liberals refused to do anything beyond instituting a Board of Trade inquiry into the facts, including an investigation of the operation of the American immigration law.[5]

The announcement of an inquiry came in an amendment to the address (the first of several during our period) demanding

[1] *Jewish Chronicle* (31 July 1891), p. 11. The meeting was addressed by the Earl of Dunraven, James Lowther (C., Kent Thanet), R. G. Webster (C., St. Pancras East), Sydney Buxton (L., Tower Hamlets Poplar), J. H. Wilson (L., Middlesbrough) and Secretary of the Seamen and Firemen's Union, and Ben Tillett, Secretary of the Dockers' Union. The organizers seem to have had some difficulty in dissuading speakers from using the meeting as a platform for more general views about foreign seamen and the nature of the capitalist system.

[2] Most loquaciously prominent among these were Howard Vincent (Sheffield Central); Captain Colomb (Tower Hamlets Bow); H. Howorth (Salford North); L. J. Jennings (Stockport); and James Lowther (Kent Thanet), like Vincent, a protectionist who, according to H. M. Hyndman in his *Record of an Adventurous Life* (London, Macmillan, 1911), 'represented quite a large number of his party alike in his sturdy conservatism of an English sportsman and in his strong prejudices against people he could not understand'.

[3] Hansard 4S H(4)826, 13 May 1892.

[4] See Chapter 5, pp. 57–8. The appearance of Israel Zangwill's *Children of the Ghetto* in 1892 may well have increased the Government's reluctance. The subject of popularly attended lectures given by Zangwill throughout the country, and later made into a play, this book evoked such widespread sympathy for the Jewish alien that, according to Louis Zangwill, the author's brother, in a letter to the *Jewish Chronicle* of 25 May 1894, at least, the Conservative party dropped the Aliens Bill 'under the direct influence of his writings'. The book reached three editions by May 1893 (the third being a cheap edition).

[5] The report showed that immigrants were kept out of the United States not because they were destitute or poor, but because they were morally or physically diseased.

aliens legislation and moved by Howard Vincent and supported from the back-benches of the Conservative party. Although one or two Liberals, like Henry Labouchere, influenced by the xenophobic fears of the Northampton boot and shoe workers, attempted to persuade the House that this was, or should be, a 'non-political subject', the amendment was opposed pragmatically by Gladstone and Mundella (President of the Board of Trade) for the Government and more positively from the Liberal back-benches by Charles Dilke. It was eventually whipped to defeat by 234 to 119 with the help of Jewish M.P.s on both sides and the Irish, who were particularly incensed that the English should become so worried about immigration, yet do nothing about a set of conditions which caused the emigration of thousands of Irishmen. They also frequently expressed a justifiable pride in an Irish history which they claimed to be uniquely characterized by the absence of anti-Semitism. The Irish House of Commons also had passed an Emancipation Bill long before the English ever dreamed of doing so.

Shortly after the defeat of the amendment, a further stage in the organization of the anti-alien lobby came with the commencement of regular meetings of a Parliamentary Immigration Committee composed of Conservative M.P.s and organized by Howard Vincent and James Lowther. By March 1894, this committee was attempting, with only moderate success, to establish contact with members of the Anglo-Jewish community, and had set up a special fund 'to enable the movement to be placed fairly before the public'.[1]

A second attempt to embarrass the Government was made in July 1894[2] with the introduction of an Aliens Bill by a Lord Salisbury concerned not only to keep out destitute aliens, but to do battle with the anarchists as well—'those who live in a perpetual conspiracy of assassination'. Rather mysteriously, the Conservative leader introduced his Bill 'in his capacity as a private member'. It was passed on Second Reading[3] over the opposition of a Liberal Government now led by Lord

[1] 'Political Notes', *The Times* (21 March 1894), quoted in *Jewish Chronicle* (23 March 1894), p. 7.

[2] Hansard 4S H(26)1047, 6 July 1894.

[3] Hansard 4S H(27)117–56, 17 July 1894.

Rosebery, but died quietly when the Liberal Whip in the Commons expressed his opposition 'in very unusually forcible language'.[1]

Salisbury's Bill, however, represents the high point of the first period of organized agitation. Although sections of the Press had apparently managed to work themselves into a minor frenzy during the three Parliamentary sessions of the Liberal Government,[2] the seeds of decline were already beginning to germinate. Thus, shortly after the demise of the Aliens Bill, Board of Trade returns at last, for all their inaccuracy, began to show what was to become a continuing trend: a decline in the comparative volume of immigration.[3] Moreover, while the Trades Union Congress did pass two further anti-alien resolutions in 1894 and 1895, both (unlike the first resolution passed in 1892) met with fierce opposition. The second scraped through by only 20,000 in a total vote of 500,000 and would have been defeated but for the absence of the Northern Miners Union.

Finally, for the first time there were signs of an organized alien and Anglo-Jewish opposition to aliens legislation. The Trades Union Congress resolution of 1894, for example, was greeted by a large protest meeting of Jewish trade unionists in Whitechapel,[4] while that of 1895 inspired them to produce a pamphlet entitled *A Voice from the Alien* which, it was later

[1] Hansard 4S H(28)889, 14 August 1894.

[2] Joseph Prag describes this in a letter to the *Jewish Chronicle* (4 May 1894), p. 14: 'Heaven knows, enough attempts were made to get up a great conflagration; we had an evening paper with a Jewish editor and a large working-class circulation coming out night after night with such placards as—"The Jewish Pauper Plague".' There were also many articles in the periodical press with such titles as 'The Alien Invasion'. The date and tense of Prag's letter, however, suggest that public interest was declining even before the introduction of Salisbury's Bill.

[3] Thus, the return for July 1894 estimated the number of immigrants 'not stated to be *en route*' to America as 3,165, as against 3,415 for July 1893 (quoted in *Jewish Chronicle* [10 August 1894]). In September, the Board of Trade reported that in the first eight months of 1894, the gross immigrant figures were 51,439, as against 98,835 for the same period of 1893; and when 'those *en route*' were subtracted, 27,140, as against 29,881 (quoted in *Jewish Chronicle* [4 September 1894], p. 6). The report for the whole year, published in May 1895, contained the following comment from the Director of the Statistical Department: 'The number of Russian and Polish immigrants is seen to have been smaller by some hundreds than in 1893 and 1892, and more than 5,000 less than 1891' (quoted in *Jewish Chronicle* [10 May 1895], p. 9).

[4] *Jewish Chronicle* (21 September 1894), p. 12.

claimed,[1] prevented any further resolutions. From 1898, spurred on by the Aliens Bill of Lord Hardwicke, the Jewish Board of Deputies began to collect facts about alien immigration 'with a view to disseminating them at the proper time'.[2] This type of activity made it increasingly difficult for members of the Jewish community to join the anti-alien agitation without seeming to be traitors.

Obscurity: 1895–1900

Although in the election of 1895 the Conservatives used the issue fairly widely over an area ranging from North Buckinghamshire to Bow and Bromley,[3] and in spite of the efforts of the 'Trade and Labour Defence League' to further connect the issue with protection, the return of a Conservative Government in July 1895 did not reverse the decline we have been describing. Throughout the next six years, Government spokesmen contented themselves with 'bearing in mind their pledges' and allowed themselves to be put off by 'the technical difficulty of legislation'. Thus private members Bills introduced into the Commons in January 1897 and July 1898, and into the Lords in May 1898, all met with Liberal opposition and no more than promissory notes from the Government front bench.

The Government's general unwillingness to appear to be associated with anti-Semitism will be analysed later. It must be remembered that these were also years of declining unemployment figures and a steady level of immigration. According to the Board of Trade Report on Emigration and Immigration for 1895, published in May 1896, an analysis of all movements into and out of England for the year 1895 showed that at the end of the year the total number of foreigners in the country had actually declined by 32.

Apart from a brief flurry in 1898, agitation outside Parliament, moreover, together with the public interest on which it depended, was also in decline, as witnessed by the paucity of space assigned to it in those years by an ultra-sensitive *Jewish*

[1] J. Finn, R.C., Vol. II, *Minutes of Evidence*, Cd. 1742, 1903, p. 732.

[2] Quoted in *Jewish Chronicle* (24 June 1898), p. 27.

[3] In a speech at Bradford, Joseph Chamberlain had declared aliens legislation part of the (unauthorized) Unionist programme (quoted in *Jewish Chronicle* [6 June 1894], p. 10), though later he is reported to have said privately that he did not think legislation necessary yet. See *Jewish Chronicle* (16 August 1895), p. 5.

Chronicle. Other sections of the Press apparently felt that the issue was sufficiently non-explosive in these years to be worth occasional satirization. The *Westminster Gazette*, with heavy Victorian irony, described 'A Deputation to Lord Owlsbury' about 'The Immigration of Destitute Gulls',[1] whilst Henry Labouchere wrote mockingly of 'The Colonization and Exploitation of England'.[2]

However, if the problem lacked a sense of urgency, it was also, in these years, subject to obscuration by other issues. For, if it is true that alien immigration arose as an issue when social reform became a dominant concern in English politics, then it too suffered the same fate as did social reform before the combined onslaughts of the Irish problem and the movement towards imperialism.

The Irish problem, particularly Irish Home Rule, of course, was the dominant question of the last two decades of the nineteenth century. It had been the immediate cause of the introduction of the closure into House of Commons procedure in 1882; it had completely dominated the elections of 1885 and 1886. Because of Gladstone's determination to leave Home Rule as a permanent memorial to himself, the issue appeared at the head of most addresses, including those in the East End, in the elections of 1892 and even more in those of 1895. The Irish question provided the excuse of pressure of other business for members of the Conservative front bench who preferred to 'bear their pledges in mind'.

Far more important, however, was the fact that the last five years of the nineteenth century were dominated by the issue of imperialism and the South African Wars. As early as April 1892, the *Jewish Chronicle* is suggesting that one of the main reasons for dropping the Aliens Bill from the Conservative programme is the fact that the Government is having to exert all its available influence to convince President Kruger of the wickedness of imposing anti-alien legislation against English settlers in the Rand.[3]

The effect of imperialism, however, went beyond mere embarrassment. For one thing, Joseph Chamberlain, who had

[1] Reprinted in *Jewish Chronicle* (4 December 1896), p. 11.
[2] *Truth*, quoted in *Jewish Chronicle* (31 December 1897), p. 19.
[3] *Jewish Chronicle* (3 April 1892), p. 6.

previously shown, and was again to show, considerable interest in anti-alienism, found his energies absorbed by the Colonial Office. More basically, even the most rabid of anti-aliens discovered that beating the imperialistic drum was a far more effective means of drawing electoral dividends out of jingoism than was crying out against the foreigner. Thus the Aliens Bill of 1897 was scarcely noticed amidst the Jubilee celebrations. Thus, also, anti-alienism scarcely appears at all in the 'khaki elections' of 1900, even in the East End. On 29 September 1900, the *East London Observer*, could announce that its area had 'voted straight on the national issue', and later on 6 October 1900, that 'khaki did its work nobly' for Major Evans Gordon in Stepney. Only an 'Old Londoner' mourned in the patriotic wilderness:

Surely, for Londoners, the election should have but one object and that above all party politics. I refer to the presence in their midst of these foreign Jews. . . . There was a time when Englishmen could be roused, but now they appear to accept everything as inevitable.[1]

Triumph: 1900–1905

The 'Old Londoner' need scarcely have worried for the turn of the century brought what Gartner calls 'a decade of turmoil'. In 1899–1900, several thousand young Jews marched out of Rumania across Europe in protest against continued persecution. A total of 2,903 reached England[2] much to the displeasure of the Jewish Board of Guardians. A further mass exodus took place in 1903, after a series of outrages in the Russian city of Kishinev; and similarly in 1904, with the flight of reservists from the prospects presented by the Russo-Japanese War; and in 1905, after the Russian Revolution and its long trail of pogroms. Added to this was the price war resulting from the dissolution of the Atlantic Shipping Ring during the period 1902–4, bringing about a situation in which it was cheaper to travel from Hamburg to New York via England than it was to travel direct. As Gartner points out:

Under these hammer blows, the semblance of orderly movement, which had been preserved for some ten years, vanished. Waves of Rumanian

[1] Letter to *East London Observer* (29 September 1900), p. 6.
[2] Gartner, p. 47.

wanderers, fleeing conscripts, pogrom victims, and, above all, Jews who simply despaired of improvement in Russia streamed into the British Isles in proportions which bewildered those who tried to organize the flow.[1]

Further than this, from 1901, unemployment figures were once more on the upswing.

Parliamentary anti-aliens, who had despaired of their brain-child ever becoming legislative reality, were not slow in seizing an opportunity made the more urgent by the steady demise of imperialism as an issue because of the dragging on of the South African War. By 1900, their numbers had been augmented considerably, notably by Thomas Dewar, M.P. for Tower Hamlets, St. George's; H. Forde-Ridley, Bethnal Green South West; Claude Hay, Shoreditch Hoxton; Harry S. Samuel, Limehouse; and, from February 1905, Harry Lawson, Mile End. More importantly, a now influential Howard Vincent (Chairman of the National Union of Conservative and Unionist Associations from 1895 and Vice-Chairman of the Primrose League, 1901), marooned in the alien desert of Sheffield Central found an ally in Major W. Evans Gordon who combined high organizational talents with the profound good fortune of sitting for Stepney, a constituency blessed with a high alien population. Finally, in 1903, Joseph Chamberlain resigned from the Government and proceeded to reinforce the long-standing connection between anti-alienism and protection.[2]

Reinforcement also came to the pro-aliens. Although Samuel Montagu had retired from Parliament in 1900, Charles Dilke found new allies from Montagu's family in the persons of Stuart Samuel (Montagu's successor for Whitechapel) and Herbert Samuel; from the Liberal party, C. P. Trevelyan; from the ranks of Labour, John Burns and Keir Hardie; and, finally, from Winston Churchill, who was on the first of several journeys across the floor of the House.

During the debate on the King's Speech in February 1901, the first signs of renewed agitation appeared in complaints about the absence of an Aliens Bill from the Government programme. This was rapidly followed by the formation of

[1] Gartner, p. 46.

[2] There is a parallel here with Enoch Powell: like Chamberlain, Powell is prepared to bolster up a basically unpopular over-all policy with an anti-immigrant plank.

the British Brothers League in May.[1] Organized by William Evans Gordon and Murray Guthrie, M.P. for Bow, the League had Howard Vincent as its 'principal honorary member' and was described by the *Jewish Chronicle* of 1 November 1901 as 'a combination of Primrose Leaguers and Radical working men'. Its aim was 'to prevent any further increase of destitute or undesirable aliens'. . . .[2] The inclusion of five East End borough councillors amongst its vice-presidents was a recognition of the fact that alien immigration was becoming an issue in local, as well as national, politics. Demands for legislation via local government rarely met with much success. Anti-alien motions were defeated by both the London County Council and the Stepney Borough Council in 1902, although the London Municipal Society endorsed them in November 1903.

August 1901 saw the organization of a 'Parliamentary Alien Immigration Committee' of fifty-two M.P.s whose first action was to send a letter to Lord Salisbury demanding legislation. His reply suggested that the anti-aliens still had some way to go, for 'the matter [was] receiving the attention of the Government'. . . .[3]

Around this time, the Jewish community also began to show signs of organizing itself. Shortly after the formation of the British Brothers, a 'Conference of Delegates of Trades Unions and other Jewish bodies' assembled in the Black Eagle, Buck Lane, Whitechapel, to decide on action against possible aliens legislation.[4] By the beginning of 1902, the conference delegates had formed the 'Aliens Defence League'.[5] Seven months later, we find this body organizing and collating evidence for the Royal Commission. Jewish organization, however, did not become effective until the Committee stage of the second Aliens Bill and did not achieve its maximum influence until after the Act had been passed. In general, it was too timid for too long, and probably its main achievement in the period up to the

[1] A second anti-immigrant organization, the Londoners League, was formed in August 1901, but no further reference is traceable thereafter.

[2] *Second Manifesto*, quoted in *Jewish Chronicle* (1 November 1901), p. 12.

[3] Quoted in *Jewish Chronicle* (30 August 1901), p. 18.

[4] *Jewish Chronicle* (7 June 1901), p. 6.

[5] *Jewish Chronicle* (24 January 1902), p. 6.

second Aliens Bill, was to make Jewish anti-alienism akin to racial high treason.[1]

By the beginning of 1902, a growing savagery seems to be characteristic of the agitation outside Parliament. In November 1901, for instance, the *Pall Mall Gazette* greeted a smallpox outbreak with an anonymous article announcing the formation of a Pink Ribbon League whose members' duty was 'to draw the public mind to a consideration of this present scourge' composed of 'the loathsome wretches who come grunting and itching to our shores'.[2] The Pink Ribbon League seems, fortunately, to have died at birth, but in January 1902, the British Brothers League held the first of two public meetings at the People's Palace in East London. The meeting was addressed by Conservative and renegade Liberal M.P.s, and an audience of 6,000 greeted with 'considerable enthusiasm' such epithets as 'rubbish', 'contents of dustbins', 'savages', and 'the scum of humanity'.[3]

It may have been this meeting which finally pushed the Government to forgo further excuses about the technical difficulty of legislation in favour of setting up a Royal Commission, as proposed in amendments to the address moved by Evans Gordon and Forde-Ridley.[4]

The seven-man Commission under Lord James sat for thirteen months, calling a wide variety of witnesses and hearing a great deal of mythology about Jewish vices and virtues, and a rather smaller quantity of reality. The case for restriction was presented first: organized by Evans Gordon, it included evidence from East End residents, shopkeepers, local councillors and J.P.s, doctors and sanitary inspectors, a substantial group of trade unionists, together with a few plain cranks. Evans Gordon also presented a remarkably objective report about conditions in Russia. The case against legislation, a mainly

[1] Thus, as early as 1903, Arnold White doubted whether legislation would be an effective remedy since it would not have the support of the Jewish community. See *Jewish Chronicle* (21 August 1903), p. 6. Also N. S. Joseph, Chairman of the Russo-Jewish Committe and anti-alien in 1890, appeared before the Royal Commission to speak against aliens legislation.

[2] *Pall Mall Gazette* (29 November 1901), quoted in *Jewish Chronicle* (6 December 1901), p. 8. (See Chapter 5 for a fuller account.)

[3] *Jewish Chronicle* (17 January 1902), p. 7. A second, more restrained, meeting was held in November 1903.

[4] Hansard 4S H(101)1290, 29 January 1902.

Jewish one, was presented by Lord Rothschild[1] during the first part of 1903.

Paul Foot's theory that the Commission was virtually forced, by its very terms of reference, to come out in favour of restrictions,[2] is a rather dubious one. It is true that the Commission was prevented from considering remedies other than restrictive legislation. It is also true that the Commission's report refuted most of the allegations laid against the newcomers—concerning disease, reduction of wages, displacement of labour, and pauperism. Yet it was no more restricted by its terms of reference than the House of Commons Select Committee had been fourteen years previously, for they were essentially the same. Moreover, restricted or not, the Commission did recommend the extension of the Public Health Act to help combat overcrowding and displacement of population, the one allegation it felt to be proven.

Basically, the majority seem to have decided in favour of limited restriction and, more curiously, in favour of establishing prohibited areas against the immigrants for four main reasons. In the first place, while, like its predecessor, the Commission tended to suggest that aliens legislation would be ineffective in excluding immigrants who arrived, it went further than the Select Committee and concluded that such legislation would 'have the effect of deterring aliens of the undesirable class from leaving their homes, and also of inducing the shipping companies to exercise greater care in selecting their passengers'.[3] Secondly, the Commission was collecting evidence and reporting at a time when immigration was not only much greater than in 1888–9, but was also on the upsurge—particularly after the Kishinev massacres in May 1903. Thus, thirdly, as Jacob Herzl, President of the Zionist Congress, suggested,[4] the Commission probably found itself in the position of either recommending legislation or running the risk of causing renewed and increased immigration by seeming to issue a tacit invitation.

Finally, while anti-alien pressure reached a peak of intensity,

[1] Both Evans Gordon and Lord Rothschild were members of the Commission.

[2] Foot, p. 91.

[3] R.C., Vol. I, *Report*, Cd. 1742, 1903, p. 43.

[4] R.C., Vol. II, p. 211.

particularly with an amendment to the address in February 1903 which attempted to force the hand of the Government before the Royal Commission had reported or even heard the pro-alien case, the pro-alien agitation outside Parliament had not yet been properly organized. In fact, pressure by the Jewish community was not to become fully effective until after the Act had been passed. But even the first halting efforts of the Jewish Board of Guardians were still eight months away when the Commission reported. Thus, as the *Jewish Chronicle* sorrowfully commented in the recess between the two sittings of the Commission:

> the agitation has never subsided or even moderated in the slightest degree. Throughout the recess, tom-toms have been beaten, the air has resounded with anti-alien incantations. . . . As no counter agitation has been raised on the other side . . . we are not at all sure that a courageous showman who managed to trap an alien, and carry him in a cage around the provinces might not reap a gold harvest.[1]

Although the Royal Commissioners were not unanimous in their recommendations,[2] the anti-aliens were not slow in taking up the opportunity provided by the majority report.

Within two weeks, the Council of the Immigration Reform Association had discovered five major alien characteristics from the minutes of evidence and given them to the world in the form of pamphlets about 'Destitute Aliens', 'Criminality Among Aliens', 'Aliens and Overcrowding', 'Aliens and Vice', and a more mysterious species of 'Fraudulent Aliens'.[3] In November, the British Brothers League engaged in a second mass exercise in fraternalism at the People's Palace. On 2 February 1904, the King's Speech announced the birth of a Government Aliens Bill.[4]

This first Bill[5] followed the recommendations of the Royal Commission. Although rather longer than any of its private predecessors, its provisions were simple and vague, and intended merely to provide a skeletal basis for Home Office regulations.

[1] *Jewish Chronicle* (13 February 1902), p. 20.

[2] Two members—Lord Rothschild and Kenelm Digby, Permanent Secretary to the Home Office—dissented mainly on the grounds that the remedies proposed in the majority report were totally unworkable.

[3] Quoted in *Jewish Chronicle* (21 August 1903), p. 6.

[4] Hansard 4S H(129)4, 2 February 1904.

[5] Aliens Bill, 1904, Number 147.

Briefly, it empowered the Secretary of State, through immigration officers, to prohibit without appeal the landing of any alien who had been convicted in a foreign country of an extradition crime in the previous five years, who was associated with prostitution, who was likely to become a charge on public funds, who was without visible means of support, or, finally, who was 'of notoriously bad character'. In all these cases, the onus of proof lay with the alien, and the expenses were, in general, to be borne by the shipping company which brought him. The Home Secretary could also order the expulsion of any alien who had been convicted of an extradition crime in a foreign country, who was 'of notoriously bad character', or had received such parochial relief as to disqualify a person from voting. Courts of Summary Jurisdiction could order the expulsion of aliens convicted of crimes carrying imprisonment for three months or more. Finally, the Local Government Board was given power to designate as prohibited those areas where overcrowding was shown to be substantially due to aliens.

The Bill was introduced under the ten-minute rule and came up for second reading on 14 April, at which time the Liberals, led from behind by Charles Dilke and C. P. Trevelyan, opposed it vigorously on the grounds that it constituted an attack on political asylum and that the problems were best met by anti-sweating legislation. The Government's defence of this ill-prepared and partially unworkable piece of legislation was both careless and inept. While the Liberals made great play with the near impossibility of even defining mysterious phrases like 'persons of notoriously bad character', 'persons without visible means of support', or 'persons likely to become a public charge', and also drew attention to the sheer unworkability of the prohibited areas clause, Government spokesmen concentrated on attempting a rather half-hearted defence of the indefensible and on denying that real refugees or aliens of good quality would be kept out at all.[1] They scarcely referred to what should have been their strongest argument—and the one offered them by the Royal Commission—i.e. the deterrent effect of such legislation.

The Bill limped out of second reading only to receive a further

[1] See, for instance, the speech of Walter Long, President of the Local Government Board, Hansard 4S H(133)1099 ff., 25 April 1904.

and, perhaps, fatal battering in May—this time from Kenelm Digby in the correspondence column of *The Times*. On 3 May 1904, the Permanent Secretary to the Home Office commented tellingly that 'no more serious injury could be done to a public department than to impose upon it duties which it cannot possibly perform'.[1] Digby's letters prompted *The Times*, so long the mouthpiece of respectable anti-alienism, to editorialize rather feebly:

> It is not easy to understand why . . . discredit should attach to the Home Office, provided the new legislation is put into operation, with no exalted expectations as to what ought to be or can be done by such means.[2]

The Government now seemed to have been at a loss. It waited two months, and then presented a motion[3] to commit the Bill to the one place where the closure could not be applied, i.e. a Grand Committee. It waited a further two weeks until near the end of the session before allowing a sentence of death to be carried out (Committee consideration began 20 June). Under the leadership of an unrepentant Winston Churchill (who is claimed to have remarked privately to Rothschild, 'Yes, I wrecked the Bill'),[4] the Liberals dutifully 'choked it with words until the time limit was reached'.[5] On 11 July, A. J. Balfour, with what was probably mock indignation tinged with relief, summarized the Grand Committee process as:

> treatment which would make it absolutely impossible to carry it into law during the course of the present session. I understand that the average rate of progress was two lines a day [Ministerial cries of 'three lines in six days'] . . . half a line a day.[6]

The Bill was abandoned, though with fervent assurances for the future.

These assurances do not appear, however, to have been trusted by the anti-alien lobby, for after the withdrawal of the

[1] Quoted in *Jewish Chronicle* (6 May 1904), p. 19. See also Digby's second letter to *The Times* (31 May 1904) in which he disposes of 'persons likely to become a public charge'.

[2] *The Times* (31 May 1904), quoted in *Jewish Chronicle* (3 June 1904), p. 7.

[3] Hansard 4S H(135)1084–132, 8 June 1904.

[4] See *Jewish Chronicle* (2 December 1904), p. 12.

[5] Evans Gordon's phrase, quoted in *Jewish Chronicle* (15 July 1904), p. 20.

[6] Hansard 4S H(137)1220–1, 11 July 1904.

Bill we find pressure for its reintroduction being carried on throughout the winter by London Unionist M.P.s and by the Alien Immigration Parliamentary Committee via deputations to Government ministers and agitation amongst constituency associations. Meanwhile, philanthropist Robert Sherard greeted the advent of 1905 by writing a vicious series of articles against the alien in the *Standard* (beginning 5 January 1905).

The Government, by now, may have had its own reasons for wishing to push the Bill through Parliament. While immigration continued to rise[1] and very bad 'winter distress' threatened to put the Opposition in a different position for resisting the Aliens Bill,[2] a series of heavy by-election defeats at the beginning of what was probably an election year, seemed to make the Government's position desperate. The result of the Mile End by-election in which the aliens had been the only issue, was not a good augury for the electoral popularity of the Bill. Here, a Government majority of 1,160 dropped to 78 in a poll of 4,198. (The Government had just lost Stalybridge and North Dorset.) Yet the Government had, at least, held the seat, an important fact in an age which did not calculate in percentage swings, and in which the electorate was often so small as to make such a calculation irrelevant anyway. The temptation to drive a wedge through the developing alliance between Liberalism and 'Labour'—via the Aliens Bill and Unemployed Workman's Bill—was probably irresistible.

Even so, the Bill did not get its first reading until mid-April and, because of the Easter recess, did not come up for second reading until 2 May. Although led by Dilke and Trevelyan with the same vigour as that shown a year earlier, Liberal opposition to the Bill was considerably less effective. Most of the front bench abstained from voting altogether on the official grounds that this was 'a different Bill', but were probably most influenced by the hesitancy of the East End M.P.s and candidates.

The Government, on the other hand, had prepared its case with much greater care than in the previous year. There was a

[1] The Board of Trade Returns for 1904 showed 95,724 aliens not described in the aliens lists as *en route*; quoted in *Jewish Chronicle* (13 January 1905), p. 7.

[2] H. Maccoby, *English Radicalism 1886–1914* (London, Allen & Unwin, 1955), p. 36.

much greater focus on the deterrent aspect of such legislation. There was, moreover, considerable truth in the Liberal claim that it was 'a different Bill'.[1] The Government had gone some way to meet Opposition objections. Although still intended to keep out 'undesirable and destitute aliens', these terms were much more closely, if not more clearly, defined, and the 'notoriously bad character' had disappeared altogether. The term 'immigrant ship' was now defined by the number of aliens it carried (twenty)[2] and 'aliens' under the Bill was confined to steerage passengers. There were designated 'immigrant ports' at which any 'immigrant ship' had to discharge its passengers for inspection. The burden of proof was still to be with the alien, but either the alien or the ship's master could now appeal to an immigration board of 'fit persons having magisterial, business or administrative experience', and the 'immigrant who proves that he is seeking admission to this country solely to avoid prosecution for a political offence' was explicitly safeguarded. Finally, while the expulsion provisions remained substantially the same as before, the unworkable prohibited-areas clause had been dropped completely, with the complete acquiescence of Evans Gordon, who had announced his willingness to drop this clause in a speech before the Constitutional Club in November 1904.

Still further concessions were to rain down upon a grateful House during the Committee stage[3]—this time a manageable 'Committee of the Whole'. The Liberals had, by now, rediscovered their backbones and with the help of a now militant Jewish community and a Jewish Board of Deputies at last in active opposition, they managed to force fairly considerable safeguards for religious refugees.[4] These came from a Government

[1] See Aliens Bill, 1905, Number 187.

[2] The figure was later subject to alteration. The Conservatives reduced it to twelve; the Liberals raised it to twenty again in 1906.

[3] In fact, there was a total of 149 Amendments put down: 95 from Conservatives, 54 from the Opposition. See Hansard 4S H(148)268, 27 June 1905; 1144, 5 July 1905; and 4S H(149)1287, 19 July 1905.

[4] In both the Committee and Report stages, the Government went to considerable lengths to meet Opposition objections on this clause. As it finally stood, the Bill (Number 277) read as follows: 'in the case of an immigrant who proves that he is seeking admission to this country solely to avoid *prosecution* or punishment on religious or political grounds, or for an offence of a political character, or persecution involving danger to life and limb, leave to land shall not be refused

embarrassed by its own conscience, perhaps by the threat of certain wealthy Jews to withdraw contributions from campaign funds,[1] and certainly by its own back-benches. Many of the latter were under considerable pressure from local Jewish congregations who had been advised by the Jewish Board of Deputies to approach their local M.P.s, using the 'form of address' outlined by the *Jewish Chronicle*. Local Jewish committees were formed to interview the sitting M.P.s and several Conservatives came out in favour of strengthening religious safeguards after such an approach, notably Robert Ropner (Stockport), M. Pemberton (Sunderland), Ernest Flower (Bradford West), Sir C. Furness (West Hartlepool), and Colonel Sadler, the M.P. for Middlesborough and a member of the Commons Immigration Committee.[2] Even Thomas Dewar, fearful for the Jewish vote, felt it necessary to write to Councillor Louis Davis about his letter on religious safeguards: 'I am in complete concurrence with the views you express.'[3]

A second group of concessions—whereby transmigrants were excluded from the terms of the Act—came as a result of continued pressure from the shipowners and their Conservative and Liberal spokesmen.[4] This was, perhaps, scarcely surprising

on grounds merely of want of means.' The Government balked only at substituting *persecution* for *prosecution*, as demanded by Dilke.

[1] See the speech of Sir William Walrond, late Conservative Chief Whip, in his constituency of Tiverton, Devon: 'Some [rich Jews] who supported the party financially and otherwise had marked their displeasure by withdrawing their patronage.' Quoted in *Jewish Chronicle* (26 May 1905), p. 27.

[2] See *Jewish Chronicle* (26 May 1905), p. 7, and (9 May 1905), p. 9.

[3] *Jewish Chronicle* (23 June 1905), p. 25.

[4] Their influence seems to have been exerted in between the two Bills and during the Committee and Report stages of the second Bill. In regard to the latter, see the annual report of the Liverpool Steamship Owners Association (tonnage: 3½ million) for the year 1904 quoted in *Jewish Chronicle* (10 February 1905), p. 11; and the Report of the Direct Short Sea Traders Association, described as being 'one of the most important bodies of shipowners in this country [who] control 50 per cent of the trade of the Port of London' (quoted by C. Fenwick [C., Newcastle-upon-Tyne], in Hansard 4S H[148]393, 28 June 1905). See also amendment on transmigrants moved by Austin Taylor (C., Liverpool), Hansard 4S H(148)450, 28 June 1905, and disliked, postponed, and then finally accepted by the Government to become part of clause I(C), Aliens Bill, Number 271—all of which, together with the wording of some of the amended clauses (e.g. VIII[A]), tends to confirm the verdict of Massingham, Parliamentary correspondent of the Liberal *Daily News* (quoted in *Jewish Chronicle* [2 June 1905], p. 14): 'Mr. Akers Douglas has promised the shipowners engaged in the immigrant trade to accept their list of emigrants without question, the big firms—Wilson, Cunard and the

since the ships engaged in the immigrant trade included most of the big lines, like Wilson and Cunard.

With the aid of the guillotine, the Bill passed rapidly through its remaining stages. The Committee stage was completed by 10 July, the Report stage by 17 July; and on 19 July, an exhausted House gave the Bill its third reading by 193 to 103. With the approach of the end of the session, it was forced rapidly, and without amendment, through the Lords, to be breathlessly offered up for Royal Assent on 10 August.

The Bethnal Green Conservative Club celebrated the passing of the Bill by distributing 10,000 copies of the telegram announcing the Royal Assent and putting on a massive display of fireworks. Whether voters in the East End felt that they were celebrating the Act, or merely burning its remains, is, however, open to question. Probably, they agreed with C. P. Trevelyan's parting shot: 'The Government had the magnificent record of having passed a Bill which would keep out five dinghy loads of tatterdemalions.'[1] Of the twelve Conservative East End M.P.s, only William Evans Gordon and Claud Hay were returned in 1906 to witness the further emasculation of the Act by the Liberal Home Secretary.

rest taking all responsibility. Strong influence has also been brought to bear in other quarters . . . this poor little Bill is really being murdered behind the scenes.'

[1] Hansard, 4S H(149)1263, 19 July 1905.

IV

The Agitation: Anglo-Saxon Attitudes

It was all very well to dissemble your love
But why did you kick me downstairs?

OLD JEWISH COUPLET[1]

The Ghetto and Its Setting

Walter Besant, writing at the turn of the century, described East London as 'above all a city of the working man'.[2] He quoted Charles Booth who, after sorting through one million people, could find only 443 heads of families and 574 women who were independent of work.[3] Apparently, Besant felt that East London had sufficient identity to be termed a city, but none the less it was 'a city without a centre, without a municipality, and without any civic or collective or local pride, patriotism or enthusiasm'.[4] The area possessed an industrial system peculiarly susceptible to the evils of sweated outwork,[5] and contained a population so densely packed that new industries, new warehouses, and new schools could only be developed if already inadequate housing accommodation was first pulled down to make room for them.[6] Reinforcing these characteristics was the fact that this 'community' of 726,000 wage-earners was in a state of constant movement. The more successful moved into the outer suburbs, leaving the less successful to face competition from a further 'remarkable characteristic of East London'—namely, 'the way in which the industrial population is constantly recruited from the country'.[7]

East London possessed, in other words, all the characteristics of what we should now call an area of urban decay; and it is

[1] Quoted in *Jewish Chronicle* (30 August 1903), p. 13.

[2] Besant, p. 22.

[3] Charles Booth (ed.), *Life and Labour of the People of London*, Vol. III (London, Macmillan, 1892–7), quoted in Besant, p. 24.

[4] Besant, p. 38.

[5] See Chapter 9.

[6] See Lipman, p. 104.

[7] Besant, p. 25.

finally significant that Besant's survey was intended as a guide-book, since to the rest of English society East London, even without its aliens, was like a foreign country. Consequently, it possessed a deep feeling of neglect and isolation which both enhanced, and was itself reinforced by, the factors outlined above. William Catmur, writing in the *East London Observer* just before the 1906 election, gave graphic and bitter expression to this feeling:

Get along, you're joking. As if East London could have any special issues or interests in a Grand Imperial General Election! The Rand, Park Lane, the Stock Exchange, the City may well have a mind and a message. The canny Midlands, the thoughtful Scotch, the determined Irish will get respect and attention. Birmingham is a reality, Mr. Carnegie's slummy town, Dunfermline, shall be cited [*sic*] as a living being by the Premier in person. East London is nothing; indeed less than nothing—wholly a vile, malodorous, irreclaimable thing, a dumping ground for undesirables, a dust bin, a forgotten garret, a neglected basement, creepy, smelly, stifling; that superior persons now and then must perforce sniff gingerly at for a short space until they may fly elsewhere to the sham respectables that their souls love, and boast of their daring philanthropic sacrifices.[1]

Into this area of urban decay, and into similar areas in other large cities, particularly Leeds, Manchester, and Salford, there came the alien Jewish immigrants; that is to say, into areas particularly in need of a scapegoat, came groups of people peculiarly suited for that role. The immigrants were drawn into areas of earlier Jewish settlement and so increased their scapegoat potential wherever they went by the formation of a ghetto. This increased their actual and imagined strangeness in habit, dress, language, and complexion, and as the *Jewish Chronicle* fearfully pointed out in 1888:

If poor Jews will persist in appropriating whole streets to themselves in the same district, if they will conscientiously persevere in the seemingly harmless practice of congregating in a body at prominent points in a great public thoroughfare like the Whitechapel or Commercial Road, drawing to their peculiarities of dress, of language and of manner, the attention which they might otherwise escape, can there be any wonder that the vulgar prejudices of which they are the objects should be kept alive and strengthened. What can the untutored, unthinking denizen of the East End believe in the face

[1] *East London Observer* (6 January 1906), p. 6. The paper was Conservative, but pro-alien.

of such facts but that the Jew is an alien in every sense of the word—alien in ideas, in sympathy, and in interests from the rest of the population, utterly indifferent to whom he may injure so long as he benefits himself, an Ishmael whose hand is against everyone, and against whom the hand of everyone may rightly be.[1]

Contemporary host accounts of the ghetto tended to confirm the *Jewish Chronicle*'s prognostications and were as much a commentary on the reactions of a homogeneous society shocked by the appearance of strangers as a description of life in the ghetto itself. Thus, Sir William Marriot, Conservative M.P. for Brighton, observed after a day excursion to the East End: 'There are some streets you may go through and hardly know you are in England.'[2] From the opposite benches, eleven years later, Mr. H. Norman (Liberal M.P., Wolverhampton, South-East) regaled the House of Commons with tales of a place where there were:

railway timetables posted . . . in Hebrew characters, the bills of places of amusement distributed in the streets in Hebrew, and the public entertainments given in Yiddish (as well as a foreign press) in which were advocated with great immunity all kinds of revolutionary doctrines.[3]

Even the internationalism of socialists could waver in the face of the sense of shock which the ghetto seemed universally to induce. The Editor of *Clarion*, taking time off from ignoring the aliens question, spent 'A Pleasant Saturday Afternoon' in the East End and discovered it to be 'a strange experience, because within half-an-hour's walk of the City Boundaries we were in a foreign country'.[4]

Residents of the East End were even more graphic, and sometimes even poetic, in their descriptions:

There is no end to them in Whitechapel and Mile End. It is Jerusalem.[5]
It is like the waves of the sea—they simply keep spreading, but they do not retreat like the waves of the sea do.[6]

The ghetto provided a point of focus for real or imagined grievances against the immigrant and made him into a visible

[1] *Jewish Chronicle* (28 September 1888), p. 9.
[2] Hansard 4S H(8)1205, 11 February 1893.
[3] Hansard 4S H(133)1110, 25 April 1904.
[4] *Clarion* (22 August 1896), p. 268.
[5] William Walker, an undertaker, quoted in R.C., Vol. II, p. 298.
[6] William Rose, a carpenter, quoted in R.C., Vol. II, p. 302.

and readily available scapegoat. It focused working-class fears of unemployment and lowered wages, and reinforced in the popular mind whatever slight connection there was between the immigrant and the sweating system. It made credible allegations that the immigrant brought dirt and disease. Above all, the presence of a highly visible immigrant quarter gave a special reality to terms like 'swarms' and 'alien invasion',[1] and made the chorus of complaint about overcrowding and displacement of population seem irrefutable.

Moreover, if things were bad because of the arrival of 'them Jews', it followed that the period before they came was a veritable golden age, when life was not merely clean and pure, but uncomplicated: for anti-alien hostility was, after all, an attempt to comprehend complexity by simplification. Thus Mrs. Ayres, a midwife, could remember that:

> It used to be a street occupied by poor English and Irish people. In the afternoons you would see the steps inside cleaned, and the women with their clean white aprons sat in summer times inside the doors, perhaps at needlework, with their little children about them. Now it is a seething mass of refuse and filth . . . the stench is disgraceful. . . . They are such an unpleasant, indecent people.[2]

The Anti-alien Case

To ask which came first, hostility or agitation, is rather like asking a similar question about the chicken and the egg. Probably, it may be assumed that the agitators gave the legitimacy of coherence to a vague sense of grievance, to what, in Magnolia Street, at least, was 'this feeling'.[3] They added a few complaints and stereotypes of their own and produced the anti-alien case.

Broadly, the argument ran as follows: England was being subjected each year to an invasion by thousands, or even

[1] The harvesting of metaphors was in itself a common result of 'ghetto shock'. Note the previous quotation: note also the Bishop of Stepney in 1902: 'The East End of London was being swamped by aliens who were coming in like an army of locusts eating up the native population or turning them out. Their churches were being continually left like islands in the midst of an alien sea.' (Quoted by Evans Gordon, in Hansard 4S H[145]717, 2 May 1905.) The most recent example, of course, is Enoch Powell: 'Like the Roman, I seem to see the Tiber foaming with much blood . . . [it is] like watching a nation building its own funeral pyre.' (Quoted in *The Times* [22 April 1968], p. 2.)

[2] R.C., Vol. II, p. 310.

[3] Organized anti-alienism seems to have been very weak in Manchester and Salford. See later, p. 69.

hundreds of thousands, of aliens, an invasion made the more serious by the growing uniqueness of England's outdatedly sentimental policy of keeping open house to all comers, and one which might, at any moment, reach catastrophic proportions should Russo-Jewish emigration develop into a general exodus.

In any case, it was argued, legislation was necessary now. The present effect on working-class employment wages, rents, and housing was quite bad enough, for the aliens were driving the natives out 'from hearth and home'. The number of immigrants was already large, and might be far larger than even Board of Trade figures suggested. How did one know that those who claimed to be in transit subsequently left this country? Even if numbers proved to be comparatively small, and even if England received fewer aliens than any other country, they none the less had a deteriorating effect out of all proportion to their real numbers because they were concentrated in a few areas and a few trades. After all, 'Ten grains of arsenic in a thousand loaves would be unnoticeable and perfectly harmless, but the same amount put into one loaf would kill the whole family that partook of it.'[1]

Apart from numbers, the other major immigrant characteristic was destitution. Here, as elsewhere, the argument became, if not less certain, then decidedly flexible. It was alleged that, since they represented those sections which had failed in the central European 'struggle for existence', the aliens were now, and were unlikely to be other than, a burden on the rates. When these charges of alien pauperism were disproved,[2] their persecutors took refuge in the idea of 'a lower standard of life', which, aided by Jewish charity, enabled them to compete with the native population in a decidedly un-Queensberry fashion and so drive on to the rates a native population already 'burdened with the education of thousands of children of foreign parents'.[3] When doubt was cast even on this,[4] the argu-

[1] Evans Gordon, Hansard 4S H(101)1273, 29 January 1902.

[2] In fact the rate of pauperism among aliens was considerably lower than that among the native population. The 1901 census found 1,753 alien paupers, which represented 0·79 per cent of alien population, as against a national average of 2·4 per cent (quoted by Walter Long, in Hansard 4S H[133]1052, 25 April 1905).

[3] Evans Gordon, Hansard 4S H(101)1274, 29 January 1902.

[4] The Whitechapel Union reported to the Local Government Board in 1893: 'There is no sufficient data upon which to found the opinion that the immigration

ment took a further step back from specificity, and its proponents gestured vaguely towards:

> a moral aspect to this competition. . . . The alien notwithstanding many virtues, seems to bring a sort of social contagion with him which has the effect of seriously deteriorating the life of those who are compelled to be his neighbour . . . the neighbourhood in which he settles speedily drops in tone, in character and in morals.[1]

Moreover, 'public opinion had shown itself behind this measure'[2] and legislation was demanded, 'rightly or wrongly', particularly by the working classes whom, after all, 'we have made . . . our masters'. Those who preached about political asylum, it was argued, should preach it to them, for 'they had no right to be generous at other people's expense'.[3]

The foregoing is the core of the anti-alien argument; it was embellished, from time to time, by other charges of less direct interest to 'our working classes'. The most common of these were the alleged connections between aliens and pestilential disease, and aliens and crime. There was also the danger of 'mongrelization'; while others argued that: 'They never assimilate. In face, instinct, language and character, their children are aliens.'[4] Another supposed problem was 'their remarkable fecundity'. Lord Salisbury seemed to believe that a high percentage were anarchists, while S. H. Jeyes felt that nearly all were 'politically unfit to be suddenly transplanted into those democratic institutions for which we have adapted ourselves by a long course of self-governing liberty'.[5] Arnold White, for most of the time, agreed with everything that anybody had ever said at any time, but felt that 'another characteristic of these poor people is pro-Boerism', and yet another, 'a tendency to, or the existence of, incendiarism'.[6]

of foreigners has indirectly been the cause of any increase of pauperism in the Union' (quoted in *Jewish Chronicle* [3 February 1893], p. 13).

[1] Rev. G. S. Reaney on 'The Moral Aspect', in Arnold White (ed.), *The Destitute Alien* (London, Swan Sonnenschein, 1892), p. 91.

[2] James Lowther, Hansard 4S H(8)1166, 11 February 1893.

[3] Claude Hay, Hansard 4S H(149)182, 10 July 1905.

[4] Rev. G. S. Reaney in White (ed.), p. 84. See, on the other hand, the Earl of Dudley, Hansard 4S H(58)274, 23 May 1898: 'They come to intermarry and this means necessarily a lowering of the whole moral and social standard of the population of those districts in which they settle. . . .'

[5] White (ed.), p. 189.

[6] R.C., Vol. II, p. 22.

Presentation and General Characteristics

The anti-alien case was capable of infinite flexibility. The arguments were not only difficult to pin down, and so simple that they required complex arguments to refute them, but they could be varied to suit the audience. A crowd of low-paid or unemployed operatives could be regaled with tales of alien blacklegs and 'the sweaters' den', or aroused by emotive phrases which accused the aliens of 'taking the bread out of English mouths', or of 'driving the native from hearth and home'. The philanthropic middle class could have its conscience titillated by stories of empty churches, alien dirt, disease, and immorality; or it could be sent scurrying to rescue both constitution and property from alien anarchists, or from those who 'may pollute the ancient constitutional liberalism of England with the visionary violence of Continental Socialism'.[1]

In a sense, the agitation managed to combine a rather extreme theory of democracy, which came very close to delegation, with a fear of democracy, specifically a fear of what the masses might do if their wishes were not granted. A major part of the justification for anti-alien legislation was that it was 'wanted by the working classes of this country'. Political asylum was all very well, but 'will the working classes permit us to continue it at such a sacrifice?'[2] Anti-alienism was a cause which could spur the Primrose League into a flurry of petition gathering,[3] could stimulate Howard Vincent to present to Parliament a petition 'signed by 50,000 working men',[4] and could persuade a host of Conservative M.P.s and peers to support legislation on the (for them) unlikely and dangerous grounds that the Trades Union Congress favoured it. But however much the agitators might misquote Robert Lowe's dictum that 'we have made the working men our masters', their argument was often clinched with the warning:

> Let the politicians look to this! The agitators have taken it up; the strike leaders are discussing it. . . . Mr. Burns and Mr. Tillett and Mr. Mann could raise a *Judenhetze* tomorrow if they liked to do it. . . .[5]

[1] White (ed.), p. 189.
[2] Ibid., p. 186.
[3] See 'Political Note', *The Times* (20 July 1898).
[4] *Jewish Chronicle* (8 March 1905).
[5] White (ed.), p. 189.

The first part of this warning was not, perhaps, entirely without foundation, for in some of the agitation outside Parliament there was, if not a revolutionary strand, then at least something that would have been 'agin the ruling class' had it not been diverted into anti-alienism. Thus James Johnson, a labourer and the Chairman of the Executive Committee of the British Brothers League, could conclude a prepared statement to the Royal Commission with the dire admonition:

> We venture to say that, if this question touched the rich, there would very soon be a stop put to it, it does not [*sic*] and some of them [the landlords] think they may grind the working man to powder, yes grind him down, he will stand it as long as the rich man becomes the richer upon his ashes; but we say, beware of the dust, it rises with a high wind, and may become injurious even to those who cause [it?] [*sic*].[1]

An analysis of the agitation as an attempt to divert popular attention from more radical movements (and from more realistic causes of misery) also perhaps partially explains a further element of dualism: the mixing of localism with jingoism. The agitators relied, in part, upon the exploitation of local grievances and upon the emphasis that this, among other things, was a local problem.[2] In this way, they were able to use the East End's feeling of neglect both as a means of working up enthusiasm in their constituencies and as a telling means of combating the arguments of their opponents. At the same time, however, the agitation possessed a strong undertone of jingoistic nationalism. Thus Thomas Benskin's address to the electors of South West Bethnal Green in 1892 observed, in part:

> I consider the time has arrived when statesmen should consider measures which will directly benefit 'John Bull' without due regard to outside and foreign interests. I am in favour of stringent measures to prohibit the whole-

[1] R.C., Vol. II, p. 228.

[2] In addition, all the East End Conservative M.P.s (like their more successful Liberal opponents) were 'good local members' who had strong local ties and/or assiduously nursed their constituencies. Several, like Spencer Charrington (Mile End), Thomas Dewar (St. George's in the East), and candidates Thomas Benskin and Rupert Guinness, were local employers (via breweries). Harry Lawson (Charrington's successor in Mile End) 'has never left the constituency even for a week to take care of itself' (*East London Observer* [6 January 1906], p. 8). Evans Gordon was 'a local resident'.

sale immigration of pauper foreigners. I warmly support the principle of maintaining 'Great Britain for the British'.[1]

Similarly, during what may have been a bad attack of over-assimilation, Lewis Sinclair (*né* Louis Schlesinger), the Jewish Conservative candidate for Romford, told his adoption meeting:

Now, gentlemen, I want to tell you that I am for 'England for the English'. I want England to come in first, second and third, and the foreigners to come a long way after. I say that the immigration of pauper aliens . . . should in every way be withstood.[2]

Others, too, shared Sinclair's particular brand of anti-alien sentiment. On the day assigned for the Second Reading of the 1904 Aliens Bill, one newspaper gave prominence to an anonymous, unisentence letter which read: 'It is hoped that every London newspaper under British control will publish a list of traitors in Parliament who vote against this measure.'[3]

Seen in this way, anti-alienism becomes one of a number of ways of beating the patriotic drum. Indeed, it is not surprising that during the period of 1892–1906 the one election in which immigration was not an important issue, even in the East End, was the 'Khaki election' of 1900. Nor is it a coincidence, nor merely the result of the linkage between anti-alienism and Protection, that by the time of the two elections of 1910 anti-alienism had been replaced by Tariff Reform as the means of exorcizing the foreign bogy. The idea of 'the refuse of Europe' flooding the British labour market was no longer present in the East End Unionist mind; rather it was:

the Protectionists in America who wish to see Free Trade maintained, so that they may continue to DUMP THEIR SURPLUS GOODS on our shores DUTY FREE and STARVE OUT THE BRITISH WORKING MAN. . . . THE BRITISH MARKET FOR THE BRITISH WORKING MAN. This Election will decide whether ENGLAND IS TO BE RULED BY THE ENGLISH.[4]

The Agitation and Anti-Semitism

Thus, we can see a connection between the agitation against the alien and a more general theme of jingoism. But to what extent

[1] *East London Observer* (25 June 1892).
[2] *Jewish Chronicle* (29 January 1897), p. 12.
[3] Quoted by Dilke, Hansard 4S H(133)1063, 25 April 1904.
[4] An address by E. Ashmead-Bartlett, quoted in *East London Observer* (3 December 1910), p. 5.

did the agitation become anti-Semitic? Is Gartner correct in assuming that 'the full depths of racism requiring not mere anti-alienism but anti-Semitism towards all Jews, including apostates and their children, were never plumbed'?[1] The central theme of the rest of this chapter, and a major theme of the rest of this book, is that Gartner may be technically, and even broadly, correct if we use Robb's definition of anti-Semitism:

An attitude of hostility towards Jews as such, that is, *not towards a particular Jew, and not towards a number of people whom, apart from having an attribute that arouses hostility, also happen to be Jewish*; the hostility to be called anti-Semitic must be associated definitely with the quality of being a Jew.[2]

The agitation, like the public opinion upon which it thrived, was, generally speaking, anti-alien. But really the question of anti-Semitism is irrelevant, for what was crucial was not whether or not the agitation was in fact anti-Semitic, but that people thought or feared it might be. The very fact that the immigrants were Jews and that the agitators were further exploiting an already universal scapegoat, dominated the discussion and exercised a considerable influence over the course of events. All who pressed for anti-alien legislation were aware of the possible support accruing to their campaign from anti-Semitism. Some came very close to exploiting it deliberately. Others attempted to raise it as a spectre of the unintended, though, perhaps, unavoidable, consequences of resisting legislation. Yet, since anti-Semitism was not merely disreputable, but also possessed the same sort of reputation as witchcraft, all went out of their way to avoid the charge of anti-Semitism and most, at least, acted as if the very success of their campaign depended upon its not being tarred with the anti-Semitic brush (as indeed it did; see Chapter V). Everyone, from Government minister to East Ender, was looking over his shoulder fearing or threatening, or being embarrassed by and denying (or some combination of all four) what others might do or be doing.

It is this general situation which seems, at least partially, to explain the curious and thoroughly ambivalent behaviour of the Conservative front bench throughout the period. The most notable example of this type of behaviour comes between 1891

[1] Gartner, p. 278. [2] Robb, p. 11. (Italics my own.)

and 1893. In July of 1891, we find Hicks Beach, President of the Board of Trade, telling the House that he does not think 'there is any sufficient reason at present' for legislation.[1] Seven months later, C. T. Ritchie, President of the Local Government Board, gives the same reply, telling one member that his figures are 'misleading'.[2] In April 1892, A. J. Balfour is still discounting charges against the immigrant.[3] However, on 6 May 1892, with an election on the way, the Government, while still mistrustful of statistics, is 'considering legislation'.[4] By 13 May, 'a Bill on this subject is in the charge of the Home Secretary' and Balfour believes 'he will be in a position to introduce it soon'.[5] Three days later, it is discovered to be 'in an advanced state of preparation'.[6] Then, suddenly, caution strikes and a sheepish Home Secretary tells the House: 'It was thought necessary to institute enquiries, not only at home but abroad, before giving definite shape to the measure.'[7] The issue is used in the election by every East End Conservative candidate and M.P., with the exception of C. T. Ritchie in St. George's. Then in February 1893, Mundella, the Liberal President of the Board of Trade, can jubilantly, and without refutation, discredit an amendment to the address with the news: 'I have made enquiries . . . but there was not a vestige or a scrap of a Bill left behind by the late Government.'[8]

We find the Conservative front bench pursuing the same wayward behaviour over the next six years. The issue is used widely and officially in the election of 1895, but, from then on, dilatory verbiage is the rule of the day. The Government bears its promises in mind, but when pressed to fulfil them, the answer is always 'not now' or 'later'. Salisbury, the initiator of an Aliens Bill in July 1894, was to become particularly adept at such answers. Similarly, Chamberlain, 'who at the General Election roared like a lion about aliens eating bread that would save our people from starvation, now coos gently as a sucking dove'.[9] Similarly, again, a private member's Bill introduced by the

[1] Hansard 3S H(356)551, 28 July 1891.
[2] Hansard 4S H(2)1661, 24 March 1892.
[3] Hansard 4S H(3)146, 1 April 1892.
[4] Hansard 4S H(4)279, 6 May, 1892.
[5] Hansard 4S H(4)826, 13 May 1892.
[6] Hansard 4S H(4)1447, 16 May 1892.
[7] Hansard 4S H(5)215, 30 May 1892.
[8] Hansard 4S H(8)1210, 11 February 1893.
[9] 'Notes', *Jewish Chronicle* (16 August 1895), p. 50.

Earl of Hardwick in 1898 was supported fervently by the Earl of Dudley for the Government but lapsed as soon as it left the Lords, for it was 'not a Government Bill'.[1] Even when finally pressed into commitment with the aid of a Royal Commission in 1904, the Government, as we have seen, does not appear either to have done much pre-natal preparation, or to have been particularly fond of its first legislative offspring when it arrived. Only in 1905, with the imminence, again, of a general election does it begin to show a real interest.

Part of the explanation for this waywardness obviously lies in the sheer technical difficulty of framing legislation that would have the desired effect of keeping out the elusive and undefinable 'pauper alien'. But this did not stop the Government in the desperate years of 1904 and 1905. Moreover, the Government was affected by its apparent anxiety not to appear to be associated with racial prejudice. This is directly suggested in a number of ways: by the fervency with which Government spokesmen dismissed such imputations about their Bills; by the fact that these spokesmen managed to get through debate after debate without ever mentioning the word 'Jew'; and, tentatively, by the *Jewish Chronicle*'s claim that the appearance of Zangwill's *Children of the Ghetto* in 1892 caused the Government to drop the idea of legislation. More conclusive evidence comes from the Government's anxiety in 1905 to meet the objections of those who claimed that the Bill excluded religious refugees, and from its insistence throughout 1904 and 1905 that this was a moderate Bill intended only to check 'undesirable' aliens and 'to give moderate powers reasonably applied'.[2] Even more interesting is an allegation made by William Stanley Shaw, former President of the British Brothers League, who in an interview with the *Jewish Chronicle* confided that, after that organization's first violent demonstration at the People's Palace, the East End Conservative M.P.s were 'threatened with the serious displeasure of high officials of the party if they appeared on the British Brothers League platform again'. According to Shaw, 'the government didn't want the League'.[3] In fact, the East

[1] 'Notes', *Jewish Chronicle* (16 August 1895), p. 50.

[2] See, for example, Walter Long, President of the Local Government Board, Hansard 4S H(133)1104, 25 April 1904.

[3] *Jewish Chronicle* (13 October 1902), p. 9.

End M.P.s took part in a later meeting in November 1903, but, significantly, this was 'on the whole a more restrained and sober performance than that of two years ago, and Evans Gordon's speech "studiously sane" '.[1]

We can see the same factors at work amongst the agitators themselves. Before we analyse their effect, however, let us first note that the argument about whether the agitation was, or was not, anti-Semitic is irrelevant in another sense from that already noted above. It draws the attention away from a multitude of other sins. It says nothing, for instance, about the exaggeration, alarmism, and violence of some of the language employed by M.P.s and candidates inside and outside Parliament. Conservative candidates in the East End were sometimes not averse to accusing their Liberal opponents of 'getting in on the alien vote'. Thus Colonel Trench, Conservative candidate for Whitechapel, at an election meeting in 1892 attributed a previous defeat in 1886 'in a large measure to the fact that the sitting member polled a large number of aliens, and it was his determination that the voice of the British elector should not be swamped at election times'; he also spoke of the Liberal registration officers' threat to put 'another 2,000 alien votes . . . on the register'.[2] Nor did some of them scruple to use their election addresses to express such sentiments as the following:

> Whitechapel, standing as it does at the very gates of the city of London, the centre of the Empire, was never destined to become a foreign pauper settlement. It is intolerable that we should have unblushingly dumped down among us the very scum of the unhealthiest of continental nations . . . an outrage to the district.[3]

The electors of Stalybridge, a town not noted for its alien population, were treated to several thousand leaflets containing this message:

> Let them all come is the Radical cry. The Radicals, by their obstruction of the Aliens Bill are evidently glad to see all foreigners who are criminals, who suffer from loathsome disease, who are turned out in disgrace by their fellow countrymen, who are paupers, who fill our streets with profligacy and disorder.[4]

[1] *Jewish Chronicle* (13 November 1903), p. 19.
[2] *East London Observer* (2 July 1892), p. 6.
[3] *East London Observer* (6 January 1906), p. 5.
[4] Quoted in Hansard 4S H(145)773, 2 May 1905.

A variation on the same theme enlivened the Chichester by-election:

there was a large placard . . . with a line drawn down the middle. On the one side there was [Campbell-Bannerman] beckoning with a very pleasant smile, to a long perspective of aliens to come here; and, on the other side of the line, there was [Asquith] and an array of British working men with their tools on their shoulders. The legend was: 'We have no room for these British working men: we want the men on the other side of the picture.'[1]

The campaign by those unconnected with Parliament was sometimes more violent still. Certain sections of the daily and weekly Press sometimes gave space to sentiments whose violence—even if construed as being anti-foreigner rather than anti-Jew—would, fifty years later, exclude them from everything but the anonymous broadsheets of the political fringe. None of this was real anti-Semitism, but this is to say very little: for what Gartner might call 'mere anti-alienism', which was respectable, sometimes came so close to outright xenophobia as to be virtually indistinguishable, in everything but terminology, from overt anti-Semitism, which was not respectable. Thus, one writer in the *New Century Review* of October 1897 felt that:

the destitute foreign immigrant is, as a rule, diseased in both mind and body. . . . Besides being a physical plague spot, the destitute foreigner is usually a bad citizen, a breaker or evader of the law, a sedition monger and, in the last resort, an enemy of this country.[2]

Launching the 'Pink Ribbon League', an anonymous writer in the *Pall Mall Gazette* attempted to connect an outbreak of smallpox with the alien immigrants, 'the loathsome wretches who come grunting and itching to our shores'. Then choosing his epithets with even more care, the writer described how:

the small-pox now creeping through London, this agony now throbbing and scorching in my arm is caused (make no mistake about it) by the scum washed to our shores in the dirty waters flowing from foreign drainpipes.[3]

Finally, we discover the most violent of all expressions of anti-alien sentiment in the *Standard* which published a series

[1] Cited by Dr. Hutchinson, in Hansard 4S H(148)863, 3 July 1905.

[2] Quoted in *Jewish Chronicle* (8 October 1897), p. 18.

[3] Quoted in *Jewish Chronicle* (6 October 1901), p. 18. In fact, the East End escaped the outbreak altogether.

of articles by a 'Special Correspondent' (also called an 'impartial investigator', but later discovered to be Robert H. Sherard)[1] who, standing in the Hamburg Emigration Halls, looked about him and then wrote:

One sees the splendid specimens of men and women—Russians, Lithuanians, Hungarians, Slavonians—clean, sturdy, open-faced, sweet creatures; these for America and Canada—to work in the fields, to work in the factories—with their strong arms, clean hearts to be put at the entire disposal of their new country. One sees, too, the very opposite of these—filthy, ricketty jetsam of humanity, bearing on their evil faces the stigmata of every physical and moral degradation; men and women who have no intention of working, otherwise than in trafficking. These for England.[2]

Some articles later, the same writer found himself in 'the alien quarters of London' where his researches revealed:

for instance, the pleasure taken by the foreigners in laughing at the homeless, unemployed English who spend their days in Spitalfields churchyard feeding on garbage. . . . They have taken the homes and they have taken the bread of the English; plump and oleaginous, they deride their victims.[3]

Apparently Sherard eventually became too much even for the *Standard*, since, after a violent interchange of letters with the *Jewish Chronicle*, the series was terminated on 14 January, a week early.

One notices from all these examples that the word 'Jew' is conspicuous by its absence, except that occasionally in Sherard's case xenophobia switches to overt anti-Semitism. Sherard claimed that he told his stories of alien sins to a Rabbi who (perhaps not surprisingly) 'laughed repeatedly'. He also claimed that the Russian pogroms were 'mild reprisals' for the sins of the Jews in Russia.

One notices also that in the absence of the usual declamations of innocence of prejudice, all three writers choose, or at least try, to remain anonymous, despite the fact that their articles could be seen as manifestations of xenophobia rather than anti-Semitism.

The trouble was that although anti-alienism was respectable, and although, consequently, one could be as rude about 'foreign'

[1] See Bibliography.
[2] Quoted in *Jewish Chronicle* (6 January 1905), p. 25.
[3] Quoted in *Jewish Chronicle* (13 January 1905), p. 14.

immigrants as one wished, other people had a habit of continually reminding the agitators that the 'aliens' also happened to be Jews. Thus, in the normal way of things, rudeness had always to be preceded by almost neurotic protestations of innocence. Such protestations, in fact, acquired the force of ritual. This was true of the agitators within Parliament:

> Before I deal further with this matter, I wish to say that, so far as I am personally concerned—and I think I am also speaking for all those who are co-operating with me in this matter—nothing could be further from our objects and sentiments than to cause pain to that injured race [the Jews] many of whose members in this country are among the most loyal and charitable subjects of the Queen.[1]

> Whatever I do in the course of this or other sessions, I wish to disclaim the slightest intention of importing into the discussion any vestige of religious feeling or prejudice.[2]

> It is said that this agitation is aimed at the Jewish race. Sir, it seems hardly necessary for me to repudiate so monstrous and groundless a charge. . . . They are objected to not because they are Jews or Gentiles, but purely on social and economic grounds.[3]

This unwillingness to appear overtly anti-Semitic can also be observed in the behaviour of the Parliamentary agitators outside Parliament, and explains their anxiety to claim and obtain the support of prominent members of the Jewish community. It explains similarly why in the course of 1893 the Parliamentary Immigration Committee got in touch:

> with some leading members of the Jewish community in the hope of finding some common line of action and with the object of removing misapprehensions that the Parliamentary movement was in any way antagonistic to Jews as such.[4]

Meanwhile, the non-Parliamentary agitators, while sometimes coming much closer to overt anti-Semitism, and even blatantly exploiting it on occasion, were, if anything, even more fervent in laying claim to a sainthood of the social norm. William Stanley Shaw, apparently, left the British Brothers

[1] James Lowther, Hansard 4S H(8)1160, 11 February 1893.

[2] Howard Vincent, Hansard 4S H(89)117, 14 February 1901.

[3] Major Evans Gordon, Hansard 4S H(101)1279, 29 January 1902.

[4] 'Political Note', *The Times* (21 March 1893). Note also the contemporary example of Alderman Griffith, who in 1962 attempted to make contact with the leaders of the Birmingham Indian Workers Association. See Foot, p. 42.

League partly because he suspected that it was becoming anti-Semitic and wrote specially to tell the anti-alien *East London Advertiser* of 5 July 1902:

> Sir, my attention has been called to a leaflet headed 'British Brothers League' and signed by Messrs. A. T. Williams, L.C.C., and F. E. Eddis in the course of which it says—'If you, or any of your friends have suffered by the Alien Jews coming here, now is the time to say so.'
>
> As the organizer of the British Brothers League, I should like to say that the first condition that I made on starting the movement was that the word 'Jew' should never be mentioned and that, as far as possible, the agitation should be kept clear of racial or religious animosity.[1]

However, of equal significance was the reaction of the League to Shaw's accusation. A. T. Williams, one of the League's most prominent members, said he had been 'informed . . . by an official of the League that this Leaflet was issued without the authority of the Executive Committee'. The League was anxious to show that it possessed clean hands. Its 'Second Manifesto' began by claiming: 'It is of no consequence whether a destitute immigrant believes in the Bible, the Talmud or the Koran. . . .'[2] Similarly, the League commenced a prepared statement to the Royal Commission with the following terms: 'In the first place, we maintain that this is not a question of politics, race or religion, nor does the country these aliens come from concern us.'[3] The essential preliminary ritual now completed, the statement went on to speak of aliens who:

> live on us like parasites, sucking out our heart's-blood, because we wish to live and will as far as possible, a little bit decent. . . . We ask are they not persecuting us? Have they not come from persecution to persecute? Are they not revenging themselves on us. . . . They openly tell us they are going to have this country.

In fact, the closer the agitators came to anti-Semitism, the more fervent were their denials. Arnold White, perhaps the strangest of all, was a man capable of accusing the Jews of practically every crime in the calendar including 'the lack of a sense of humour' (the *Jewish Chronicle* called this a 'white lie'),[4] one who could, at times, discover the world to be 'in pawn' to

[1] Quoted in Robb, p. 202. [2] *Jewish Chronicle* (1 November 1901), p. 12.
[3] James Johnson, in R.C., Vol. II, pp. 286–8.
[4] *Jewish Chronicle* (29 October 1899), p. 12.

'rich and powerful Hebrews',[1] and who confided to the Royal Commission:

The first evidence that we are importing a criminal Jewish population is shown by the fact that the Government, without mentioning the matter in the House of Commons, are building Synagogues at Wormwood Scrubs, Parkhurst and Pentonville.[2]

Yet this same person could reveal a veritable persecution complex when accused of prejudice before the Select Committee:

I should like to say that I absolutely refuse to regard this as a Jewish question, and that I have not gone into the religions of these people and do not intend to do so. I think nothing can injure the question more than doing that. . . .[3]

[Q.] You mean to say that you do not know these people are Jews? [White] I am quite ignorant as to the religions of any of these people; it is not a question I put.

[Q.] Do you know of any society who assist these Jewish immigrants after they arrive here? [White] If you mean these foreign immigrants, there are two institutions. . . .[4]

In a sense, Arnold White is a microcosm of the neuroses of the agitators as a whole. Unadulterated hostility towards the alien Jew was an impossibility, and White, their most long-standing, if not most effective, enemy, had apparently to show himself their dearest friend. As the *Jewish Chronicle* commented, and not without amusement:

He is, at once, apologist and accuser, a strange mixture of frowns and smiles, a veritable Janus at the gates of Jewry. . . . Mr. White seems to love us and to hate us in a breath, to at once kiss us and scratch us with proverbial feminine inconsistency.[5]

[1] *Jewish Chronicle* (17 December 1897), p. 19.
[2] R.C., Vol. II, p. 21.
[3] R.S.C., Vol. II, p. 66.
[4] Ibid., p. 85.
[5] *Jewish Chronicle* (1 April 1899), p. 19. A later issue of the *Jewish Chronicle* (17 January 1908) carried the following comment: 'Some of his closest friends, added Mr. White, were Jews.'

V

Public Opinion and the Accusation of Prejudice: More Anglo-Saxon Attitudes

I do not believe that public opinion in this country would permit the grosser forms of race hatred.

CHARLES BRADLAUGH[1]

The anti-aliens were almost as united in claiming the unprejudiced nature of their mass support as they were in declaring their own purity. Most Liberals would, undoubtedly, have agreed with Charles Dilke's verdict when he told the House: 'An anti-Jewish feeling has been aroused. It is impossible to close our eyes to the fact.'[2] Indeed, some of the agitators were not above occasionally threatening that, at some time in the future, and, in some way unconnected with their own wishes or activities, public opinion in the East End might become anti-Semitic, particularly if either a reluctant Government or an obstinate Jewish community were to block anti-alien legislation. Thus, Forde-Ridley managed both to wash his hands of the matter and look meaningfully over his shoulder in claiming:

This is not a question of Jew or Gentile. It is unfortunate that the racial question should be introduced into the matter but it is difficult for us to enlighten the uneducated classes of this country upon the subject . . . you cannot persuade them it is not a racial question when they are being turned out of their homes. They naturally take a hatred to the Jewish people. It is for the Government to prevent that anti-Semitic feeling which, if something is not done to check the influx of aliens, . . . must inevitably result in an outbreak of very grave proportions.[3]

Similarly, Evans Gordon warned that if the Jewish community 'ranged themselves against the natural and rising feeling of the people on this subject then, indeed, there is a grave risk of anti-Semitic colour being imported into this controversy'.

[1] *Jewish Chronicle* (16 May 1890), p. 7.
[2] Hansard 4S H(133)1075, 25 April 1904.
[3] Hansard 4S H(101)1288, 29 January 1902.

However, most of the agitators, for most of the time, were as anxious as the Earl of Dudley that their support should not appear to possess even the potentiality towards anti-Semitism:

> it cannot be doubted that there is a very strong feeling amongst the English population in the East End against this intrusion. It is said by some that this feeling must be put down to race hatred, that it is an aspect of the anti-Semitism that we find on the continent. . . . I do not, for one moment, believe this to be the case. The feeling is not against the Jew as a Jew.[1]

Indeed, Evans Gordon even went so far as to suggest that his support could not possibly be anti-Semitic since it was multi-racial and, as far as the first British Brothers meeting was concerned: 'No such gathering representing all classes and creeds and every shade of political opinion and religious belief has ever come together on any question before.'[2]

If we now turn from self-interested theory about public opinion to fact, we shall find that it is dominated by the Jewish aspect of the problem in a way very similar to that in which the agitators were themselves affected.

Pro-alienism

However much the *Jewish Chronicle* might gloomily prognosticate about a hardening of the Englishman's heart, an influential and coherent section of the public was still deeply attached to the tradition which saw England as the haven for the religious and political refugee, a tradition which dated from the reception given to the Huguenot and Palatine refugees, and which had become part of the Victorian ark of covenant during the revolution, reaction, and restoration cycles of the mid-nineteenth century. Although by the end of the century the tradition was beginning to loss its hold in the face of a growing nationalism, its influence was still considerable, particularly since those seeking asylum were the most persecuted race of all time, fleeing from the worst type of persecution. And even in the eyes of late Victorians, the persecutors were the worst in Europe—the Russians.

Thus, during the course of our period, we find a number of motions against immigration control emanating from the

[1] Hansard 4S H(58)270, 23 May 1898.
[2] Hansard 4S H(101)1280, 29 January 1902.

middle-class suburban conscience. The Stoke Newington Vestry in 1893 defeated a motion in favour of immigration control at a meeting where its proposer:

> met . . . with not a single supporter out of an attendance of about forty gentlemen. Speaker after speaker pulled his statements to pieces and gloried in the fact that this country was able to supply a resting place for the victims of oppression. They resented the motion as an insult to the principles of Christianity and all spoke in the highest terms of the Jew in his character of husband, father and loyal citizen. On being put to the vote even the seconder of the resolution voted against it, and there was only one hand held up in its favour.[1]

Similarly, in 1895, 'the Parliamentary Debating Society of Birmingham . . . which comprises a large sprinkling of professional men and has only six Jewish members' defeated a motion in favour of restriction.[2] The 'Hampstead Parliament' defeated a similar motion in 1896, and in 1900 threw out an Aliens Bill 'without a division'.[3]

We can see similar processes at work, perhaps on a slightly wider social scale, when we examine the reception given not only to the book *Children of the Ghetto* (which reached its third and cheap edition within a year of publication), but also to its author, Israel Zangwill, when he embarked on a lecture tour of the country in November 1896. Zangwill visited, among other places, the Leeds Theatre Royal where he found an audience of 3,000; the Hampstead Conservatoire where there was 'a record house'; the Music Hall, Sheffield, with 'hundreds standing round the wall'; and the Royal Institute where in 'a crowded meeting . . . more than one eye was tear-dimmed'.[4] All these lectures on the ghetto were heard by 'mainly Gentile' audiences.

Certain sections of the country were probably particularly sympathetic to the tradition of religious asylum. It was, perhaps, no surprise that during the Committee stage of the second Aliens Bill, Mr. Spear, Liberal M.P. for Devon Tavistock, should tell the Government that he felt very strongly 'that his

[1] Joseph Prag, in a letter to *Jewish Chronicle* (24 February 1893), p. 7.

[2] *Jewish Chronicle* (25 January 1895), p. 20. Birmingham was also the political base of Joseph Chamberlain.

[3] *Jewish Chronicle* (28 February 1896), p. 21, and (26 January 1900), p. 5.

[4] *Jewish Chronicle* (20 November 1896), p. 8, and (27 November 1896), p. 7.

constituents would object to the passage of the Bill if it prevented this country from continuing to be the refuge of the victims of religious persecution'.[1]

It is more significant that Mr. Duke, Conservative M.P. for Plymouth and a man not otherwise opposed to the Aliens Bill:

could not help thinking that there must be some modification of the terms of the clause, which would enable the Government to meet a sentiment which . . . would find a powerful echo throughout the country . . . among the masses of the people there was an honest desire that they should do nothing to deprive themselves of a source of national pride.[2]

However, it was not merely the Liberal West Country, nor the literate middle class, who could be roused to display sympathy with the Jewish refugee. Protests against the Aliens Bill, as an erosion of religious or political asylum, also emanated from areas which acted as major centres for immigrant influx. Thus, Manchester, which possessed 'after London the largest settlement of Jews in any city in the United Kingdom', seems to have been almost totally free of organized anti-alien hostility. 'Happily, the anti-Semitic crusade has not so far spread to it with the virulence apparent in the metropolis.'[3] In 1904–5, Manchester appeared to be the main national centre for protests against restriction. In June 1904, we discover:

A largely-attended meeting to protest against the Aliens Bill . . . held . . . in Stephenson's Square, Manchester. The large majority of the audience belonged to the English working-classes.[4]

Even more significant, in a sense, is 'a largely-attended meeting of Jewish and Christian Workmen' held a month earlier in the Labour Hall, Strangeways, the main area of Jewish concentration.[5] There are also reports of 'a meeting of citizens' in the Midland Hotel, on 28 June 1905, chaired by Joynson Hicks, Conservative candidate for North-West Manchester, and supported by several gentlemen from both political parties, which passed several resolutions against the Aliens Bill.[6]

[1] Hansard 4S H(149)166, 10 July 1905. See also Wills, Liberal M.P. for Dorset North, Hansard 4S H(148)842, 3 July 1905.

[2] Hansard 4S H(149)166, 10 July 1905.

[3] *Jewish Chronicle* (23 January 1903).

[4] *Jewish Chronicle* (24 June 1904), p. 25.

[5] *Jewish Chronicle* (6 May 1904), p. 28.

[6] See *Jewish Chronicle* (30 June 1905) and Hansard 4S H(148), 3 July 1905.

We can also find manifestations of sympathy with the alien even in the East End. Lord Monkswell, during what was admittedly a slack period for anti-alienism, reported that he had:

gone to Toynbee Hall in the middle of Whitechapel, where, if anywhere, there ought to be a strong feeling against destitute aliens, and . . . on two occasions addressed a working-class audience there . . . on both occasions the room was packed and the result of the voting was two to one against any restrictions whatever.[1]

Monkswell's evidence is open to the charge of partiality on two counts: (a) he was a Liberal peer, and (b) Toynbee Hall represented what C. Russell called 'the more intelligent working man'.[2] This is not, however, the case with the evidence of Reverend Wilfred Harold Davies, the Rector of Spitalfields and a mild anti-alien, who (at a time when anti-alienism was once more on the upsurge) told the Royal Commission:

There is no question about it that there is a very strong feeling on the part of the English people, not only against the alien Jewish population, but also in their favour. A very large section of the English people have a great respect for the Jewish people. . . . I am speaking entirely from my knowledge of Spitalfields.[3]

Similarly T. E. Williams of the Stepney Working Men's Union Club, and 'of an advanced school of political thought', said 'opinion in his club was evenly divided on the aliens'.[4] Several witnesses told the House of Lords Sweating Committee that they 'liked to work with them [Jews] and found no bad feeling against them'.[5]

In all these examples, we may well be talking about only 'the advanced section of the working class'. Even so, the extent and fervour of middle- and working-class pro-alienism, as some of the evidence quoted indicates, was partially determined

[1] Hansard 4S H(58)282, 23 May 1898.

[2] C. Russell and H. S. Lewis, *The Jew in London* (London, T. Fisher Unwin, 1900), p. 86.

[3] R.C., Vol. II, p. 317.

[4] Ibid., p. 651.

[5] See Annie and Jane Sessions, machinists, in House of Lords Select Committee on the Sweating System (hereafter, S.C.), *Report and Minutes of Evidence*, Vol. I, S.P. 1888, XX, p. 881. See also Factory Inspector Lakeman who found 'no feeling', in S.C., Vol. II, S.P. 1889, XXI, pp. 472 ff.

by the fact that the immigrant could not only be assumed to be a refugee, but was also a Jew.

The Extent of Anti-alienism

On the other hand, there was undoubtedly a significant section of opinion—particularly among the working classes—which was, or became, strongly anti-alien. How large this was, and to what extent it reached beyond the areas affected by immigration, is very difficult, if not impossible, to determine. We know that the Trades Union Congress passed hostile resolutions in 1892 without either discussion or vote, and again by a fair majority in 1894 and by a very small one in 1895; and thereafter ignored the question. These resolutions may well have been passed partly as the result of log-rolling and partly because of a tendency to confuse the deliberately imported foreign blackleg with the immigrant. Apart from this, and apart from the occasional resolution from a Trades Council, there seems to have been little organized hostility to the alien from trade unionists not affected by alien labour.

Outside the ambit of trade unionism, the evidence is, naturally, even scarcer. The Conservatives certainly used the issue in constituencies outside the East End in the election of 1892, and far more widely in that of 1895 when even the rural voters of North Buckinghamshire and Roxburghshire were warned to prepare themselves against the alien flood. . . .[1] Arnold White stood as a Unionist against J. A. Pease in Northumberland, Tyneside. Nine years later, at the height of the alien-hunting season, we find Evans Gordon reinforcing the case for a successor to the 1904 Aliens Bill with the news that after the Horsham by-election, alien immigration 'was one of the most live issues in Sussex' and the matter 'had been discussed in all parts of the country and he had been honoured with requests to address meetings . . . in places where an alien had probably never been seen'.[2] The issue was also used in

[1] According to a Liberal pamphlet published in 1900, the issue also appeared in the 1895 election addresses of candidates in Birmingham (Chamberlain), East Manchester (A. J. Balfour), Croydon (C. T. Ritchie), Liverpool, West Derby, South Birmingham, South Lanark, and West Wolverhampton. See *5 Years of Tory Government* (London, Liberal Publication Department, 1900). The *Jewish Chronicle* claimed it was used in Hythe Boroughs.

[2] Address to Constitutional Club quoted in *Jewish Chronicle* (25 November 1904), p. 12.

by-elections in Chichester, Stalybridge, and Whitby where Stuart Samuel (Liberal M.P., Whitechapel) found:

> the walls and hoardings covered with placards and literature dealing with aliens . . . and Tory orators in moving terms . . . [appealing] to people who had never seen an alien and did not know whether he was flesh, fowl or good red herring.[1]

Whether these tactics had any electoral effect is again very difficult to say. The voting figures, like those in the East End, are very unreliable guides; but if they suggest anything, it is that the effect was minimal. The Liberal majority on Tyneside remained resolutely stable until 1900, by which time Arnold White had taken his spectres elsewhere. At Stalybridge in 1905, a Conservative majority of 79 gave way to a Liberal one of 951 (a swing against the Conservatives of 12·6 per cent).[2] At Horsham, a Conservative, unopposed in 1895 and 1900, kept his seat by only 784.[3] Whitby, which returned a Conservative unopposed in 1900, returned his successor to private life in June 1905 on a minority of 445.[4] The Conservative, unopposed in 1900, just held Chichester in 1905.[5] These figures are not significantly different from those in by-elections untroubled by the alien menace.[6]

The available evidence of the extent of anti-alienism in the East End, while rather more plentiful, is almost equally difficult to use. All that can be said with any certainty is that hostility to the alien was not confined to the tiny minority as Liberals sometimes wishfully suggested. Even in 1898, the Primrose League claimed to have collected 2,630 signatures in favour of restriction from Bethnal Green (with a total voting population of 15,000). The first demonstration of the British Brothers League (claimed by a disgruntled ex-President in 1902 to have never had a membership of 'above 12,000') was claimed by

[1] *Jewish Chronicle* (26 May 1905), p. 17.

[2] 1900: 3,321 (C.), 3,240 (L.); 1905: 4,029 (L.), 3,078 (C.)

[3] 1905: 4,388 (C.), 3,604 (L.)

[4] June 1905: 4,547 (L.), 4,102 (C.)

[5] 1905: 4,174 (C.), 3,762 (L.)

[6] In January 1905, the Liberals captured North Dorset with a swing of 9·9 per cent. Again in April, they captured Brighton by 8,209 votes to the Conservatives' 7,392, after not having contested the seat in 1900. In June, East Finsbury went Liberal with a swing of 15·3 per cent.

Evans Gordon to have attracted an audience of 6,000, and the second was admitted by the *Jewish Chronicle* to have entertained 4,000. Although any interpretation of evidence given before the Royal Commission is complicated by the division of the argument into an anti-alien case and a rather disorganized pro-alien case, it is evident that most of the Gentile witnesses from the East End before both the Select Committee and the Royal Commission were, to varying degrees, hostile to the alien; there is a suggestion, too, that a greater savagery of feeling existed in 1902–3 than in 1888.

In most of the elections from 1892 to 1906, the issue was used by Conservative candidates in all the East End constituencies,[1] but its effect on voting behaviour, once again, does not allow easy measurement. The task of relating electoral swings to the effect of any given issue is a hazardous one even for modern elections. It is even more difficult in this case owing to the size of East End electorates, which was small even by turn-of-the-century standards, and which was partly accounted for by the large (and mostly unregistered) alien population. Thus in 1906, against an English average of 11,440 voters per constituency, East End constituencies, with the exception of Poplar and Bow,[2] ranged from 4,421 in Whitechapel to 7,874 in North East Bethnal Green. The effect of even a small number of voters on the swing increases proportionately with the decrease in size of the constituencies. Thus, unless differences between swings are very large indeed, it is almost impossible to make significant comparisons of either the movement of opinion from constituency to constituency within the East End, or the swings in the East End and the country as a whole.

However, so far as it is possible to judge, in spite of the alarmed and alarming prognostications of local Liberal M.P.s and candidates—or perhaps because of them—only on rare occasions does the issue appear to have been so salient in the electoral mind as to be associated with a statistically significant electoral effect. Thus, in the election of 1906,

[1] In this context, I take the following eleven constituencies to comprise the East End: the seven divisions of Tower Hamlets, the two divisions of Bethnal Green, and the two divisions of Shoreditch (Hoxton and Haggerston). North, South, and Central Hackney, and East and West Ham are not included.

[2] 9,687 and 11,196, respectively.

out of eight East End Conservative M.P.s—all of them anti-alien—only two survived: William Evans Gordon in Whitechapel and Claude Hay in Hoxton. Only in these two constituencies was the swing to the Liberals significantly reduced. While much of the East End was recording swings ranging between 11 and 25 per cent, there was only a 3 per cent leftward swing in Stepney, and Hoxton actually produced a 7 per cent swing to the Conservatives.[1] That these differences were associated with the aliens issue is, perhaps, tentatively suggested also by the fact that in the election of January 1910—by which time the issue was dead—Stepney and Hoxton were the only two East End constituencies to produce a large swing to the left.

Apart from this, however, and whatever the feelings of the East End, anti-alienism does not seem to have paid very handsome electoral dividends, even under the most favourable electoral circumstances. The test case is really the Mile End by-election of January 1905—a time when unemployment distress was at its height, and the interim period between the Liberal destruction of the first Aliens Bill and the introduction of the second. Yet in spite of these circumstances coupled with an election fought wholly on the aliens issue, the Conservative candidate found his much-loved predecessor's 'safe' majority of 1,160 turned into a razor-edged 78.[2] The swing (14·5 per cent), moreover, was not noticeably or significantly different from those of other by-elections outside the East End at this time.[3]

[1] *Stepney*

1900: 2,783 votes to Evans Gordon (C.), and 1,718 to H. Steadman (L.), giving a Conservative majority of 1,065.

1906: 2,490 to Evans Gordon (C.), and 1,853 to D. Stokes (L.), giving a majority of 637.

Hoxton

1900: 2,866 to Hay (C.), and 2,595 to Stuart (L.), giving a majority of 271.

1906: 3,849 to Hay (C.), and 2,753 to Ward (L.), giving a majority of 1,096.

Liberal Haggerston (next door to Hoxton) recorded a 4 per cent leftward swing which may be significant, but here the issue was not used until 1906. Whitechapel also recorded a 4 per cent swing, but since this invariably Liberal constituency never recorded more than a 5·7 per cent swing either way in all the elections from 1885, this is scarcely significant.

[2] 1900: 2,440 to Spencer Charrington (C.); 1,280 to Goddard-Clarke (L.)

1905: 2,138 to H. Lawson (C.); 2,060 to Strauss (L.)

1906: 2,295 to Strauss (L.); 2,169 to Lawson (C.)

[3] For example, North Dorset 9·9 per cent, and East Finsbury 15·3 per cent.

Public Opinion and Anti-Semitism

Our conclusions as to the extent of anti-alien hostility even in the East End must remain very tentative. All we can say is that it was not as insignificant as some of the pro-aliens liked to believe. There may well be some discrepancy between the amount of feeling and its translation into electoral behaviour—a discrepancy which may, in fact, be connected with the factor that helped prevent the translation of anti-alien feeling into violence or other types of action: for voting is, in a sense, a 'public act', and, at least in public, the Jewish aspect of the problem seems to have exercised as strong an influence over the anti-alien public consciousness as it did over that of the agitators and the pro-aliens.

Many contemporary observers certainly seemed puzzled by what they saw as a discrepancy between the amount of feeling and the extent of its expression. A German writer, for instance, discovered, in Leeds, 'a slumbering anti-Semitic feeling . . . not outspoken, sometimes indefinite, sometimes denied'.[1] The Reverend Arthur E. Dalton, Rector of Stepney, is typical of many observers in discovering 'a very strong feeling indeed against the aliens' and in wondering 'that it does not show itself more than it does in action'.[2] The Reverend Ernest Carter, Vicar of St. Judes, agreed as to the strength of feeling and in attempting to give that feeling legitimacy, perhaps answered, his fellow cleric's query; for it was:

> not the least sort of feeling that exists on the continent. . . . It is not the sort of feeling that caused such trouble in France a few years ago. We are all absolutely wishing to be right and just in the matter but we cannot help observing what we do observe.[3]

The last sentence is crucial, for it suggests that there was, even amongst the most hostile East Enders, a general lip-service to the ideals or social norms of tolerance and interracial brotherhood. Moreover, while the wave of anti-Semitism on the Continent might increase the intensity of this feeling amongst some people, for most the kind of anti-Semitic feeling

[1] Oscar T. Schweiner writing in *Daily Mail* (29 June 1909), and quoted in *Jewish Chronicle* (2 July 1909), p. 12.

[2] R.C., Vol. II, p. 332.

[3] Ibid., p. 337.

expressed in such stark issues as the Dreyfus case and the pogroms in Russia merely served to reinforce this lip-service, to increase the disreputability of anti-Semitism, and to heighten public consciousness of the fact that the immigrant was a Jew and that hostility towards him might be construed as anti-Semitism.[1]

Therefore, the success of a playlet entitled *Jew and Gentile* at the Paragon Music Hall, Mile End, during the second Dreyfus trial, need not surprise us. Performed before a large Jewish and Gentile audience, it centred around the Roman destruction of Jerusalem. The *Jewish Chronicle*'s description of its grand finale speaks for itself:

> 'Do you think this cruel work will unite Jew and Christian?' asked one of the Hebrew victims, and the entire audience thundered back with an approving shout.[2]

It may be argued that such an audience represents merely the pro-alien section of the East End working class. This may be so, but the lip-service to tolerance, or, at least, the wish to be dissociated from intolerance, is found in juxtaposition to even the most hostile of anti-alien sentiments, and seems to have affected behaviour in a number of ways. A landlord in Manchester who let a house unknowingly to a Polish Jew and then tried to turn him out 'repeatedly asserts that he has no prejudice against Jews, but merely objects to the particular class to which Gleik [the tenant] belongs'.[3] Another middle-class example is that of James Bairstow, owner of a wholesale clothing firm in Huddersfield and agent of Central South London Free Church Council, who told the Royal Commission, 'as having to do with the clothing trade, I am of the opinion [*sic*] that what are commonly called anti-Semitic methods or Jew-baiting . . .

[1] In contrast (and, perhaps, as proof by opposite) the Irish version of anti-Semitism, while not widespread, when it does occur possesses a certain cheerful and unashamed rumbustiousness, perhaps because the attitude of the Catholic Church gave it respectability. In 1886, for instance, posters appeared in Dublin headed 'INVASION OF IRELAND BY GERMAN JEWS AND ORGAN-GRINDERS AND STREET MUSICIANS' and advocating: 'a trade boycott of all Jews from this day until the last Jew leaves our shores. —IRELAND FOR THE IRISH—Beware of the money lenders who advertise to lend without bail. They are Jews, but use Irish names.' (Quoted in *Jewish Chronicle* [29 October 1886], p. 6.)

[2] *Jewish Chronicle* (11 August 1899), p. 20.

[3] *Jewish Chronicle* (3 February 1899), p. 13.

are objectionable'. He then went on to accuse the 'aliens' and 'foreign tailors' (amongst other things) of supporting houses of ill fame.[1]

Again, reading through the minutes of Royal Commission evidence, one is struck by the care with which many hostile witnesses steered clear of any reference to the racial background of the aliens or foreigners. Others, like James Francis, a haberdasher, pointed out to the Commissioners that they possessed 'friends in all races' and carefully distinguished between 'Anglo-Jews' and 'even old established alien Jews' on the one hand, and 'these latest importations [which] I cannot respect',[2] on the other. It found expression with equal frequency in a series of variations on the theme of 'it's the neighbours'. In describing 'the feeling in the East End', witness after witness took up a strangely detached attitude, pointing fearfully over the shoulder at a feeling which was somehow potentially violent, which no one owned to feeling himself, which many thought lay in others. Thus, for Mr. Brown, a resident of Stepney:

> The feeling is rapidly becoming very desperate, and, if something is not done very soon, I should not be surprised if the people took the matter into their own hands.[3]

Alfred Walmer believed:

> The feeling is so intense that, if a powerful leader was to come forward, it might have very serious consequences . . . you may go where you like, in any street, and go among the people and hear expressions which are anything but Parliamentary.[4]

A Hoxton costermonger told the Commissioners: 'If something isn't done before long, there will be some of our chaps doing murder.'[5] And William Rose, a carpenter, apologized: 'The racial feeling, I am sorry to say, is very bad.'[6]

We can find a similar form of lip-service to toleration, and the necessity (even the desirability) of the tradition of religious asylum, among audiences at all the anti-alien meetings. At the first meeting of the British Brothers League, a correspondent writing in the *Jewish Chronicle* found that the agitators' disavowals of racial or religious animosity were 'always received

[1] R.C., Vol. II, p. 527. [2] Ibid., p. 295. [3] Ibid., p. 87.
[4] Ibid., p. 176. [5] Ibid., p. 267. [6] Ibid., p. 301.

with great cheers'.[1] Indeed the constant attempts of the agitators to separate the Jewish aspect from the economic and social aspects of the immigration question were probably as much dictated by their audience's need to see that separation, as by the necessity felt by both agitator and follower to advertise the non-anti-Semitic nature of the campaign. This idea is implicit in the following set of rhetoric and response recorded at an anti-alien meeting in Hoxton in February 1905:

Their opponents were trying to turn the movement into a religious one [shame], to raise bitter feelings between Jew and Christian. The only reason why it could be said that they were trying to do the Jew any harm was that, at that moment, the aliens arriving in this country largely consisted of Jews, but it was only throwing dust in their eyes to say that, because they were calling for legislation to deal with this evil, they were persecuting the Jews [cheers]. He admitted that he should regret that political refugees should suffer, but he did not think that need be so [cheers].[2]

Only with these preliminaries complete, did the speaker apparently feel able to commence, or his audience to listen to, the anti-alien peroration:

He was pleased to see that they might exclude the criminal and the diseased. But that was not why they were gathered that evening. Cries of 'all the lot' and 'they are all undesirable'.

The general impression that such pieties were, in part, the fulfilment of a popular need, and that without them the agitation might have foundered, is, perhaps, suggested by a pamphlet issued by the British Brothers League in February 1902. This pamphlet was printed in Yiddish as well as in English, and was, therefore, perhaps mainly intended for a Jewish audience. Nevertheless, it is interesting, if only as a commentary on the mentality of its authors, and as a revelation of the differing respectabilities of anti-alienism and anti-Semitism. It may also have been intended to clear the 'dust' being thrown into Gentile eyes. 'Do not be deceived by people who are trying to make you believe that "alien" means "Jew". It does not! Alien means "foreigner". Religion has nothing to do with it!'[3]

[1] *Jewish Chronicle* (17 January 1902), p. 7. For a similar example at the beginning of the period, see *Jewish Chronicle* (22 April 1887), p. 5.

[2] Hon. Rupert Guinness, chairman and Conservative candidate for Haggerston, quoted in *Jewish Chronicle* (17 February 1905), p. 12.

[3] Quoted by William Stanley Shaw in a letter to *East London Observer* (5 July 1902).

Charles Braudlaugh was, therefore, saying more than he realized when he reassured the Anglo-Jewish Association: 'I do not believe that public opinion in this country would permit the grosser forms of race hatred.' The overt anti-Semite was a rare being, even in the East End. Stallholder Walter Trott's opinions about Jews were distinguished not merely by their violence and specificity, but by his willingness to own them:

I heard a statement made that they do not drink. No, they are too lousy to buy three pennyworth of Scotch; they make it. You never see an Englishman with an illicit still; an Englishman goes and has three pennyworth. . . . I say, let these Jews have an island to themselves and let them live on one another. . . . [They] live like rats in a hole—I cannot find words bad enough for them myself.[1]

In general, even the few prepared either to talk publicly in terms of invasions by 'these foreign Jews', or to tell the *East London Observer*: 'I am now definitely anti-Semite',[2] preferred the anonymity of such pseudonyms as 'Old Londoner' and 'Stepneyite'. If, as Robb suggests, violent and overt anti-Semitism is associated with social and psychological isolation, that isolation would seem to be as much a result as a cause of anti-Semitism. For in the East End, perhaps, as in Magnolia Street:

Jessie Wright's rosy cheeks got rather sick and yellow when the question of the Jews came up. She embarrassed the other people in the Private Bar. . . . They looked the other way when Jessie Wright started talking about the Jews.[3]

For most people, the fact that the immigrant was a Jew tended to complicate rather than simplify their attitude towards him, particularly in public;[4] and it probably em-

[1] R.C., Vol. II, p. 299.

[2] Quoted in *Jewish Chronicle* (26 June 1903), p. 24.

[3] Golding, p. 54.

[4] And, in this situation, perhaps, private acts at least had a habit of becoming public property. An interesting example of this process in action is observable in September 1911, when the Bethnal Green Board of Guardians decided not to award a milk contract to the lowest tender (from a Jew) and awarded it instead to an English milkman. Several members of the Board apparently said that they 'would not vote to give a contract for milk to a Jew'. A report of this meeting appeared in the *Hackney Gazette* (16 September 1911). The following week, a spokesman for the Board (one of those, moreover, who had made anti-Semitic remarks) stated that the failure to give the contract to the lowest tender was a mistake and had now been rectified. It was denied that any Jewish boycott was intended. (Cited in Robb, p. 204.)

barrassed more people than it made additionally hostile. In fact, in a situation where most people—whether agitators, followers, or potential followers—feared being thought anti-Semitic, the accusation of anti-Semitism became as potentially powerful a political weapon as the use of prejudice itself. This was so, partly because such an accusation exercised a strong effect over the Jewish community itself and made life very difficult for the Jewish anti-aliens. Thus, A. T. Williams of the London County Council and the British Brothers League, complains:

> The difficulty of getting witnesses up before this Commission is very great. From the very first, when there was an agitation started in the East End to press upon Parliament that these aliens should be kept out, the Jewish press has always endeavoured to persuade its readers that this was an anti-Jewish, and not an anti-alien question.[1]

However, the charge of anti-Semitism was not merely a handicap in gaining Jewish support for the anti-alien cause. For, as Arnold White noted:

> The disinclination of every Englishman worthy of the name to harass the persecuted Russian Hebrew, or to run counter to enlightened Jewish opinion by undertaking the invidious task of advocating restriction makes it difficult for a mere private person to obtain trustworthy evidence; and it has left the case for restriction in the hands of violent and unreasonable men, who neither appreciate the enormous weight of the reasons advanced for leaving things as they are, nor refrain from exaggerating the evils that exist, and who therefore weaken the case for restriction by exaggeration.[2]

White shows that he is partially aware that this process was, in fact, something of a vicious circle: the greater the predominance of violent and unreasonable men amongst those agitating for restriction, the greater the suspicion of anti-Semitism and the greater the embarrassment of the agitators. Councillor Belcher of Stepney told the Royal Commission that if it were a religious or racial question, 'I should have nothing to do with it'.[3] A. T. Williams took such convictions further. He was, apparently, so perturbed that Arnold White's 'violent and unreasonable men' might undermine his reputation as 'an Englishman worthy of the name', that he actually dissociated himself from the British Brothers League, the organization

[1] R.C., Vol. II, p. 105. [2] Ibid., p. 105. [3] Ibid., p. 146.

which he had helped to form. In a speech to the predominantly Jewish Whitechapel Costers Union he stated that 'certain members . . . had taken up an anti-Jewish position', and for this reason 'he could not throw in his lot with them'.[1]

Life in many ways would have been much easier for the agitators if only the immigrant had not been a Jew. The immigrants' racial background may have made him a more conspicuous candidate for the role of scapegoat, but as the agitators sometimes realized with remarkable clarity:

> It was a question if undesirable aliens were to be admitted because they were Jews, for the chief difficulty was the Jewish element.[2]

[1] *Jewish Chronicle* (14 February 1902), p. 8.

[2] A. T. Williams proposing an anti-alien resolution to the London County Council, 15 October 1901; quoted in *Jewish Chronicle* (25 October 1901), p. 16.

PART III

ALIEN IMMIGRATION AND THE LIBERALS

VI

The Liberals: Ideology and the Immigrant

> Liberalism in its Victorian plenitude had been an easy burden to bear for it contained . . . a various and valuable collection of gold, stocks, bibles, progressive thoughts, and decent inhibitions. . . .
>
> But somehow or other, as the century turned, the burden of Liberalism grew more and more irksome; it began to give out a dismal rattling sound; it was just as if some unfortunate miracle had been performed upon its contents turning them into nothing more than bits of old iron, fragments of intimate crockery, and other relics of a domestic past.
>
> GEORGE DANGERFIELD[1]

For the Liberals—as for the agitators—the fact that the immigrant was a Jew created a special situation: just as it embarrassed and blurred the hostility of the agitators, so did it help to make it almost inevitable that the Liberals should welcome him. Although it was possible to attack the Aliens Bill—as the Liberals often did—purely on the pragmatic grounds that it was an unworkable piece of window-dressing, the driving force behind the Liberal attitude lay in their ideology. The immigrant was poor; he was a religious refugee; he was a Jew. As such, he carried with him attributes that inevitably aroused in the Liberal bosom every one of those emotions and attitudes which, even at times of maximum intra-party difference, had provided Victorian Liberalism with its unity, its emotional dynamism, and the fundamental tenets of its faith. At a time, moreover, when almost without exception those tenets were in other contexts being called into question (and at a time when the Liberals were threatened with no longer being the party of the left), the Liberal defence of the alien became a means of rediscovering identity, an act of nostalgia, harking back to a time when every Englishman 'was something of a Liberal at heart'. To attack the destitute Jewish immigrant was to attack Liberalism.

[1] Dangerfield, pp. 7–8.

The Liberals and Anti-Semitism

It was partly for this reason that, in the first place, anti-Semitism (or the suspicion of it) came to occupy a special place in the Liberal calendar of devilries. Specifically, of course, this prejudice offended one of the deepest and oldest of Liberal principles, that of religious toleration. This 'leading principle amongst Liberals'[1]—one which they liked to think was peculiarly their own—found its origins in the events of 1688 and in the Whig friendship with the Dissenters, and had since been reinforced by the influx of non-conformists (together with their consciences) into the party during the course of the nineteenth century. While it did not necessarily prevent a few local stalwarts from occasionally using anti-Semitism against Jewish Conservative opponents,[2] in general the sentiment made Liberals peculiarly susceptible to Christianity's guilt complex about the Jew. The *Manchester Guardian* was wont to remind its readers:

> Christians have reason to walk humbly in the presence of a Jew, for, if they associate themselves at all with the deeds of their ancestors, or take upon themselves the historical reputation of the faith they possess, they have a debt to bear which can never be discharged.[3]

Finally, as Jewish Liberals never tired of reminding their co-religionists, particularly if the latter had suffered such unforgivable absence of mind as to become Conservative, it had been the Liberals who had campaigned for, and, in 1859, finally carried into legislative effect,[4] the removal of Jewish

[1] Samuel Montagu's phrase, quoted in *Jewish Chronicle* (31 August 1888), p. 9.

[2] See, for example, the case of N. Cohen, unsuccessful Conservative candidate: 'On the mere rumour of my willingness to stand as the Unionist candidate for the Borough of Penryn, Falmouth, and Flushing, the local organ of the Liberal Party (owned by the Chairman of the Liberal Association) published an half column of sneers and gibes at my religion. A series of attacks followed week by week, not so much on me as on my religion . . . a reference to the "unscrupulous and deceptive character of the Hebrew"; then the readers were told in effect, that to vote for me was "to smite the Lord of Life in his face" and that, "If Mr. Cohen had the mind of a Bacon . . . it should not suffice to aid him in legislating for this country which owes so much to the Christian religion" and so on.' N. Cohen in letter to *Jewish Chronicle* (26 October 1900), p. 6.

[3] Quoted in *Jewish Chronicle* (22 May 1891), p. 6.

[4] The Act was, in fact, finally carried under a minority Conservative administration.

disabilities. The mere thought of so excellent an achievement could cause even Liberals trained to the emotionless objectivity of the English legal system to become quite carried away—as it did Mr. Atherley-Jones, member for North West Durham and a leading pro-alien, who, on the fiftieth anniversary of the Act under discussion, told an audience in Newcastle-upon-Tyne that:

> he was proud to be a member of the political party which was not merely the pioneer of the movement for the emancipation of the Jews, but was the instrument under Divine providence, for effecting that noble purpose.[1]

It was, therefore, more of a reflex action than the conscious use of a political weapon that caused the Liberals to attempt to discredit the anti-alien movement by tarring it with the brush of anti-Semitism. For whatever reason, however, they used this accusation constantly and with relish.

Charles Dilke, for instance, in language which revealed the special qualities that anti-Semitism was believed to possess over other forms of inter-group hostility, felt that he 'must warn those Conservatives who have thrown themselves into this agitation that they have raised a devil which they will find it difficult to lay'.[2]

Charles Trevelyan, the other spearhead of the Parliamentary pro-alien cause, was, if anything, more charitable, and told the House of Commons: 'Among many people already—not many in this House, but many people outside it—there is a frankly anti-Semitic movement.'[3]

As we shall see in Chapter VIII, the accusation of anti-Semitism also deeply embarrassed those Liberals who felt that the safety of their seats depended upon their conversion to anti-alienism. It meant that they had to declaim their innocence of anti-Semitism even more loudly and frequently than those who led the anti-alien movement. Yet, because of the almost equal embarrassment of at least a large section of grass-roots Liberal opinion even in the East End, the accusation also provided them with the opportunity—if they wished to take it—of, at least, excusing Liberal Parliamentary opposition to the

[1] Quoted in *Jewish Chronicle* (15 January 1909), p. 30.
[2] Hansard 4S H(133)1063, 25 April 1904.
[3] Ibid., 1082.

Aliens Bill by portraying it as a battle against anti-Semitism. For some, the accusation was even a reason for, and a means of, escaping the anti-alien embrace altogether. *Reynolds's News*, the mouthpiece of Liberal Labourism, which had, in 1895, been a strong and even violent supporter of the anti-alien cause, was given to complaining:

> . . . in the end, the native has to suffer; the bread is literally taken from his mouth by his alien competitor, and he finds himself wandering about the streets and roadsides of his native land, a starving and helpless outcast. Is it right? The urgency of taking steps to regulate and control foreign immigration has now become a matter of supreme importance.[1]

From May 1904, however, the same editor was writing long editorial after long editorial denouncing the Aliens Bill, under the caption 'THE TORY ANTI JEW BILL'.[2]

Closely connected, of course, with religious toleration was the Liberals' special attachment to the tradition of giving sympathy and hospitality to the persecuted of all nations—as they significantly termed it, 'the doctrine' of religious and political asylum. It was this, perhaps, which stirred the leading Liberal pro-aliens more than anything else. Thus, one of the two grounds on which the Liberal motion opposed the Second Reading of the 1904 Aliens Bill was that:

> this House . . . desires to assure itself before assenting to the Aliens Bill that sufficient regard is had in the proposed measure to the retention of the principle of asylum for the victims of persecution.[3]

The same sentiment provided the focus for many of the Liberal amendments during the Committee stage in 1905, as well as the grounds for Dilke's unrepentant opposition to the very end.

Quite apart from other considerations, the aliens were fleeing from anti-Semitism and as such were, in Dilke's words, 'the victims of the most cruel religious persecution . . . of all the persecutions of modern times'.[4] While the Russian pogroms

[1] Quoted in *Jewish Chronicle* (26 July 1895), p. 12. It is probably a not insignificant fact that, at this time, the editor of *Reynolds News*, W. M. Thompson, was standing as Liberal candidate for Limehouse against H. S. Samuel, a leading anti-alien.

[2] See, for instance, *Reynolds News* (23 April 1905), p. 1.

[3] Hansard 4S H(133)1062, 25 April 1904.

[4] Hansard 4S H(8)1188, 11 February 1893.

brought protests from all sections of English society, none had quite that special quality possessed by Mr. Gladstone's 'thunder' at its choicest:

> Russia must be regarded as a standing menace to civilization and progress. And the world must wage a crusade against her. Her sons, wherever met, must be reminded that, in spite of her thin veneer of Parisian culture, they are members of a barbaric community; that their Government is the incarnation of inhumanity, intolerance and irreligion.[1]

Here again, in defending the Jewish immigrant from this standpoint, the Liberals were also defending party history and mythology. In holding up the Huguenot as proof that the Jew would make good, they were remembering in the first place that it had been the Whigs who had welcomed the Huguenot and Palatine refugees in the late seventeenth and early eighteenth centuries. Secondly, they were paying obeisance to the memory of Lord Palmerston, whose career had spanned and dominated some thirty-five years of the mid-nineteenth century. Palmerston (though he had been a Liberal in very little else) had been a Liberal *par excellence* in the matter of making England the haven for the persecuted of all nations. For it was he, in fact (*circa* 1860), who had erected a mere principle into:

> *that law*[2] of hospitality by which we have invariably been guided with regard to foreigners seeking asylum in this country. Any foreigner, whatever his nation, whatever his political creed, whatever his political offences against his own Government . . . may find in these realms a safe and secure asylum as long as he obeys the law of the land.[3]

We may note here that with regard to religious and political asylum, as with toleration, there was by no means a clear-cut conflict between the consequences of extending Liberal ideology to embrace the alien, on the one hand, and the assumed interests of that section of the grass-roots affected by his presence, on the other. Nobody really wanted to exclude the refugee; and had anyone suggested that one should, there would, perhaps, have been indignation even in the East End. Even the anti-

[1] Gladstone's contribution to the *Jewish Chronicle*'s 'Darkest Russia' supplement (4 September 1891).

[2] Writer's emphasis.

[3] Quoted by Rosebery, Hansard 4S H(27)129, 17 July 1894.

aliens, after all, preferred to argue that the alien was not a refugee at all. Moreover, when we come to consider the interactions between the levels of the party, we shall find East End Liberal M.P.s, candidates, and their audiences at least going through the motions of pressing for amendments safeguarding the principle of asylum. It was upon this lip-service that the Liberals were able to rely when, in the course of administering the Act of 1906, they relaxed its provisions.

Free Trade

A less direct, but equally crucial, factor in determining the Liberal attitude towards the alien was the long- and dearly-held belief in the doctrine of free trade. This was a principle and an achievement which, by stretching the facts a little (the Peelites, including Gladstone, had, after all, ultimately joined the Liberals), the Liberals could claim to be peculiarly their own. If one refused to protect British goods from foreign competition, then one could hardly protect the labour which produced them from the competition of foreign workmen. The latter step was not only illogical, not only bad for British labour, but was also an insidious movement in the direction of the former. In any case, the Liberals believed, England had 'gained most among the nations of the world from the free circulation and competition of labour'.[1] Finally, it was far better that the cheap goods produced by the aliens should help the export trade, rather than having such goods flooding the British market from abroad—which was what would happen, the Liberals argued, if the alien was turned away.

There were also other factors which reinforced this purely logical connection. In the first place, just as there was a strong link in personnel between the protectionist and anti-alien causes, so, too, were several of those who felt most strongly about free trade amongst the prominent leaders of the pro-aliens. Thus, Winston Churchill, who boasted that it was he who had murdered the 1904 Aliens Bill in its Committee stage, had crossed party lines on the issue of free trade but two months previously. In 1900, Major J. E. B. Seely, one of Churchill's chief partners in the aforementioned crime, had

[1] Asquith in reply to a Trades Union Congress delegation, quoted in *Jewish Chronicle* (18 January 1895), p. 7.

performed a similar manoeuvre for similar reasons (and had been re-elected by his constituents on the Isle of Wight).

Secondly, free trade had also provided the one issue around which the Liberals had been able to unite (with some assistance from Joseph Chamberlain) after their total disarray about imperialism and the Boer War. This disarray, moreover, had been the lowest point at the end of some five years of mutual recrimination. A party which had rediscovered its *raison d'être* around the generality of a principle which was, for the first time since its inception, under serious attack, could scarcely begin eroding it in any of its particulars.

Finally, let us note that free trade was also a very popular doctrine. When aliens legislation was presented as a measure to protect labour 'against the competition from good men coming from other parts of the world', trade unionists made, at least, the disapproving noises that were expected of them.[1] If, then, restriction could be presented as an erosion of free trade, or, still better subsumed altogether under that heading—as was the tendency of Liberal election literature (see Chapter VIII)—popular protests might well be loud and indignant. Thus, Joseph Chamberlain's remark that he regarded the second Aliens Bill less as a means of keeping out undesirables than as 'a step towards much greater things',[2] not only caused some red faces on the Conservative front bench; it also 'prevented a certain number of [Liberal] members from voting for the Bill who otherwise would have done so'.[3]

The Poverty Line

Perhaps, the least obviously nostalgic Liberal objection to the Aliens Bill was that it was unfair: it was aimed at the so-called destitute alien, undesirability was to be determined not by a

[1] Witness the exchange between Herbert Asquith, Home Secretary, and a Trades Union Congress delegation pressing their organization's anti-alien resolution of 1894: 'When I am asked in vague and indefinite terms to assent to the exclusion of foreign labour [cries of "No"]. . . .' Quoted in *Jewish Chronicle* (18 January 1895), p. 7.

[2] Hansard 4S H(145)764, 2 May 1905.

[3] Emmot, Liberal M.P. for Oldham, ibid., 768. In fact, only one Liberal, Samuel Smith, voted with the Conservatives, and he was voting against 'the foreign women who infest our streets and the vile men who live upon their earnings'. All the other Liberal anti-aliens joined the Liberal leadership in abstaining, in spite of at least Buxton's pre-Chamberlain intention of voting for the Second Reading.

man's character or capability, but by the amount of money he possessed. The Bill was a means of drawing 'a line between rich and poor. Poverty was to be more loathsome than lunacy, idiocy and disease.'[1] It proposed 'to keep out a Jew when he is poor and admit a Jew when he is rich'.[2] It was 'the one great fault' which Campbell-Bannerman could discern even when all amendment was done, and which caused him to lead his party into the Opposition lobby against the Third Reading in July 1905.

This was neither an obviously, nor totally, backward-looking objection. In part, of course, it was the normal reaction of any humanitarian party of the left, of any party which aspired to monopolize sympathy for the underdog. The arguments were, on the surface, no different from those used by 'the representatives of labour' against such legislation—although the latter were generally just as concerned to keep rich foreigners out as to let poor ones in. Indeed, when some Liberals became really carried away, they could sound remarkably socialistic when taking this line. Thus, Major Seely felt that the Bill would destroy a happy situation where 'we can now say that where a man is naked we clothe him; when he is a stranger, we take him in';[3] and, two months later, he could be heard hailing:

> the still higher doctrine of the great commonwealth of humanity held by honourable members on that side of the house, and it was because they believed that humanity could be regarded as a great commonwealth that they opposed the policy of exclusion of the poor and miserable.[4]

In spite of Seely, however, for most Liberals, the argument about the poverty line was, to a greater or lesser extent, a nostalgic one. And here we find a continuous linkage with the other Liberal objections to the Bill: for, when the Liberals objected to the exclusion of a man merely because he was poor, they were not basing their arguments on the egalitarian assumptions of the Socialists. When they spoke of England having 'reaped marked and permanent advantage' from her tradition of hospitality to all comers, when they envisaged the alien following in the steps of the Huguenot and succeeding just

[1] Churchill, Hansard 4S H(148)290, 27 June 1905.
[2] Major Seely, Hansard 4S H(145)757, 2 May 1905.
[3] Ibid., 759.
[4] Hansard 4S H(149)1261, 19 July 1905.

as he had done, and when they objected to the protection of British workmen, in all these cases, they were implicitly thinking of the sort of society upon whose assumptions Liberalism—at least in its nineteenth-century form—had been founded. Here, as in their idealization of the Jew which we are about to examine, they were harking back to the society and social values envisaged by Samuel Smiles.

Samuel Smiles

Smiles might almost be called the prophet of mid-century. The ideas which he broadcast in a series of sensationally popular best-sellers[1] over the third quarter of the nineteenth century, were by no means original. In a sense, he merely translated the Protestant ethic into the vernacular.

He believed that competition was 'the great social law of God'; that, in other words, it was both natural and moral. Its ill effects neither could, not should, be in any way ameliorated, except by the universal exercise of individual self-help; for it was only when the latter was absent that the former became apparent. Charity was, therefore, dangerous, and 'the truest philanthropists are those who endeavour to . . . help the poor to help themselves'.[2]

In fact, upward social mobility was within the grasp of everyone who liked to put his mind to it. All that was needed were the presence of one precondition and the exercise of two basic qualities. The precondition, apparently, was poverty. However, while 'the poor were often the happiest of people', they were only happy so long as they looked upon their state as 'a necessary stimulus to work' and as a temporary stage on the way to higher things. After all, 'the happiest part of men's lives is while they are battling with poverty and gradually raising themselves above it'.[3]

The qualities necessary for success in this battle were simple, almost prosaic; but then:

[1] His first and best-known work, *Self Help*, published in 1859, had sold 55,000 copies by 1865, 150,000 by 1889, and 250,000 by 1905—'sales which far exceeded those of the great nineteenth-century novels'. Asa Briggs, *Victorian People* (London, Odhams Press, 1954), p. 45.

[2] Samuel Smiles, *Thrift* (London, 1875), p. 304.

[3] Ibid., p. 301.

the men who have most moved the world have not been so much men of genius . . . as men of intense mediocre abilities, and untiring perseverance.[1]

The first of these qualities was industry, a composite of 'attention, application, accuracy, method, punctuality and despatch' and seen in 'the repetition of little acts'. As such, it was 'the main root and spring of all that we call progress in individuals and civilization in nations'.[2] Without it, life was 'worthless', 'a mere state of moral coma'. The poor man who laboured diligently and energetically would not only make short work of 'irksome drudgery and dry details' but would soon discover that:

Practical industry, wisely and vigorously applied, always produces its due effects. . . . All may not rise equally, yet each, on the whole, very much according to his deserts.[3]

For this to happen, however, a second quality was needed: thrift. Like industry, this was a habit essential to the well-being both of society and of the individuals who composed it, for 'it is only when labourers begin to save that the results of civilization accumulate'.[4] Money itself was valueless, but saving it gave rise to independence and self-respect, which 'is the root of most of the virtues—of cleanliness, chastity, reverence, honesty and sobriety'.[5] For this reason, 'a few pence or shillings laid aside' could be a wonderful means of 'securing moral elevation'.

Basically, anyone—even the poorest labourer—was capable of being thrifty: 'Let no man say he cannot economise. There are few persons who cannot contrive to save a few pence or shillings weekly.'[6]

It was 'merely a matter of self denial and private economy', a mode of living which 'dispenses with everything which is not essential and avoids all methods of living that are wasteful and extravagant'.[7] The trouble was that few were prepared to follow this wise course of action. There was far too much misery and social degradation in the world, and it was 'for the most part, voluntary and self-imposed—the result of idleness, thriftlessness, intemperance and misconduct'.[8] Those 'mob

[1] Smiles, *Self Help* (London, 1859 and 1959), p. 117.
[2] Ibid., p. 265. [3] Ibid., p. 264. [4] Smiles, *Thrift*, p. 8.
[5] Ibid., p. 22. [6] Ibid., p. 13. [7] Ibid., p. 16. [8] Ibid., p. 39.

orators' who encouraged millions to cry 'Who will help us?' should remember that: 'society mainly consists of two classes . . . the provident and the improvident, the thrifty and the thriftless, the Haves and the Haves not [*sic*].'[1]

If the working classes were poor, it was because they:

> very much underestimate themselves. Though they receive salaries or wages beyond the average earnings of professional men, yet many of them have no other thought than that of living in mean houses, and spending their surplus time and money in drink.[2]

To waste money in this way was, to Smiles, an act of extreme folly; for if only men would stop this kind of wastefulness, they could 'easily become capitalists'. This was the centre-piece of the Smilesean edifice. It was the carrot which Smiles constantly dangled before the noses of his readers. For, as he reminded them over and over again:

> One of the results of industry and thrift is the accumulation of Capital. Capital represents the self-denial, the providence and enterprise of the past. The most successful accumulators of capital have, in all times, risen from the ranks of labour itself. They are the working men who have shot ahead of their fellows, and who now give employment instead of receiving it.[3]

The Smilesean Symbol

Although Smiles himself was to live until 1905, the relevance of his advice to the social and economic circumstances of his readers declined considerably during the last quarter of the nineteenth century. The industrial system steadily became less competitive and far more impersonal, and, consequently, Smiles's worker-to-small-capitalist ideal became less the far-off prize and more the infrequently remembered dream. As Dangerfield puts it: 'The independent small entrepreneur—that dream of Liberal economics—had vanished from the earth.'[4] Moreover, great ostentation increasingly accompanied great wealth, and even the working classes began to expect a certain 'standard of life' which was above the level of mere subsistence. As Smiles himself noted unhappily in 1887: 'We no longer know how to live upon little.'[5]

[1] Smiles, *Thrift*, p. 9. [2] Ibid., p. 55. [3] Ibid., p. 184.

[4] Dangerfield, p. 219.

[5] Samuel Smiles, *Duty* (London, 1881 and 1905), p. 76.

In *Duty*, which was more of a personal commentary on the times than an exhortation, Smiles also accurately discerned another factor, one which he regarded as the main evil of our time. Towards the turn of the century, there was:

a widening chasm which divides the various classes of society. The rich shrink back from the poor, the poor shrink back from the rich. The one class withholds its sympathy and guidance, the other withholds its obedience and respect.[1]

Smiles wrote this in 1887, the very year that the arrival of the alien Jews was first noticed in Parliament. He provides the clue to, perhaps, the most important ideological reason for the almost inevitable welcome that the Liberals were to give the immigrant. Partly because of the characteristics that the immigrant brought with him, partly because of certain characteristics of Anglo-Jewish society, and most importantly because of the sort of party that the Liberals—for all their protestations of sympathy for the working classes—still remained, the Jewish immigrant took on a symbolic role. As I hope to show, he became, in the first place, the symbol of the slowly crumbling but still nostalgically satisfying Victorian economic and social morality which we have just summarized. Secondly, he became the inverse image of all that many Liberals, secretly or openly, felt was wrong with 'our working classes'. If, after 1906, 'the Liberals advanced upon social reform with noisy mouths and mouse-like feet', one reason was that they still believed that Smiles was right and that reforms merely performed the tiresome task of helping those who left self-help unheeded, those who wilfully rejected the capitalist ethic.

Let us first note that the alien Jew in many ways fitted the Smilesean ideal very closely. He was perhaps, the only working example of the principles of *laissez-faire* and individual self-help that had ever existed. He was industrious; he worked long hours for low wages; he was thrifty. He was very sober, very law-abiding, and so religious that he was given to denouncing the Anglo-Jew for moral laxity. He was intensely competitive, and his great ambition, and, frequently, his crowning achievement in life, was to become 'a small master', with the minimum of delay. Anglo-Jewish charity, it is true, was

[1] Smiles, *Duty*, p. 296.

extremely generous, but its sole aim—that of giving a man the means of making himself independent—was one of which Smiles, if he noted it, must heartily have approved. Moreover, the Jewish community as a whole—probably for the very reason that it was a community—seems to have remained relatively isolated from the processes of social cleavage that Smiles, unhappily, noted going on elsewhere.

The parallelism, needless to say, was not complete. Not every alien Jew was 'typical' and, of those who were, many, perhaps, came close to Smilesean caricature. Even Smiles, deeply as he believed in the value of competition, had softened his conception somewhat with notions of 'self-sacrifice', 'duty', and 'gentlemanly character'. Thus, he would scarcely have favoured, for instance, the degree of ruthlessness that the Jewish immigrant often brought to the struggle—something which Beatrice Potter interpreted as a total absence of social morality, and which Herbert Samuel attributed to the ghetto mentality. Nevertheless, the identity between actuality and image was sufficiently close to encourage the nostalgia of anyone who felt so inclined, and the Liberals, as we shall now see, most certainly did.

As far as the Parliamentary Liberals were concerned, some of the most persistently enthusiastic of the symbolizers were to be found not surprisingly amongst the Liberal peers. Thus, whilst serving on the Sweating Commission, for example, Lord Thring, much to Arnold White's disgust, drew the following inference from the latter gentleman's statements:

> I want to get this clearer; I understand you to say that these men, paupers though they be, are men of unparalleled industry, that the majority of them get up in the world?[1]

Similarly, no Liberal speech in the Upper House was really complete without some fairly strong Smilesean overtones. Lord Ribblesdale, in the debate on the Aliens Bill of 1898, spoke of the immigrants being the source of 'small inventions'; they were 'a very feeble but what may prove a very useful folk'.[2] Lord Farrer waxed eloquently about a man who was 'a very efficient and able workman who would be a credit to English industry, and a man whom English employers would

[1] S.C., Vol. I, p. 47. [2] Hansard 4S H(59)736, 20 June 1898.

be glad to have in their factories';[1] and Lord Thring spoke warmly of how the aliens became 'some of the best workmen to be had in the East End of London'.[2] Meanwhile, earlier in the debate, Lord Grey had made perfectly clear what was on everybody's mind when he objected to religious refugees being called 'the meanest of their race', and alternatively described them as:

the people possessing the best enterprise and endowed with the best brain power. These men, when they arrive, may come destitute, but the evidence goes to show that, after a few years' stay . . . when they become assimilated to our English life, they form an industrious portion of the community, contribute to the taxation of the country and become a source of wealth.[3]

Equally enthusiastic idealizations in the same terms could be heard reverberating from the Liberal benches in the Commons. If they did not always make such explicit reference to Smilesean virtue, Liberal speakers, almost without exception, projected the Jew in the image of the Huguenot, and, in doing so, sometimes showed the special significance that the previous waves of immigrants possessed for the Liberals. For instance, James Joicey, M.P. for Chester-le-Street and company chairman,

personally knew some gentlemen who had arrived in this country as alien poor and to whom this country owed very much. These gentlemen had become wealthy and respected citizens.[4]

The two most prominent pro-alien leaders, Dilke and Trevelyan, were radicals of the most modern kind. (Dilke was by 1902 virtually fellow-travelling with the Labour party, and Trevelyan was later to become the first Labour President of the Board of Education in 1924 and again in 1929–30.) Thus they were presumably unsympathetic to much of the capitalist ethic that produced such nostalgia amongst rank-and-file Liberals. Yet even they watered down the symbolism only to the extent of giving it a little less prominence and occasionally referring to Jewish vices as well as Jewish virtues. Trevelyan remembered that they were gamblers, as well as being 'fairly sober and industrious'.[5] Dilke went further and spoke of 'the regular lives led by these destitute aliens, and the

[1] Hansard 4S H(59)744, 20 June 1898. [2] Ibid., 746.
[3] Ibid., 734. [4] Hansard 4S H(148)844, 3 July 1905.
[5] Hansard 4S H(133)1081, 25 April 1904.

total absence of drinking among them',[1] and significantly singled out only the quality of thrift when he told the Commons:

I know a good deal about them, having travelled in their country, and seen them at home, and I can say that these persons . . . are a thrifty class. . . .[2]

For many other more conventional Liberals, indulgence in the imagery of perfection was even more tempting. Mundella, in 1893, informed his fellow M.P.s that:

Since 1886, he had been in constant communication with the foreigners in his own constituency and he could testify that, as a rule, they were fairly intelligent, exceedingly industrious and extremely sober.[3]

Eighteen years later, among other Liberals, we discover George Harwood—M.P. for Bolton, cotton magnate, extreme militant pro-alien',[4] and something of a radical in a way that Liberals were allowed to be[5]—revealing both his own and perhaps his party's basically Smilesean soul, by arguing that:

. . . there was no ground for the contention that the class of people who come here were paupers. . . . There were fewer paupers amongst these people than in any other class of the community. And why? For the simple reason that they have been strained through the filter of self-denial. They were a superior class, and to talk of them as paupers was monstrous. He [Harwood] came from a community that had learnt its business from alien immigrants, the people of Lancashire having got their industry from the Huguenots. He, therefore, was against committing a suicidal act.[6]

However, although they may sometimes have referred to a 'superior class', the Parliamentary Liberals, no matter how excited they became, never explicitly drew any favourable comparison between Gentile and idealized Jew. Liberals outside of Parliament, on the other hand, were inhibited neither by working-class votes, nor by the fabled odiousness of such exercises.

It is, perhaps, neither surprising nor, from our present point

[1] Hansard 4S H (133) 1081, 25 April 1904.
[2] Hansard 4S H(8)1188, 11 February 1893.
[3] Ibid., 1211.
[4] Harwood seems to have taken over the leadership of the pro-aliens after 1906, and had been the only Liberal on the Grand Committee to refuse assent to the Liberal 'compromise' Bill to exclude criminal and diseased aliens.
[5] He was in favour of land nationalization.
[6] Hansard 4S H(148)823, 3 July 1905.

of view, particularly significant that Jewish Liberals should have been making these sorts of comparisons. Their doing so, in part, merely fits into the general picture of rising Jewish militancy that we shall be describing in the following chapter. What is more interesting is that it should be a common and sometimes quite savage practice amongst Gentile counterparts.

Sometimes, such comparisons were no more than Aesop-like strictures to 'our working classes' to read, mark, and inwardly digest the shining example held before them.[1] Mary Hancock Thompson told the West of Scotland Women's Liberal Association that the aliens:

> soon find ways of supporting themselves by their industry and they show a good example to their English neighbours by their thrift and by their remarkable freedom from drunkenness.[2]

Similarly in September 1895, a leader in the Liberal *Echo* had pondered the problem of why the East End Jew was apparently more successful than his Gentile neighbour and hit upon the answer:

> It is rare for a Jew to be arrested for crime or disorder, and still more rare for one of them to be found in our workhouses. While agitating against these immigrants, our own poor would do well to learn from them the virtues of thrift, perseverance, orderliness and endurance.[3]

More often, these comparisons were more direct and sometimes took the form of pseudo-sociological explanation—and here we see the influence of Social Darwinism in giving a sort of freakish death-bed vigour to the doctrine of *laissez-faire*. This is found in its mildest form in an article by George R. Sims in the *Tribune*, significantly the only Liberal paper agitating for the outright repeal of the Act. According to Sims:

[1] It is significant that the tendency to believe the foreign workmen superior, or at least, to hold up the foreign workmen as an example to their English counterparts, was in itself a Smilesean characteristic. As Smiles himself noted in *Thrift* (p. 231): 'One thing . . . remains to be said of foreign workmen generally. Although they do not work so hard as the English, they take much better care of their earnings. They are exceedingly frugal and economical. Frenchmen are much soberer than Englishmen and much better mannered. They are, on the whole, greatly more provident than English workmen . . . [and] much more independent.'

[2] *Jewish Chronicle* (17 February 1899), p. 10.

[3] *Echo* (10 September 1895), quoted in *Jewish Chronicle* (13 September 1895).

It is to their sobriety and their devotion to their children that the Jewish aliens largely owe their early success in a strange land, which enables them to push on and, gradually improving their condition and adding to their means, to displace and dispossess a less sober and less domesticated people... slowly and surely, the sober race is ousting the intemperate race.[1]

Such pontifications, however, were sometimes delivered in much stronger terms, and here the idealized Jewish immigrant tended to become as much a stick with which to beat the Gentile population of the East End in particular, and the working class in general, as an object of sympathy. Thus an 'Ulster Liberal' indignantly asked the readers of the *Newcastle Daily Chronicle*:

Can it really be maintained that men who work for low wages . . . are injuring their neighbours . . .? How is it that they are willing to work for lower wages than other people round about them, and how is it that they can get through more work in a day? The facts are simply these. Jews are not addicted to drink; they can therefore afford to work for lower wages than their less temperate neighbours; and they are more frugal and industrious than most English working-class people are in these days.[2]

In the face of defenders such as these, even militant Jews must have occasionally wondered whether they did not need saving from their friends. They must have pondered the problem still harder when they came across this final example of rampant Liberal pro-alienism. For Charles Rolleston, writing in what was laughably called the *New Liberal Review*, showed just what could be done on the Jewish immigrants' behalf when Samuel Smiles was allied with Charles Darwin in the Liberal pro-alien mind. In doing so, he summarizes for us just what it was that basically attracted many Liberals to the Jewish immigrant.

Rolleston discovered 'amongst the submerged' of the East End 'two distinct orders, the very poorest section of the Jews, and a decadent non-Jewish population'. Both were poor, but whereas the Gentiles were almost invariably hopeless degenerates, brutalized and worthless, they were gradually being replaced by a better type of Jewish alien who:

enters the lists of the national struggle . . . endowed with a more than average capacity for work, together with an intense instinct for gain.

[1] The *Tribune* (18 February 1907), quoted in *Jewish Chronicle* (22 February 1907), p. 32.

[2] Quoted in *Jewish Chronicle* (30 December 1898).

Neither a loafer nor an idler, he appreciates the value of time and money; he is sober, self-denying and intelligent, working with the supreme object of placing himself in a wealthier and better position . . . he is not a hopeless degenerate, but very progressive. . . . When this man gets on in life so as to afford better food and healthier surroundings . . . [he becomes] in the second and third generations . . . a self-respecting businessman, thoroughly English in sentiment.[1]

One Liberal, in fact, carried his nostalgia to its ultimate conclusion, and decided that the whole anti-alien agitation was 'at the bottom got up by trades unionists . . . partly a trades union conspiracy against freedom of labour, partly a socialist attack upon industry and thrift'.[2] Inaccurate though this description was, it provides us with a clue (as we shall see in Chapter X) to the point at which the pro-aliens of the old left parted company with those of the new.

[1] *New Liberal Review* (March 1904), quoted in *Jewish Chronicle* (11 March 1904), p. 15.

[2] T. Dundas Pillans, *Liberty Review* (March 1904), quoted in *Jewish Chronicle* (1 April 1904).

VII

The Liberals: Administering the Act

> By a strange irony, the Liberal party which displayed so unsympathetic a demeanour towards the Aliens Bill is now called upon to inaugurate the operation of the Aliens Act.[1]

> These are democratic days.[2]

In general, the Liberal Government's administration of the Aliens Act was consistent with the party's previous attitude towards the Bill. However, it was in some ways a rather uneven performance, and it is significant that in spite of pressure from several Liberal back-benchers, the Labour party, and the Jewish community, the Act was neither repealed nor amended. In fact, the over-all verdict on Liberal policy[3] must be that whilst it largely nullified the effect of the Act upon all but a small minority of those migrants who came to England, it did little to modify those provisions which deterred many from coming at all. Thus, one really needs to ask two questions: Why did Liberal consistency go so far? Why did it go no further?

Administering the Act

Herbert Gladstone, the new Liberal Home Secretary, advanced upon the Aliens Act with a demeanour that was at once resigned, contemptuous, and patronizing. He believed that nothing but odium awaited those who had to operate the Act, and that its framers had, in any case, made that task an impossibility. However, since 'he had to recognize that the Act was the law of the land', he was at least ostensibly determined—rather like a cat with a piece of stale fish—'to get as much good as he could out of it'.[4] This was the only way, for: 'If the Act is a

[1] *Jewish Chronicle* (15 December 1905), p. 9.

[2] *Jewish Chronicle* (17 April 1908), p. 11.

[3] Here I am largely excluding consideration of the clauses relating to the expulsion of criminal and diseased aliens about which there had always been considerable bi-partisan agreement.

[4] Hansard 4S H(153)158, 5 March 1906.

bad Act, we cannot prove that to the satisfaction of all parties unless we have experience of its working.'[1]

In fact, his first actions were, at least from the point of view of the anti-aliens, interpretable more as a search for proof of the Act's inoperability than as a means of obtaining 'good out of it'. For, having signed the regulations drawn up at the instruction of his predecessor, Akers Douglas, and having clarified them by a memorandum of his own, Gladstone then proceeded to modify them fairly radically.

In the first place, from 20 March 1906, reporters were allowed to attend all meetings of the Immigration Boards—which represented a fairly important concession since much of the campaign against the Act was being conducted via the publication of hair-raising examples of its cruelty in the columns of the Jewish and Liberal Press. However, of more importance was a second appendix to the regulations directing that only vessels carrying twenty or more aliens (rather than twelve or more, as had previously been the case)[2] were to be classified as 'immigrant ships' within the meaning of the Act.[3] In effect, this meant that aliens could now enter the country without being subject to inspection if they came in groups of nineteen, rather than, as previously, in groups of eleven.

By far the most crucial modification in the operation of the Act, however, had been made some two weeks earlier when Gladstone, in a circular letter to the Immigration Boards, had attempted to increase the flexibility of the clause intended to safeguard religious and political asylum. Because of the Conservative Government's eagerness to reach bi-partisan agreement on this issue in the Committee and Report stages of the Bill, this clause had, from the start, provided a fairly sizeable loophole. For it stated that:

> in the case of an immigrant who proves that he is seeking admission to this country solely to avoid prosecution or punishment on religious or political grounds, or for an offence of a political character, or persecution

[1] Hansard 4S H(153)1322, 14 March 1906.

[2] The Act had originally fixed the number at twenty, 'or such number as shall be fixed by order of the Secretary of State'. Akers Douglas had subsequently altered this to twelve.

[3] *Regulations made by the Home Secretary under the Aliens Act*, 'Appendix', Cd. 2879, 1906 (S.P. 1906, XCVI, pp. 279 f.), Sections II, III, and IV.

involving danger of imprisonment or danger to life and limb, on account of religious belief, leave to land shall not be refused on the ground of want of means.[1]

Now, partly under the influence of the wholesale Jewish massacres following in the aftermath of the Russian Revolution, that loophole became a yawning gap. For, in his letter, the Home Secretary, whilst prepared to realize the difficulty of obtaining corroboration for an immigrant's claim to be a refugee, expressed the hope, nevertheless, that:

having regard to the present disturbed condition of certain parts of the Continent, the benefit of the doubt, where any doubt exists, may be given in favour of any immigrants who allege that they are fleeing from religious or political persecution . . . and that leave to land may be given.[2]

In the case of the Immigration officers, over whose deliberations the Home Secretary had more control than he had over the Immigration Boards, this expression of hope became an instruction.

This was not all, for the opening paragraph of the letter appeared to widen the categories of those exempted from the provisions of the Act to the point of allowing admittance even to some of those about whom there could be no 'doubt' at all. Parliament, Gladstone felt, had 'never intended' that the provisions of the Act should be applied in such a way as to exclude 'considerations as to whether refusal to land would involve great personal hardship or suffering'. Specifically included here, apart from refugees, were women and children, and immigrants who were seriously, though not infectiously, ill.

Those anti-aliens who had survived the electoral massacre at the beginning of the year saw these changes as drastic and fundamental. Meetings of protest were organized in the East End and some 150 Unionist Associations held a meeting to decide how best to organize public opinion against such administrative rapine. Evans Gordon bewailed what 'amounted, in fact, to a repeal of the main provisions of an Act of Parliament which had not yet been three months in operation'.[3] The actual

[1] Aliens Bill, 1905, Number 277, Clause I, 3(c).

[2] *Regulations Made by the Home Secretary Under the Aliens Act*, p. 30.

[3] Hansard 4S H(153)1312, 14 March 1906.

effect of these modifications is very difficult to measure, however, because we do not know how many immigrants would have been rejected under a Conservative Home Secretary.[1] Moreover, the regulations drawn up under Akers Douglas were in operation for two months only before being modified by Gladstone's circular, and during that period the officials may well have been marking time. What we can say definitely is that during the first five years of its operation (see Table, p. 107) in terms of the number of people actually rejected, the Act rather affirmed the misgivings of the Jewish Liberal who described it as being 'an elephant engaged to catch a flea'. The ratio of those rejected to those liable to inspection was generally low. In 1906, the year of maximum persecution and immigration, and presumably of maximum benefit of the doubt, it was very low indeed. Moreover, if one excludes from the reckoning those rejected because they were suffering from infectious disease (the one reason for exclusion about which there had never been much disagreement)[2] the ratios became lower still.

At this point, Liberal policy can, in fact, be seen as a brave gesture to consistency. Although for the extreme pro-aliens there still remained a number of unremedied grievances, including, for some, the very existence of the Act itself, the Liberals probably did about as much as was possible to soften its effect without actually amending or repealing it. Even where cases of injustice still occurred, the Home Secretary could have done little to remedy or prevent them without taking powers over the deliberations of the Immigration Boards which were not granted to him by the Act. Moreover, although the Liberals did little directly to nullify the deterrent effect of the Act, it is reasonable to assume, in the first place, that, in 1906, they could at most have only half believed in its efficacy. Secondly, even assuming that they did believe in deterrence, it is arguable (again from the vantage point of 1906) that Gladstone's letter possessed a manifestly even chance of seriously eroding it. Further than this, in the years that followed 1906,[3] although Russian and Polish Jews were entering England at an average

[1] The Act came into operation on 1 January 1906.

[2] In 1904, after the rejection of the first Aliens Bill, the Liberals had produced a Bill to exclude diseased and criminal aliens—a compromise rejected by the Government.

[3] A year in which 12,832 'Russians and Poles' arrived.

Ratio of Immigrant Rejection to Admission Before and After Appeal 1906–1910

	1	2	3	4	5	6	7
	Number of alien steerage passengers not accounted for as trans-migrants, sailors, etc.*	Total of column 1 rejected in first instance	Total rejected on appeal to Immi-gration Boards	Total of column 3 rejected because of means	Total of column 3 rejected because of disease	Ratio of column 2 to column 1	Ratio of column 3 to column 1
1906	38,527	931	489	360	129	1/41	1/79
1907	27,541	974	802	404	398	1/28	1/34
1908	21,776	720	608	360	248	1/30	1/36
1909	20,471	1,465	1,347	920	427	1/14	1/15
1910	19,143	1,066	922	713	209	1/18	1/21

* Figures include residents returning.

Compiled from the *Annual Reports of Her Majesty's Inspectors under the Aliens Act.*

rate of some 5,000 per year and, in spite of spasmodic demands from the anti-aliens, the Liberal Government never considered the possibility of even revoking 'the benefit of the doubt', let alone further restricting the flow.

Anti-alienism Embarrassed

In assessing the reasons for such praiseworthy stiffness of back-bone, let us first note, however, that the Liberals, in many ways, were very fortunate in the circumstances which prevailed in the first few years of aliens administration. In the first place, the anti-alien forces in the House of Commons had been very seriously denuded by the election of 1906. Of the original group of standard-bearers, only William Evans Gordon, Claude Hay, and Howard Vincent remained; and, of these, Evans Gordon retired in May 1907 and Howard Vincent died in April 1908. Others attempted to fill the vacuum. But al-though Leverton Harris, another Conservative of anti-alien inclinations, was elected to Evans Gordon's seat in Stepney, Harris possessed neither the stature nor the capacities of his predecessor. Meanwhile, the spectacle of such men as Anthony Fell, C. Coates, Lord Turnour, and W. W. Ashley bewailing the disastrous effects of alien immigration on the British working class from the vantage point of constituencies in Yarmouth, Lewisham, Sussex Horsham, and Blackpool, respectively, no longer carried either the authority or the conviction that the urban, particularly the East End, anti-alien M.P.s had carried in the happy days before the Act was passed. In fact, though it had learnt nothing and forgotten nothing, anti-alienism seemed once more what it had been dismissed as in the early 1890s: an atavistic agitation of the backwoods Conservative squirarchy.

This impression was confirmed by the fact that their indignant complaints against Liberal iniquity, and their occasional demands that the Act be strengthened, found very little support from the Conservative front bench. Thus, no prominent Conservative spoke in support of Evans Gordon's protest against Gladstone's circular, whilst in a speech that the Liberals never forgot and the anti-aliens, perhaps, never forgave, Sir Edward Carson said that the Home Secretary was doing a good job.[1] Similarly, an amendment to the address was debated before a virtually empty House in February 1909, and received only lukewarm and rather vaguely stated support from Akers Douglas, who terminated his speech in vigorous style by noting 'an agreement between the two sides of the House that this Debate shall conclude this evening'.[2]

In part, the Conservatives were embarrassed by their own inconsistency. A Labour amendment to the Aliens Bill to exclude foreign contract and 'blackleg' labour in 1905 had been refused on the only partially credible grounds that it came outside the purpose of the Bill. Worse still, in 1906, an Aliens Bill of similar intent passed through the Commons, undebated and unopposed, only to meet instant, and Conservative-engineered, death in the Lords. Conservative concern for the consequences to British workers of unfair competition by foreign labour, it seemed, was only election-deep.

[1] During a debate on the Estimates. Hansard 4S H(153)1312–27, 14 March 1906.

[2] Hansard 5S H(1)955–81, 25 February 1909.

It was also difficult to oppose Liberal policy without seeming to be uncharitable. The Russian Revolution had occurred in November 1905, and, in its wake, came pogroms savage even by Tsarist standards—so savage, indeed, that even a hardened correspondent of the *Jewish Chronicle* felt impelled to describe them as 'an open campaign of annihilation against the Jews'.[1] The Liberals could, therefore, claim with some justice that their actions were determined solely by the desire to let in religious refugees. In contrast, the anti-aliens were reduced to dividing their time between denying that the immigrants were refugees at all and attending meetings in the East End to protest against Russian barbarity.[2] As we have seen, religious and political asylum indeed aroused deep loyalties amongst the middle classes and amongst sections of the working class, and at least lip-service amongst even the Gentile population of Stepney and Whitechapel. In this atmosphere, the Liberals stood to gain far more unpopularity by leaving the Act as it was, than by softening its effect.

Coupled with and partly reinforcing these circumstances was the simple probability that popular anti-immigrant protest was itself beginning to lose momentum. In the first place, although, as stated earlier, some 12,832 'Russians' and 'Poles' entered England in 1906, and although an average of 5,000 continued to do so thereafter until 1914, it was apparent that the rate of immigration was, if not declining, then, at least, remaining stable. Moreover, in spite of the unreliability of Board of Trade statistics, it was also becoming apparent that very similar things were happening to the total immigrant population—and happening for reasons unconnected with the Aliens Act. Thus, the *Annual Report on Emigration for 1905*,[3] showed that as a result of the various comings and goings, the total foreign population of the British Isles had been reduced by 4,833—a reduction which became 18,000 when one took into account foreign sailors included in the arrivals, but not in the departures. The writer of the report, even with that caution conceived in statistical unreliability, felt able to note:

[1] *Jewish Chronicle* (22 June 1906), p. 10.

[2] For example, Evans Gordon, Harry S. Samuel, and Harry Lawson attended such a meeting in Stepney. See *Jewish Chronicle* (29 December 1905).

[3] Published July 1906.

> . . . it can probably be said with some degree of certainty that the alien population of the United Kingdom either decreased in 1905, or, if it increased, it increased to a much lesser degree than in former years.[1]

This impression was confirmed by the later reports of the Inspector under the Aliens Act, who, for instance, in 1909, having subtracted foreign sailors and probable deaths from the alien arrival and departure figures, concluded that Britain's foreign population was a stationary quantity.[2] If these facts did not permeate the consciousness of the East End, it was only because the anti-aliens could not exploit them.

Whilst the alien population remained stable, the problems associated with its presence had begun to die away. There is some evidence, for instance, that the sweating system was at last beginning to lose its hold upon the industrial system of the East End. Thus, by 1907, one factory inspector could observe that:

> The transformation from the state of things [in Whitechapel] as I first knew it [in the late 1880s] from the room which constituted the nursery, the sleeping apartment, the kitchen and the workshop, to the well-ventilated and sanitary domestic apartments separate from the workshop needs only to be seen to be appreciated. . . . I can only say that the improvement in the condition of the people does one's heart good.[3]

Moreover, even if such prognostications were rather optimistic, the Liberals had proved by the Trades Boards Act of 1910[4] that they had meant what they said in 1904–5 in their argument against the Aliens Bill: namely, that the evils of sweated labour were much better 'met by legislation to prevent sweating'.[5]

[1] Quoted in *Jewish Chronicle* (20 July 1906), p. 22.

[2] With 534,805 alien passengers arriving and 524,577 leaving, the excess of arrivals over departures was 10,228. When the 9,380 foreign seamen included amongst the arrivals were also assumed to have left, and with the subtraction of deaths, the excess could be assumed to have cancelled out.

[3] Herbert Evans, interviewed in *Jewish Chronicle* (16 August 1907), p. 12.

[4] The culmination of the work of Charles Dilke, this Act provided for the establishment of Trades Boards composed of Government officials, masters, and men in the ready-made and wholesale bespoke tailoring trades, and a number of others. The Boards were to fix a minimum rate of wages for time work and, 'if they think fit', general minimum rates of wages for piecework for their trades. The Bill had been recommended by the House of Lords Sweating Commission twenty-two years previously.

[5] Liberal amendment to the Second Reading, in Hansard 4S H(133)1062, 25 April 1904.

Still more importantly, even before the passing of the Aliens Act, it was becoming apparent that the many-sided problem of overcrowding in the East End—perhaps the crucial cause of anti-alien resentment—was easing rapidly. As early as July 1904, Dr. Thomas, the Medical Officer of Health for the Borough of Stepney (as distinct from the constituency), was drawing attention to the large number of empty houses in his area.[1] By the end of June 1907, London County Council return revealed 2,450 unoccupied houses and 108 vacant warehouses (there were 62 in March 1904) in Stepney and Bethnal Green. It also showed that the average weekly rent for new accommodation in that area had fallen from 3*s.* 10½*d.* in 1902, to 3*s.* 5½*d.* in 1906, whilst key money had disappeared altogether.[2] A week later, Dr. Thomas was reporting that the number of cases of overcrowding detected by his department had fallen from 1,489 in 1904 to 805 in 1906.[3]

Rampant Pro-alienism

Whilst the anti-aliens found themselves rather sheepishly trying to argue that the immigrants were not refugees at all, their protagonists, backed by all the force that popular moral indignation at Jewish massacre could muster, agitated for amendment[4] and repeal. Within Parliament, there was strong and consistent pressure from the Labour party together with a small but vocal contingent of Liberals and Radicals led by George Harwood, M.P. for Bolton. Outside the precincts of Westminster, many Liberal newspapers, most notably that paragon of official Liberalism, the *Daily News*,[5] took their lead from the *Jewish Chronicle* and published full accounts of the often rather harrowing proceedings of the Immigration Boards, and used them to back up their campaign for radical amendment

[1] Cited in *Jewish Chronicle* (22 July 1904), p. 7.

[2] Cited in *Jewish Chronicle* (26 July 1907), p. 27.

[3] Cited in *Jewish Chronicle* (2 August 1907), p. 12. In fact, this was merely the re-establishment of the old pattern. For the first time in four decades more people were moving out of the East End into the outer suburbs than were moving into it.

[4] Normally, they demanded the removal of the poverty clause so as to leave only exclusion on grounds of disease and expulsion on grounds of criminality, while others (e.g. Harwood and Seely) would only assent to the exclusion of criminals.

[5] Also the *Daily Chronicle*, the *Daily Graphic*, the *Westminster Gazette*, and, most fervently of all, the *Tribune*.

of the Act. In Manchester, a mass meeting of protest in December 1905 gave rise to the Jewish Protest Committee which, under the presidency of George Harwood, was to press for amendment at least, and repeal if possible. In London, some three months later, a meeting of prominent Liberals and Socialists formed a 'Watch Committee' whose purpose it was to prevent injustice by keeping Parliament and the public informed upon the working of the Act and, if possible, to bring forward a test case. Although the anti-aliens also began to organize at this time, their organization was neither active nor particularly long-lived, and Evans Gordon, in a significant comment, inadvertently acknowledged just how the tables had been turned:

> The facts were that a campaign had been organized ever since the Act came into force. . . . It was organized in order to prejudice the public in every possible way against the working of the Act.[1]

Jewish Militancy

However, what gave the pro-alien movement much of its dynamism and most of its impact upon the Liberal leadership, was not just the outraged sensibilities of what may broadly be called the nonconformist conscience; it was also, and perhaps far more, the militancy of an increasingly large and influential section of the Jewish community. For whatever misgivings there may have been up until about 1902 with regard to the benefits conferred by alien immigration, the Jewish community reacted to the Aliens Act, and to the manner of its passing, with a unanimous sense of outrage.

This feeling found expression in a number of ways: through numerous protest meetings in the East End, and through motions passed by Jewish trade unions. It can be seen, too, in the impatience which greeted the often rather timid gestures of official Jewry, as represented by the Jewish Board of Deputies—and in the fact that these gestures were made at all. The feeling can be observed in its most bitter and most coherent form, however, in the editorial columns of the paper which had long since established itself as the sole journalistic spokesman for Anglo-Jewry, the *Jewish Chronicle*.

[1] Hansard 4S H(153)137, 5 March 1906.

Throughout the first five years of the operation of the Act, the *Chronicle* devoted one or two pages per week to the proceedings of the Immigration Boards, those 'obscure little tribunals set up by a reactionary law'.[1] Satisfied neither with the timidity of the Jewish Board of Deputies, nor with the Gladstone circular, it felt that 'the community should strive for nothing short of repeal'.[2] On 11 October 1907, having watched the Act in operation for some two years, the paper published a vitriolic series of two-page editorials which began by calling the Act:

> An un-English piece of legislation, saturated with class prejudice from almost the first clause to the last, and divorced from almost every true democratic instinct. It has proved itself arbitrary, tyrannical and cruel. . . . It has laid down the preposterous proposition that a half-witted or criminal alien with a ten pound note in his pocket is a worthy resident in these islands, while a sane, honest and industrious foreigner with less than five pounds in his possession is a menace to the national peace.

It concluded four weeks later, by contemptuously dismissing the Act as 'cruel where it is not impotent, and impotent where it is not cruel'.[3]

Finally, even as late as 22 July 1910, although now 'too sad for tears', the *Chronicle* gave no sign of having relented. Commenting on a recent case of an immigrant refused leave to land, a lead editorial ended with the remark:

> The Devil must grin when he perceives such a stroke of his handiwork, perpetuated in a land bursting with wealth and luxury, and priding itself on its devotion to the God before whom all his creatures are equal.

The Jew Becomes an Englishman

The indignation went beyond the mere outpouring of vituperation. It changed, at least for a while, the whole basis of Jewish political thinking and behaviour. This, in turn, affected the whole relationship between the Jewish community and the Liberal party.

Ever since the development of universal suffrage, regular and frequent attempts had been made in every constituency where Jews resided to attract 'the Jewish vote'. Sometimes this went

[1] *Jewish Chronicle* (19 November 1909).
[2] Ibid. (2 February 1907), p. 12.
[3] Ibid. (8 November 1907), p. 19.

no further than careful steps taken so as not to offend that vote. Indeed, it provides us with another reason why, apart from the prevailing norm of tolerance, there was so much anxiety not to appear anti-Semitic. Thus A. J. Hollington, a local employer standing as candidate for Alderman to the Ward of Portsoken, felt it necessary to take up one and a half pages of the *Jewish Chronicle* in 1891, to publish a list of Jews working for him, so as to refute 'the assertion . . . that I object to the employment of Jewish labour'.[1]

Sometimes, on the other hand, such efforts took the form of Jewish candidates canvassing for support on grounds of common religion. Until 1906, this kind of appeal was comparatively infrequent, and certainly few were as direct as was Mr. John Harris in an advertisement appearing in the *Jewish Chronicle* on 11 January 1889:

COUNTY COUNCIL
WHITECHAPEL DIVISION

Every Jewish Elector should give One vote to
MR. JOHN HARRIS
ON JANUARY 17TH[2]

More frequently, prominent members of the Jewish community were found appealing to their co-religionists on behalf of Gentile party colleagues. Joseph Prag, writing in 1898, could recall that:

> five, ten, fifteen and twenty years ago . . . in every constituency where Jews resided, Jewish speakers of influence were procured to speak to them, and addresses were sent out to Jews, signed exclusively by Jews; . . . special Jewish canvassers were employed and the highest placed in the community did not disdain to issue an appeal on behalf of a particular candidate. . . . I have myself seen Jewish ministers canvassing, acting upon what were practically orders from high quarters; canvassing Jews in districts which were five and six miles from where these ministers lived; districts, too, in which they had no interests whatsoever, and candidates which they did not even know.[3]

[1] 'To the Jewish Electors of the Ward of Portsoken', *Jewish Chronicle* (19 June 1891), pp. 19–20.

[2] Harris was standing as a Moderate; for his later activities see p. 122.

[3] Letter to *Jewish Chronicle* (21 January 1898), p. 8. The last phrases of the quotation are perhaps an interesting indication of what was, and what was not, tolerable as far as the exertion of political influence by ministers was concerned.

Prag's picture may be a little exaggerated. He is almost certainly inaccurate in implying that such appeals had subsided to any considerable extent. Very few elections, either before or after 1898, were allowed to go by without an appeal to Jewish voters, from a Rothschild, or a Montefiore, or a Cohen, 'to give their suffrages' to all Conservative candidates in general and to certain of them in particular.

Moreover, Prag was a prominent Liberal, and his *bêtes noires* in this respect were presumably Tories. However, throughout this period far more frequent and direct appeals were apt to emanate from, and on behalf of, members of his own party. Conservatives tended to claim that Jewish emancipation was 'the work of time' or that Liberal concern with this question was only a means of getting the Jewish vote. In fact, because of the Liberals' predominant part in the long campaign for the removal of Jewish disabilities, they saw themselves as the natural and God-designated custodians of both Jewish rights and Jewish votes. Thus, Jesse Collins said that he always 'took it for granted that a Jew was a Liberal'.[1] But memories were, perhaps, short; and with so glorious a past, no reminder of it could either be too direct or too frequently made. James Haysman, the Liberal candidate for Mile End and a Gentile, whom the *Jewish Chronicle* described as 'one of our many true and faithful Christian friends',[2] even went so far as to publish a special address:

TO THE JEWISH ELECTORS OF MILE END

REMEMBER that it was the Liberal Party which agitated for years in favour of, and ultimately secured JEWISH EMANCIPATION and that it was the obstructive Tories who, as strenuously, opposed the measure.

Do not forget that it was a Liberal Administration under Mr. Gladstone, which created the first Jewish Peer in the person of Lord Rothschild.

Then on all grounds vote for MR. HAYSMAN, THE LIBERAL CANDIDATE.[3]

Normally, however, the task of memory-jogging was left to Jewish Liberals. They performed it with relish. Indeed, they both portrayed and genuinely looked upon their Conservative co-religionists as being compounded, in equal parts, of wilful foolishness, gross ingratitude, and downright wickedness.

[1] Quoted in *Jewish Chronicle* (18 June 1885), p. 10.
[2] *Jewish Chronicle* (22 June 1906), p. 27.
[3] Ibid. (1 July 1892), p. 5.

Ernest Hart, Liberal candidate for Mile End, typically reminded them that:

they would not have been recognized as Englishmen at all, they would not have possessed any of the rights of Englishmen, had they been left to the tender mercies of the Tory party.[1]

Samuel Montagu declared himself sorry to discover that:

When a Jew is a Conservative, he frequently considers that he may sacrifice the interest of his relatives and friends on the altar of Toryism, and endeavours to divert the gratitude of the Jews from that great party which has given them religious liberty.[2]

Some Jewish observers quite failed to understand 'why these gentlemen [are] so anxious to lick the stick that formerly beat them;'[3] was it, perhaps, as others suggested, that they had 'got all they want . . . from the Liberals'?[4] All, however, agreed that it need never have happened for: 'if they cannot see sufficient reason for supporting a Liberal they should remain neutral in the conflict.'[5]

The *Jewish Chronicle*, however, normally greeted such activities with a mixture of scorn and foreboding, and an attitude that almost amounted to proselytizing non-partisanship. Time and again, before and during every general and local election, it warned its readers against the 'energetic endeavours [which] will be made by Radicals and Unionists alike to capture the Jewish electors "*en masse*" '.[6] With equal frequency, it devoted long editorials to dismissing 'the absurdity of the myth about special Judaic sympathies in politics',[7] and expended some of its choicest irony upon those who disagreed:

Surprise or no surprise, Jews actually do support Radicals; wonder or no wonder, Jews are often Tory. The fact is that Jews have become so thoroughly English that they regard their responsibility as voters entirely as Englishmen.[8]

[1] Quoted in report of an election meeting in *Jewish Chronicle* (6 November 1885), p. 7.

[2] Ibid.

[3] H. S. Leon, M.P., in letter to *Jewish Chronicle* (16 March 1894).

[4] Strauss, Liberal candidate for St. George's, in letter to *Jewish Chronicle* (12 October 1900), p. 9.

[5] Harry Harris, quoted ibid., p. 7.

[6] *Jewish Chronicle* (11 June 1892), p. 5.

[7] Ibid. (8 July 1885).

[8] Ibid. (26 November 1885), p. 9.

Indeed, by 'sinking the Jew in the Englishman', Jews were apparently making themselves more English than the English had ever dreamed of being. But, even had the *Chronicle* realized this, it would have made no difference, because 'the evil of the opposite course'[1] was unthinkable. It led to anti-Semitism.

In regard to the idea of Jews voting for Jews as Jews, the *Chronicle* was, perhaps, a little more ambiguous. Although denouncing the idea as vigorously as it dismissed that of the partisan bloc vote, it understandably came close to advocating it during school board elections:

> The undivided support of the Jewish ratepayers ought to suffice to secure his return by a large majority. . . . Apart from his connection with the community, Mr. Raphael is entitled in virtue of his opinions to the suffrages of his co-religionists.[2]

It also, possibly, laid itself open to a certain amount of suspicion by devoting several pages at every general election to the pictures and potted biographies of all the Jewish candidates standing, and by gleefully hailing those who were successful. Here, however, it could claim that it was doing no more than fulfilling the duties of any good 'house magazine', and that there were often very few Jews in the constituencies of Jewish candidates. In general, it denounced the idea of communal back-scratching as being as ridiculous as it was dangerous.

To what extent the *Jewish Chronicle* was factually correct in its rejection of the idea of a partisan bloc vote is clearly impossible to measure accurately. However, although some Liberals obviously believed otherwise, there does seem to have been at least a very significant Jewish Conservative minority. Certainly, this was true of the East End. For example, in 1886, the *Jewish Chronicle* discovered to its own unbounded relief that the theory of the solid Jewish vote had 'once again been triumphantly disproved' by significant numbers of Jews working for Colonel Trench, Samuel Montagu's Conservative opponent in Whitechapel.[3] Where the Conservative candidate was a Jew, there were sometimes good grounds for believing

[1] *Jewish Chronicle* (20 November 1885), p. 9.

[2] Ibid. (16 November 1888).

[3] Ibid. (9 July 1886), p. 4. Trench, however, attributed his defeat to the clannishness of Jewish voters.

that the Jewish vote 'was cast almost wholly in his favour'.[1] However, even in the case of Evans Gordon in 1900, we learn that 'the Conservatives anticipated that a fair proportion of the Jewish vote would be in their favour'[2]—an anticipation gloomily confirmed by a local Jewish Liberal who noted that 'the West Ward of Stepney, packed with Jews, is a hotbed of Toryism'.[3] Outside the East End, it is significant that in 1892, for the first time, among Jewish candidates there were actually more Conservatives (7) than there were Liberals (4), and thereafter numbers remained roughly equal—another fact in which the *Jewish Chronicle* found considerable reassurance.

Meanwhile, if many Jews did not vote Liberal, many more, in the East End at least, failed to vote at all. In some constituencies outside the area of alien settlement, the Jewish electorate was sufficiently large to cause considerable trouble to any returning officer who decided to hold the election on a Saturday. Within the East End it was by no means an inconsiderable quantity in constituencies which possessed electorates of no more than a few thousand, and whose parliamentary representatives generally counted themselves lucky if they obtained majorities of over 500. However, the most significant fact about the Jewish vote in the latter case was just how tiny a percentage it represented of the total Jewish population. Thus, whereas aliens represented some 28 per cent of the population of St. George's, the Jewish vote—although the highest in any East End constituency—amounted to only 11 per cent of the total electorate.[4] To at least one anti-alien, this was 'perhaps a matter for satisfaction'.[5]

In fact, as Israel Zangwill noted, the East End Jew—with

[1] This was the *East London Observer*'s conclusion, on the evidence of party agents, about Nathaniel Marks in 1895 (22 September 1900). See also the beautifully frank remark of the President of the St. George's Conservative Association about the 1900 election: '. . . if we don't capture the Jewish vote, my name isn't Joe Abrahams'. *East London Observer* (25 September 1900), p. 3.

[2] *East London Observer* (6 October 1900), p. 5.

[3] *Jewish Chronicle* (12 October 1900), p. 3. A further pointer to the probable absence of a Jewish vote—at least one that was any longer very responsive to Liberalism's historic appeal—is the fact that James Haysman in 1895 did not think it worthwhile to repeat the experiment of 1892 that we noted earlier (see p. 115).

[4] In 1900, there were 350 Jews in a total electorate of 5,004. The 1901 Census showed a total population of 49,068, of whom 13,746 were aliens.

[5] Alderman Silver, R.C., Vol. II, p. 96.

his background of Russian ghetto and Tsarist autocracy—was 'only slowly becoming a political animal'.[1] This was true even of the registered voters. During the election of 1886, the *Jewish Chronicle* discovered that in Whitechapel:

Many of the foreign Jewish electors appear to have had conscientious scruples against placing a cross by the side of Mr. Montagu's name. As a substitute for the cross, we have been assured that they marked the paper with [a] Hebrew letter.[2]

Even as late as 1900, one witness—admittedly a partial one—noted that many Jewish voters 'don't know the meaning of the words Liberal or Conservative'.[3]

Thus, at the turn of the century, the Jewish vote was something to be allured and manipulated, to be ignored, occasionally not to be offended; and to the *Jewish Chronicle*, it was something that was, above all, English. The passing of the Aliens Act, however, produced a complete change in the general situation. As a result, the Jewish vote became organized; it became Liberal, at least for a time; it became militant.

As early as 1900, in fact, there had been signs of a certain limited Conservative awareness that anti-alienism might offend Jewish susceptibilities. Forde-Ridley, for example, published election addresses in the *East London Observer* and the *Jewish Chronicle* which were identical except for the fact that Jewish readers were not treated to a summary of the candidate's views on the aliens question.[4] Similarly, Evans Gordon told a Jewish audience that he was 'not in favour of legislation to restrict alien immigration'.[5]

There are also at this time a few indications that such fears were not entirely unjustified. Thus, Lord Rothschild and Sir Francis Montefiore, who had given ostentatious support to Thomas Dewar because of his views on South Africa, rather sheepishly withdrew that support when, at the last moment, they

[1] Zangwill, p. 244.

[2] *Jewish Chronicle* (16 July 1886), p. 5.

[3] Harry Harris, a Jewish Liberal, quoted in *Jewish Chronicle* (12 October 1900), p. 7.

[4] See *Jewish Chronicle* (28 September 1900), p. 4, and *East London Observer* (22 September 1900), p. 8.

[5] Quoted in *Jewish Chronicle* (28 September 1900), p. 10. However, the election addresses of both Evans Gordon and Thomas Dewar, published in the *Jewish Chronicle*, contained their views on alien immigration—Dewar's in heavy type.

'discovered his views on alien immigration'.[1] Again, both in 1900 and after the setting-up of the Royal Commission in 1902, there is some speculation about the possibility of organizing the Jewish electorate on the question, as well as some realization that the Jewish vote, though small, 'is large enough to decide an election'.[2]

Generally, however, in these first two or three years of the twentieth century, the Jewish attitude seems to have been that of the *Jewish Chronicle*: namely, that although 'unhappily' some Jewish representation may be desirable on the issue, 'this is hardly a question that goes deeply to the dividing lines of party'.[3]

In fact, the real change in Jewish political attitudes does not come to the surface until the actual introduction of the first Aliens Bill in 1904. The Bill received its First Reading on 29 March, and two weeks later Dr. Dreyfus, Conservative Councillor and leading Zionist in Manchester, could be discovered declaring his absolute intention of working and speaking in the coming election against A. J. Balfour in Central Manchester, 'a constituency where he [Dr. Dreyfus] had some little influence'.[4] The *Manchester Evening News* noted, presumably with some glee, that this promise had 'aroused considerable misgivings amongst Unionists'.[5]

The major part of the movement towards the organization of the Jewish vote, on behalf of the Liberals, however, probably occurred as a by-product of the phenomenon that we witnessed in an earlier chapter,[6] i.e. the militant, widespread, and very effective actions of Jewish congregations during May and June 1905 in pressing for the amendment of the second Aliens Bill. Certainly, the correspondence columns of the *Jewish Chronicle*, from this time onwards, contained an increasing

[1] See *Jewish Chronicle* (5 October 1900), p. 9.

[2] 'OIE', in letter to *Jewish Chronicle* (7 March 1902), p. 6. See also the issue of 12 October 1900 (p. 7), for a report on Jewish Liberal Harry Harris's suggestion of a 'Jewish Parliamentary Association, which should have for its object the organization of all Jewish voters and to teach them who are their guiding stars—Liberal or Conservative . . . and work in connection with the Liberal Club of the district'.

[3] *Jewish Chronicle* (28 September 1900), p. 17.

[4] Quoted in *Jewish Chronicle* (13 May 1904), p. 32.

[5] Quoted ibid. Balfour lost Central Manchester, a financial constituency, in 1960.

[6] See Chapter III.

and largely uncontradicted number of letters giving voice to such sentiments as the following:

Hitherto, we have everywhere voted according to our individual leanings and have consequently stultified ourselves as a political power. If we can but alter this, and, within the next few weeks, wield ourselves into a solid party, ready to support at the next General Election those candidates who agree with us on the matter and to oppose those who differ, I venture to predict the present Bill will share the fate of its unhonoured predecessor.[1]

These writers do not seem, moreover, to have been in any way placated, even by the very considerable concessions somewhat sheepishly granted by the Conservative Government. Their letters continue in very much the same vein until January 1906, on the eve of the election, when we find the *Jewish Chronicle* noting for the sake of brevity (as well as political guidance):

We have received several letters from Liberals and Conservatives alike in which the writers urge that Jewish electors irrespective of their views on general politics, should work and vote against candidates especially those in the East End, who were conspicuous in the last House of Commons by their strenuous advocacy of the Aliens Bill, and largely contributed to its passing.[2]

That this was more than just the isolated ranting of extremists is suggested by more than one event during the election itself. In Stepney, according to the *East London Observer*:

The fear is entertained [by the Unionists] that the Jewish vote is more than shaky. In fact, the feeling about the Aliens Act is so strong that [Liberal] supporters are more confident now than at any period during the campaign.

The paper also noted that although most of the foreign Jews in the constituency did not possess votes, 'they have influence with their co-religionists and this counts for a good deal'.[3]

If Evans Gordon, however, was worried by the probable reaction of his Jewish constituents to his activities, Captain Kyd, the Conservative candidate for Whitechapel who chose to

[1] *Jewish Chronicle* (9 June 1905), p. 6.

[2] Ibid. (12 January 1906).

[3] *East London Observer* (13 January 1906), p. 5. The fact that Evans Gordon won against the general trend is, therefore, a doubly eloquent tribute to the popularity of the Aliens Act amongst the Gentile voters in his constituency.

describe the aliens as 'the very scum of the unhealthiest of foreign nations',[1] must have had reason positively to regret such boundless enthusiasm for the anti-alien cause. At a meeting (presumably of Jews) organized in his support, the unhappy Kyd was confronted by John Harris, an angry Jewish Conservative Alderman, who, arriving from nowhere, proposed an amendment declaring the former unfit as Conservative candidate. It was passed 'amid a scene of great enthusiasm during which Alderman Harris was carried shoulder high'.[2]

There are also indications from outside the East End that Jewish militancy was being translated into political action at this time. Thus Winston Churchill, standing in North-West Manchester, laid claim to the Jewish vote as just reward for services rendered; and according to his canvassers, received some five-sixths of it.[3] On the other hand, Conservatives, not unnaturally, went through rather less happy experiences. The Balfour brothers seem to have been particularly unlucky in this respect. While Arthur, as we have already noted, was having trouble in Central Manchester, Gerald, across the Pennines in Central Leeds, found himself opposed not only by the Liberals, but by the Leeds Jewish Electoral League as well. This organization was led by Edward E. Burgess, a Jewish Liberal who was 'recognized in the local press as the "official" Jewish political organizer'.[4] According to the *Jewish Chronicle*, Balfour's defeat was 'largely brought about by the votes of Jews who were indignant at [his] support of the Aliens Act'[5] (90 per cent of the Jewish voters are claimed to have voted Liberal and 5 per cent to have abstained from voting).[6] The paper noted, moreover, that what had happened in Leeds was merely symptomatic of communal indignation and action throughout the country:

[1] Election Address, *East London Observer* (6 January 1906). (Not printed in *Jewish Chronicle*.)

[2] Ibid., p. 19; Kyd was defeated by Stuart Samuel, the sitting member, by 356 votes. (The Liberal majority had been 41 in 1900.)

[3] Out of 460 Jewish voters in the Cheetham District (which in 1900 returned a Conservative unopposed), 406 were pledged for Churchill who won a seat by 1,241. In the constituency as a whole the Jewish electorate numbered approximately 1,000 out of a total of 11,411 in 1906.

[4] *Jewish Chronicle* (2 February 1906), p. 20.

[5] Ibid. (19 January 1906), p. 9.

[6] Ibid. (2 February 1906), p. 20.

We do not think that the Jewish members who either timidly opposed, or actively assisted in the passing of the Aliens Bill, realized the strength of communal feeling in relation to it, especially in the great provincial centres . . . it brought large numbers of Jews into the political field to deal a blow at the promoters of such legislation.[1]

This quotation is also indicative of another equally crucial point: a movement on the part of official Jewry in general, and the *Jewish Chronicle* in particular, away from the emphasis upon the Jew as an Englishman before all else. In its regular diatribes against the idea of the Jewish vote, the *Jewish Chronicle* had sometimes admitted that in exceptional circumstances 'politics might impinge upon Jewish interests',[2] and communal political action become necessary. In 1905, and in the years that followed, these diatribes increasingly assumed the role of rather infrequent formality, and the exception became the rule.

There were, in the first place, signs that as the 1906 election approached, the paper was finding its non-partisanship an increasingly irksome burden to bear. Letters advocating all sorts of unholy alliances found their way into the correspondence columns, without eliciting either comment or criticism. Meanwhile, the editorial columns found space for remarks which bore an interesting resemblance to advice disguised as commentary. When the Liberal leadership abstained from voting on the Second Reading of the 1905 Aliens Bill, the *Chronicle* saw fit to hint that there were more things in Heaven and Earth than merely the votes of East End Gentiles:

Influenced by a craven fear of giving their opponents a popular cry at the polls, they [the Liberals] may lose the best opportunity afforded them in modern times of obtaining the whole-hearted support of Jews as a body.[3]

Two months later, with the Act passed and the Liberals having now redeemed themselves, the paper nearly burst its non-partisan seams altogether in observing that it was 'perhaps a fortunate thing that the earlier years of the administration of the Act are likely to be years of Liberal predominance in English politics'.[4] On the eve of the election, as we have seen,[5] the

[1] *Jewish Chronicle* (19 June 1906), p. 10.
[2] Ibid. (12 May 1892), p. 11.
[3] Ibid. (12 May 1905), p. 7.
[4] Ibid. (18 July 1905), p. 7.
[5] See p. 121.

Chronicle dryly spoke of the large numbers of letters it had received advising its readers to vote against anti-alien candidates. Jubilantly hailing the result of the election, the paper noted that it 'installs a ministry in power which is thoroughly friendly to our people'.[1]

This general change of attitude can also be seen in the increasing tolerance, and even benevolence, shown by the *Jewish Chronicle* towards the large number of appeals to purely sectional loyalties that were emanating from the mouths of Jewish candidates at this time. Among the most direct of the latter variety came in the form of a circular from R. S. Strauss, Liberal candidate for Mile End:

> As a co-religionist, I ask for your vote for a reason which is above mere party politics. The repetition of the Russian atrocities should be made impossible and this can best be done by returning Jews to Parliament.[2]

Such a request, had it been made five years previously, would have been utterly crushed under at least two columns of admonition in the best *Chronicle* tradition of over-Anglicization. Now it merely produced the dry comment:

> . . . judging from the circular [Strauss] addressed to the Jewish residents in the constituency . . . [he] will not be afraid to champion the interests of his co-religionists in Parliament.[3]

North-West Manchester and Beyond

Although important in the election of 1906, the political expression of Jewish militancy did not reach its peak until after the election had passed. It did not really culminate, indeed until the North-West Manchester by-election, held as a result of Winston Churchill's promotion to Cabinet rank as President of the Board of Trade. Although the efforts of the Jewish community on that occasion ultimately achieved rather less than had at first seemed likely, the by-election is important, first, as an indication of the sort of pressures that were being exerted upon the Liberal party in the first years of the Act's administration. It is also important in showing the continuing and crucial effect of the Aliens Act on Jewish political thinking.

[1] *Jewish Chronicle* (19 January 1906), p. 10.
[2] Quoted in *Jewish Chronicle* (26 January 1906), p. 27. [3] Ibid.

Following Gladstone's letter of February 1906 to the Immigration Boards, Jewish spokesmen, while not necessarily relinquishing the hope of ultimate total repeal, had centred their immediate opposition to the Act around four main grievances. In the first place, they demanded the establishment of receiving-houses at all immigration ports, where the preliminary proceedings under the Act could be carried out and where the potential immigrant might stay whilst awaiting either return to his country of origin or the hearing of his appeal to an Immigration Board. Secondly, they objected to the absence of uniformity in the proceedings of the Boards themselves—a failing which was ascribed to the faulty composition of bodies whose personnel had been appointed by a Conservative Home Secretary,[1] and which led, it was alleged, to the frequent refusal of the benefit of the doubt. As a partial remedy, they proposed the establishment of proper judicial procedure and the appointment of a legally trained person to each Board.[2] Thirdly, strong exception was also taken to the method of collecting and interpreting evidence laid down under the Act. Particularly at issue was the principle that an immigrant, who frequently could not speak English and who was granted no legal representation facilities, had to prove eligibility (rather than ineligibility having to be proved against him). And finally, partly as a consequence of the foregoing, the objectors wanted the right of appeal from the decisions of the Immigration Boards to the King's Bench Division of the High Court.

Quite apart from Churchill's new position and his previous activities in relation to the Aliens Act, two factors made it inevitable that these grievances should figure so largely at North-West Manchester. Firstly, there was the simple fact that a constituency which possessed an electorate of 11,914 and which had given its members a majority of 1,241 in 1906, also contained some 1,000 Jewish voters. The second factor was the reply of the Home Secretary to a letter from the Jewish Board of Deputies in which that body, as well as requesting the abolition of the naturalization fee of five pounds, had set

[1] It was even alleged that many Board members were publicans who objected to the Jewish immigrant on account of his much vaunted temperance.

[2] The Act only stipulated that one member be a magistrate.

out the grievances against the Aliens Act which we have just examined. Gladstone's letter (dated 31 March 1908) arrived, as it turned out, just over three weeks before the by-election, and was a disappointing one, at least by most Jewish criteria.[1] While recognizing the desirability of receiving-houses, the Home Secretary declared that he could not establish them 'unless further powers are conferred upon him by legislation'. On the composition of the Boards, he was generally discouraging although 'always willing to receive suggestions from responsible quarters for additions to any of them. On the interpretation of evidence, Gladstone ignored altogether the point about the immigrant's proving eligibility and merely contented himself with repeating his offer 'to consider any authenticated cases of default'. Moreover, it would be impossible, he said, to grant an appeal to the High Court without further legislation, a remedy which had 'obvious practical difficulties'. Finally, Gladstone refused to abolish the naturalization fee.

Gladstone's letter, disappointing though it was, was soon superseded. Even before Churchill's appointment and the resultant by-election had been officially announced, a correspondent in North-West Manchester was noting that 'speculation is rife as to what attitude the Jewish voters in the constituency will take up'.[2] Now, as this three-cornered contest[3] opened, a 'self-elected' and all-party committee of forty-three was set up;[4] it was composed of representatives from every prominent local institution. With a healthy disregard for both superstition and traditional Jewish political custom, this body sent a deputation of thirteen to see the Liberal candidate 'with a view to eliciting his views and those of the Government in regard to questions particularly affecting Jewish interests'.[5]

[1] 'The Board asked for the very driest of dry bread; it was given the hardest of hard stone.' *Jewish Chronicle* (24 April 1908), p. 7.

[2] J. Dulberg, President of the Manchester Jewish Working Men's Club in a letter to the *Jewish Chronicle* (10 April 1908), p. 15. He was later to be a rather unwilling member of the deputation to see Churchill. The *Jewish Chronicle* published a large number of letters on the subject, mainly advocating a vote 'as one man' in Churchill's favour, both on grounds of past services and because 'it is always well to have a friend at court'.

[3] William Joynson Hicks stood as Conservative candidate, and Dan Irving as a Socialist.

[4] The committee consisted of 21 Liberals, 20 Conservatives, and 2 Socialists.

[5] *Jewish Chronicle* (4 April 1908), p. 10. As well as the four points in relation to the Aliens Act already discussed, and the question of naturalization fees, the

Churchill had evidently got wind of these developments, for he had been in contact with the Home Secretary. Thus, his backward progress from Gladstone's letter was fully prepared and sanctioned before the deputation arrived.[1] The result was a clever mixture of official revision, changed emphasis, and personal view. Firstly, on the matter of receiving-houses, the new President of the Board of Trade 'was authorized to say on behalf of the Government' that, where it could be shown that such houses were necessary, they should be set up 'even if legislation were required to set them up'. Meanwhile, grievances relating both to the composition of the Boards and to the interpretation of evidence 'could be dealt with administratively' and 'he could say that the Government was prepared to improve and alter the composition of the Boards . . . by putting on them a number of members satisfactory to the Jewish Community'. Churchill also promised 'a full service of interpreters' and 'in his opinion', the immigrants ought to have the right to be legally represented if they chose. In regard to appeals, he 'was personally in favour of [and] the Government has no objection, in principle, to allowing the right of appeal from the decisions of the Immigration Boards to the King's Bench Division of the High Court'. Finally, while the last Cabinet did not see their way to doing anything about naturalization fees, that decision 'does not necessarily bind the present Cabinet'; but in this case, he was not sure that he could persuade his collegues to agree with him.[2]

The deputation left the meeting, not unnaturally, well pleased with it's day's work. The original committee met, agreed, and issued a report on the meeting in the form of a manifesto which ended with this fervent exhortation:

It is the duty of every Jew, on the present occasion, to sink all party differences, and to vote as Jews only, because, since Mr. Churchill became the member for North West Manchester, he had exerted to the utmost his

deputation also raised matters concerning the Sunday Opening of Shops Bill and the Education Bill, which were both before Parliament and were both issues for which Churchill's replies were considered satisfactory.

[1] For a verbatim report of the meeting, see *Jewish Chronicle* (15 May 1908), pp. 13–15.

[2] But, as he told an election meeting afterwards: 'If you can think of anyone who will be of more use and more influence, then support him.' *Jewish Chronicle* (24 April 1908), p. 10.

strength and influence on our behalf and he assures us that he will 'continue to take a special interest in questions affecting the welfare, representation and education of the Jewish people'.[1]

The manifesto was ratified by a 'packed' and enthusiastic meeting in the local Jewish Working Men's Club, to which all 1,000 Jewish electors in the constituency had been invited.

The campaign itself must, at times and in places, have borne a rather strong resemblance to one of the Jewish festivals. There were quite open appeals to sectional sentiment. The daily Press carried uncontroverted reports of a notice to the effect that 'Dr. Gaster, Chief Rabbi of the Sephardic community should advise all his brothers to work and vote for Mr. Churchill'.[2] At another point, the Jewish voters were treated to a circular giving them the news that:

SIR ALFRED TURNER, A FRIEND OF THE JEWS, SAYS: ANY VOTE GIVEN BY A JEW TO MR. JOYNSON HICKS IS A VOTE GIVEN FOR ANTI-SEMITISM. VOTE FOR CHURCHILL; THE FRIEND OF THE JEWS.[3]

The extent to which the campaign had contrived to capture the imagination of Jews, whatever their country of origin, may be gauged from the *Jewish Chronicle*'s special correspondent who returned from a visit to Cheetham with the distinct impression that:

Never before have the Jews of Cheetham been seized by such tumultuous and turbulent excitement as that which is reigning here this week . . . not a thought is spared for any other topic. Instead of greeting one another with 'Good Yomtov!' as is customary, this week the children of Manchester's Ghetto stop each other and inquire 'Nù vot are you? Tsetsill?' Tsetsill, it should be explained, is one of the several local modes of pronunciation of the name of the President of the Board of Trade.[4]

Although Churchill, in fact, lost the North-West Manchester by-election,[5] and although at least one letter-writer ascribed his defeat, in part, to a sort of Gentile backlash,[6] it is strongly indicative of the toughness of Jewish political thinking at this

[1] Quoted in *Jewish Chronicle* (24 April 1908), p. 10.

[2] Ibid. (1 May 1908), p. 13.

[3] Ibid. Turner was a prominent English Zionist.

[4] Quoted in *Jewish Chronicle* (24 April 1908), p. 19.

[5] The results were Joynson Hicks, 5,417; Churchill, 4,988; Irving, 276; thus giving Hicks a majority of 429.

[6] The letter described a feeling of exasperation among the English that candidates were induced to devote so much of their time to 'the Jewish vote, the Catholic vote, the Irish vote', yet there was 'never a word about the English vote'.

time that over 50 per cent of the letters which flowed to the *Jewish Chronicle* in the months that followed, expressed no regret whatever at the events that had led some 900[1] Jewish voters to support Winston Churchill at the polls.

Thus, J. Loewy, also a member of the Labour Electoral League, told the readers of the *Jewish Chronicle* that in spite of what had happened, he was 'an absolutely unrepentant sinner. I glory in my share of the work, and, under similar circumstances, shall act in a similar manner.'[2] Several other committee members expressed similar sentiments; and in answering those who seemed to think that the Jews of North-West Manchester had thrown themselves into the same bottomless pit as persons who shouted at cricket matches, 'A Conservative Elector' pointed out that:

> . . . this sectional support of candidates for election to the House of Commons has always been a recognised practice . . . the Jews in Manchester holding the views they did . . . acted strictly within their constitutional rights as English citizens and voters in supporting [Churchill].[3]

Even amongst those who critized these actions, several did so merely on the grounds that:

> . . . if the organized vote is in any given case desirable, it is better to arrange it quietly, by personal canvass instead of by meetings reported in the Press.[4]

Meanwhile 'Politicus' expressed the new spirit of Anglo-Jewry at its most militant and most coherent. His remarks are worth quoting at length since they illustrate the nature of the change that had taken place. To this writer, North-West Manchester represented:

> practically the first time in the history of English politics that the importance of the Jewish vote has been recognized by either of the great political parties

[1] The evidence for this comes from J. Loewy, one of the original all-party committee; see his letter to *Jewish Chronicle* (8 May 1908), p. 12. See also Joynson Hicks, quoted in *Jewish Chronicle* (22 May 1908), p. 17. In a speech to the Maccabeans, he 'very strongly deprecated the attitude taken up by the bulk of the Jewish community in Manchester'. He too placed the Liberal Jewish vote at 900.

[2] *Jewish Chronicle* (8 May 1908), p. 12.

[3] Ibid. (29 May 1908), p. 22. The *Jewish Chronicle*'s own comment (15 May 1908) is equally interesting. In its eyes, the by-election 'marked the emergence of a new spirit and the breaking of an old superstition'. The paper had been taken over in January 1907 by L. J. Greenburg, a prominent Jewish Liberal; but, as we have seen, its conversion began long before.

[4] J. Dulberg, in *Jewish Chronicle* (1 May 1908), p. 13.

in the State, and the first time that the Jewish community has had brought home to it so convincingly the power that it can wield by means of an organized franchise. . . . Jews are expected to act as no other section of the population ever dreams of acting. . . . The Jew always votes as an Englishman, but, if he is true to his Judaism, he will vote *as an Englishman who is a Jew.*

We do not know our own power; the sooner we realize it and exert it in the interests of political freedom the better it will be [for everybody]. . . . Our patriotism will be called in question, it is said, if we put forward the question of Jewish interests. My reply is: it will be questioned by those who are determined to find fault with us whatever we do.[1]

By the end of the first week in May, the Government had already begun to show signs of backsliding somewhat from the promises and emphases given and placed in North-West Manchester, and was to continue to do so, at least until Churchill's appointment as Home Secretary in February 1910.[2] The *Jewish Chronicle*, as well as other organs of the Jewish community, expressed its disappointment angrily and often, and showed signs of returning to its former emphasis on Jews voting 'as their conscience dictates, with sole regard to the welfare of the country'. What is significant, however, is that the reason for this attitude was now quite different; it was no longer dictated by the dangerous wickedness of sectionalism, but by the fact that:

The Jew cannot be tied to the chariot wheels of Liberal or Conservative . . .

[1] *Jewish Chronicle* (1 May 1908), p. 18. Emphasis in original text.

[2] See Gladstone's replies to Hay, in Hansard 4S H(187)1657, 4 May 1908.

The Government, however, did not backslide to the extent that the *Jewish Chronicle* liked to make out. Receiving-houses began to be established towards the end of 1909 and, having been incorporated in Churchill's Port of London Act of 1909, were eventually extended to the capital in May 1910. Gladstone announced himself ready 'to take all steps to remedy any defect in the present arrangements for the interpretation and presentation of evidence', and this was apparently settled to the satisfaction of the Jewish community because there were no further complaints.

Although Gladstone ignored the point, Churchill as Home Secretary announced himself ready to allow legal assistance 'providing the immigrant pays for them himself'. (Gladstone had merely noted: 'the Act makes no provision for legal assistance . . . at the public expense'.) This concession enabled Jewish organizations to provide it. See *Jewish Chronicle* (10 June 1910), p. 25.

No appeal was allowed to the High Court in this period because it would require legislation 'which, in the existing circumstances, cannot be undertaken' and the Government 'only undertook to consider it'. Both Gladstone and Churchill announced themselves willing to alter the composition of the Boards, though Churchill was the more enthusiastic. The naturalization fee was not reduced.

both parties are almost equally tarred by their attitude towards the Aliens Act. . . .[1]

The extent to which Jews, as a whole, took heed of even this advice in the two elections of 1910, is difficult to measure. What visible indications there are seem to show that, on the whole, they remained Liberal. Certainly, this seems to have been true in Leeds, where 'a large and enthusiastic meeting of Jewish electors' formed a Jewish section of the Liberal Federation in September 1909.[2] In Central Leeds, the Jewish vote seems, once again, to have bulked large, and the Liberal candidate, Robert Armitage, the man who had defeated Gerald Balfour in 1906, gave every indication publicly that he believed that the Jewish vote had again contributed considerably to his success of January 1910. This was:

evidenced by the acknowledgement the honourable member publicly made after the poll. A notable feature of the contest was the frequent reference to, and quotations from, the *Jewish Chronicle*, and it was not unusual to see a speaker holding a copy and reading extracts therefrom in order to substantiate his assertions on questions immediately affecting Jews.[3]

The most ironic and most significant tribute to the power of organized Jewish militancy, however, was yet to come. Having contributed to keeping the Liberal nose to the pro-alien grindstone, the alluring quality of the Jewish vote now, in the second election of 1910, brought about the final neutralization of the Unionists. Fittingly enough, the scene of the wheel's completing its full circle was North-West Manchester. Here, Lord Rothschild, in a public letter of support for Bonar Law, the Conservative candidate, wrote in the tones of one who had presumably received assurances beforehand:

I have no doubt that if you and the party you represent are returned to power, the provisions of the Act will be carried out in such a way as to give satisfaction to the Jewish community.[4]

[1] *Jewish Chronicle* (14 January 1910), p. 9.

[2] The reasoning of the Chairman at the inaugural meeting is an interesting variation of a familiar theme: 'Jews had a perfect right to organize themselves, and to be prepared for the political fray. By doing so, no matter to what political party they attached themselves, they would prove that they did not live in exclusiveness, but were as ready and prepared to share the interests and fate of the State as non-Jewish citizens.' See *Jewish Chronicle* (10 September 1909), p. 14.

[3] *Jewish Chronicle* (21 January 1910), p. 11.

[4] Quoted in *Jewish Chronicle* (2 December 1910). Rothschild had hinted at this, though much less strongly, in December 1909 at an election meeting in St. George's

Thus Far, No Further

Although the Liberals administered the Aliens Act with considerable humanity and left as many loopholes as was possible for a party which did not wish to be accused of breaching the absolute authority of Parliament, they refused, however, either to amend or repeal it.[1] Although they remained 'opposed to the whole conception of the provisions of the Aliens Act'[2] and although by February 1907 they were aware of the Act's deterrent effect—'the effect of the Act is not to be judged from the mere figures showing alien immigrants to whom leave to land has been refused'[3]—they did nothing, after 1906, to try to lessen it. Moreover, by 1909, in his anxiety to disprove the charge that he had administered the Act out of existence, Gladstone could be discovered showing, if not enthusiasm for deterrence, then certainly a recognition of its permanent existence: 'The administration of this Act has had a very deterrent effect abroad . . . it is only right that I should make that admission to the authors of this Act.'[4] On occasion, he even growled ominously about people who were 'slipping through the net'.[5] Even Churchill, when he succeeded Gladstone, although insisting that his opinions had not changed and revealing no remorse for the rude things he had done to the first Aliens Bill, signified final acceptance of the coming of age of its successor when he spoke benevolently of 'another and stronger infant, which has now grown up to manhood, and taken its place in the legislative and administrative machinery of the country'.[6] Finally, the Liberals never attempted to answer the most effective argument put forward by those who sought the Act's total annihilation: namely, that, whatever

Town Hall. See *Jewish Chronicle* (31 December 1909), p. 18. The Liberals won back North-West Manchester in January 1910, and retained it in December.

[1] This was the real reason why the Jews remained unsatisfied by the Home Office's attempts to remedy their four minimum grievances.

[2] Campbell-Bannerman, quoted in *Jewish Chronicle* (2 August 1907), p. 18.

[3] Hansard 4S H(169)308, 14 February 1907.

[4] Ibid., 5S H(1)975, 25 February 1909. This effect originated partly from the tendency to select only those with visible means of support so as to avoid having to bear the cost of carrying them back.

[5] In fact, the definition of an immigrant ship was, for a while, reduced to two at Hull, where the Government suspected systematic importation.

[6] Hansard 5S H(19)1320, 20 June 1910.

a Liberal Home Secretary might do now, there was no telling what an anti-alien holder of that office might do in the future.

In part, the reason for Liberal acceptance of the Act was the strong convention that governments do not destroy the legislative work of their predecessors. In part, it was because the rampant pro-aliens themselves never really faced up to the problem of deterrence. Gladstone may also, to some extent, have been captured by his own officials.

Winston Churchill, however, put his finger somewhere near the central reason when he told a Jewish audience in North-West Manchester that the Act could not be repealed because such legislation would be obstructed by the Conservatives and thrown out by the House of Lords. Of course, the matter went deeper than this. The real point was that, at a time when the Liberals were girding themselves to do battle with the Lords over their obstruction of the less positively popular aspects of the Liberal programme, they dared not risk giving that body (or the party that controlled it) the chance of obstructing something definitely unpopular.

The Liberals probably administered the Act in as generous a spirit as was possibly without further legislation. They also probably went as far as popular lip-service to, and even enthusiasm for, the ideals of tolerance and sympathy for the persecuted would allow them to go.[1] The Conservatives could not oppose such action without seeming to threaten the sacred cow of religious and political asylum. But, although it had been possible, perhaps, to oppose the Bill and still remain within the bounds of lip-service, to repeal the Act, to destroy the barriers once established, would have laid the Liberals open to the charge of throwing back the flood-gates, of welcoming 'the riff raff', of 'letting them all come'.

[1] Their actions also fitted into the ambiguity of the trade unions. (See Chapter IX.)

CHAPTER VIII

The Liberals: Front Bench, Back-Bench, and Grass-Roots

> It is all very well for the Right Honourable Gentleman, safe in the sylvan seclusion of the Forest of Dean, to philosophize on the traditions of England, and extol the beauties of free and unrestricted asylum to all and sundry. What part of the burden which this asylum imposes has he borne . . . ? Will he undertake to house 10,000, 20,000 or 30,000 foreigners in the homes of his constituents and seek to pacify them with speeches about the open door? Sir, the open door is a very fine thing so long as it is someone else's.
>
> WILLIAM EVANS GORDON[1]

Official Liberalism went a long way towards obeying the dictates of party ideology. On the whole, it vigorously resisted the move towards restrictive legislation, and, from 1906, administered the result of that move with reasonable liberality. Not all sections of the party, however, were quite so certain about the unalloyed nature of the benefits accruing from having several thousand paragons of Liberal virtue running round on the loose.

East End Liberals and Others

There is limited but fairly significant evidence that among large sections of local party organizations in areas affected by his presence there was a decidedly less than friendly attitude towards the immigrant. In Leeds, for instance, in 1898, there occurred 'a very ugly and disagreeable incident' when two billiards matches were arranged between the Jewish Young Men's Club and the Central Ward Liberal Club:

> The first was duly played in the Jewish club rooms, and the Gentile visitors were loud in their praises of the warm welcome and hospitality they received. But, when the return match was about to be played at the Liberal Club, the Committee of the latter suddenly stepped in and forbade it, on the grounds

[1] Hansard 4S H(133)1088, 25 April 1904.

that the Jews could not be allowed to enter their premises and mingle with their members.[1]

It is obvious here that the hostility was, by no means, unanimously felt. Moreover, when the matter was 'exposed' by the Conservative *Yorkshire Post*, and private nastiness became public knowledge, the Liberal Committee hastened to obey the normal rules of Anglo-Saxon racialism by putting up one of its members to deny that anti-Semitism was in any way connected with the incident.

Let us note, however, that, in spite of what we have said here and in a previous chapter about the disreputability of anti-Semitism, there was a section of East End opinion that was not merely anti-Semitic, but apparently unashamedly so. It is difficult to believe, for example, that the Bethnal Green Liberal and Radical Club thought that the following blatantly worded resolution, passed by a majority, would remain a secret: 'That, in future, no candidate will be accepted as a member if he be one of the Jewish race.'[2]

In at least one constituency resentment against the Jewish alien also seems to have extended beyond the social side of East End Liberalism, and to have become a calculation which dictated the choice of candidates for election. In 1903, the Executive Committee of the St. George's and Wapping Liberal and Radical Association unanimously rejected one of the candidates put forward by the local Labour party for a united ticket on the ground that he was a Jew. In announcing this decision, John C. Barrett, Honorary Secretary of the organization, wrote a letter to the Labour party that was a somewhat bizarre mixture of oddly directed apology and typically pessimistic conclusions about the extent and catastrophic effect of anti-Semitism in others:

Firstly, let me say that there was no attack upon Mr. Lyons in regard to his personal character, but it was owing to his being of the Jewish persuasion that the Committee came to the decision they did. I think it is a

[1] *Jewish Chronicle* (4 March 1898), p. 25.

[2] Quoted in *Jewish Chronicle* (18 October 1901). The President of the Club, however, strongly dissociated himself from this resolution in a letter to the *Jewish Chronicle* (15 November 1901). *Club Life*, the organ of the Working Men's Clubs movement which published the resolution, also condemned it and suggested that the majority of affiliated Clubs were against such action. In spite of the *Chronicle*'s expectation, it is not recorded whether and/or when the ban was withdrawn.

well-known fact that there is a very bitter feeling against the Jewish population here in St. George's, and we feel positively that, in the event of a candidate running who is a Jew, it means defeat for the list on which the person is running.

I have been assured by some score of Liberals in St. George's who have informed me that they will neither work nor vote for our candidates if we attempt to run a person of the Jewish populace.[1]

As it turned out, none of the ticket were elected, and the successful Conservative list demonstrated how great could be the gap between assumptions about racial hostility on the one hand, and the reality on the other, since it included a Jew, Louis Davis.

In fact, this type of pessimism seems to have been particularly characteristic of this Association. Other Liberal associations in the East End were much less chary about adopting Jewish candidates: both Limehouse and Mile End adopted Jewish candidates for the London County Council elections of 1904; Mile End chose B. Strauss for the Parliamentary by-election of 1905 (he was finally elected in 1906), and Whitechapel was represented by Samuel Montagu throughout this period. Moreover, the Secretary of St. George's Liberal Association was the only East End Liberal official of those interviewed by the *East London Observer* in 1905 who, at least openly, admitted to the gloomy feeling that: 'We shall lose a lot of votes on that account [i.e. removals]. A great many of our people are being ousted by the foreigners.'[2]

[1] Quoted in *Jewish Chronicle* (20 October 1903), p. 20. J. Pam claimed that he too had been rejected by the same Association 'on the ground that I am a Jew'. See *Jewish Chronicle* (23 October 1903), p. 6.

The Chairman of the Association, who had apparently not been present at the selection meeting, later wrote to the *Chronicle* 'to emphatically dissociate [himself] from any resolution passed by the . . . Association with reference to the Jewish Community'. See *Jewish Chronicle* (30 October 1903), p. 6.

[2] *East London Observer* (2 September 1905), p. 7. For the opinions of Liberal agents elsewhere in the East End, see p. 141, note 3.

Anti-Semitism also seems to have been associated with election candidates more overtly in the constituency than in any other. The Liberal candidate in 1900, Bertram Strauss, claimed that it was used against him in that year by his opponent's canvassers. There were also well-authenticated charges that the sister of the Liberal candidate (Miss Wedgwood Benn) made fairly open use of the sentiment in 1906 and 1910. This may have helped to account for whatever degree of popular respectability the sentiment possessed. St. George's also had more Jewish residents than any other constituency except Whitechapel—and more Jewish voters than even Whitechapel.

However this may be, the atmosphere of popular hostility towards the alien—and probably also the suspicion that far more lay under the surface than met the eye—affected the behaviour of Liberal M.P.s and candidates in these areas (and even outside them) in a number of ways. Some became quite definitely and even violently anti-alien, both inside and outside the House. Thus, during the debate on the anti-alien resolution of 1893 Henry Labouchere 'was constrained, keeping his eye on the vote of the Northampton shoe trade, to support Mr. Lowther'.[1] Similarly, Sydney Buxton and Henry Norman seem to have felt that working-class opinion in both Poplar and the country at large necessitated not only anti-alien behaviour within Parliament, but also their saying some very rude things indeed about aliens from the platforms of the British Brothers League:

> Let the nations burn their own smoke [Cheers]. Let them disinfect their own sewage. Englishmen . . . [will] not have this country made the dumping ground for the scum of Europe.[2]

The examples of Labouchere, Buxton, and Norman show that the violence of anti-alien sentiment among individual politicians was by no means proportionate to the number of aliens in their constituencies; this is, perhaps, partly symptomatic of the fact that one's impressions of the degree of racial hostility might be formed quite independently of the reality of the situation. Indeed, it is doubtful whether most of the voters of Wolverhampton South, or even Northampton (in spite of the boot trade) had ever seen an alien;[3] while Poplar, though part of the East End was never an area of alien settlement,

[1] London correspondent of *The Scotsman*, quoted in *Jewish Chronicle* (22 November 1895), p. 1. Labouchere supported the motion by speech and vote, and voted for the Second Reading in 1904. Though there were very few aliens in Northampton, Labouchere had received a violently anti-alien letter from the secretary of the Bootmakers union, and this union seems to have been the most actively anti-immigrant of all the East End unions. (See Chapter IX.)

[2] Henry Norman, quoted in *Jewish Chronicle* (17 January 1902), p. 7.

[3] Although Norman's later behaviour (see p. 145) suggests that he was anti-alien by what he thought to be political necessity rather than by belief, several of those who voted for the Second Reading of the first Aliens Bill in 1904 possessed constituencies so far from the nearest immigrant as to point to a genuine belief in the necessity of keeping him out. See, for example, Vaughan Davies (Cardigan), Cathcart Wason (Orkney and Shetland), and C. D. Rose (Cambridge Newmarket).

and none of Buxton's Conservative opponents ever openly used the issue against him at an election. Moreover, his majority was a large one by East End standards, never (except in 1886 before the agitation began) falling below 800, and sometimes rising as high as 2,000.

Several other local politicians, however, with rather more reason,[1] followed Buxton's line. Thus, Liberal candidates like Stopford Brook in Bow and Bromley, Durham Stokes in Stepney, and William Pearce in Limehouse, on occasion, openly boasted to East End audiences of their anti-alienism. Meanwhile, all the East End Liberals—with the possible exception of Samuel Montagu in Whitechapel and his successor Stuart Samuel—showed at least some signs of strain, some signs of finding the pro-alien halo a difficult burden to bear. And with the sole exception of Stuart Samuel, every one of them appended his name to a petition addressed to the Liberal leadership in May 1905:

> We . . . believing that the present Aliens Bill can be made to satisfy the legitimate demands of East London, express the hope that the Second Reading of the Bill will not be opposed by the Liberal party.[2]

We can see this ambiguity of attitude most clearly, however, if we look at the way the issue was handled at election times. For example, in all the elections between 1885 and 1910, the present writer has been able to discover only three occasions when the issue was mentioned by a Liberal candidate in his official election address—and addresses were often very specific. In one of these, William Pearce, the candidate for Limehouse in 1906 and a local manufacturer, expressed his feelings about the aforementioned petition in the following terms:

> The invasion of DESTITUTE FOREIGN JEWS has rendered the Aliens question a special trouble in this district. In April last, I joined in a successful appeal by East End members and candidates to the Liberal Leaders to prevent

[1] Poplar may, of course, have been subject to what seems to be a characteristic of the present situation whereby the population on the fringe of an immigrant area are more hostile than those in the area of settlement itself. Buxton was the earliest anti-alien of all, and his attitude was probably affected by his early background as a carpenter and his continuing membership of the Amalgamated Society of Carpenters and Joiners.

[2] Quoted in *Jewish Chronicle* (5 May 1905), p. 25.

party opposition to the Aliens Exclusion Bill. . . . The progress of the Bill was greatly facilitated in consequence.[1]

Other than this, only in Whitechapel in 1892 and 1895 do we discover, in an election address, any sign that the Liberal candidate was even aware that aliens were living in the East End. Moreover, in 1895, even Samuel Montagu, the bravest of the East End Liberals, sailed into battle with his anti-alien opponent, Sir W. H. Porter, by reminding his constituents at the end of his address that:

I continue my exertions in diverting, as far as practicable, the stream of Foreigners to those places which are more suitable for them than this crowded country.[2]

In general, candidates not only failed to mention the alien in their election addresses, but tried to ignore him at their election meetings as well. Even when forced to acknowledge him, moreover, even the most courageous Liberal brethren could say some decidedly ambiguous things about their intentions towards the immigrant.

This type of behaviour is most starkly observable in the Mile End by-election of January 1905. It was the only election fought solely on the Aliens issue—although the Liberal candidate did try to place his main emphasis on the free trade issue, running on the motto 'HANDS OFF THE FOOD OF THE PEOPLE'. After the cliff-hanging Conservative victory had been announced, the *Jewish Chronicle* proudly drew its readers' attention to 'the manly way Mr. Strauss [the Liberal candidate] conducted the fight'.[3] Taken as a reference to Bertram Strauss's early pronouncements, this assessment of moral virility was a fairly accurate one. He had begun by contemptuously telling one of his audiences that if he were beaten:

You will have an Aliens Bill and you will have some poor wretches prevented from coming in here. Some people in Mile End will benefit but I do not believe the nation will benefit.[4]

[1] *East London Observer* (16 January 1906), p. 5.

[2] *Jewish Chronicle* (5 July 1895), p. 3, and *East London Observer* (4 July 1895), p. 4. Montagu was closely involved with communal efforts to persuade the immigrants to settle in America, and later in 1903, also founded the Jewish Dispersion Committee which attempted to settle immigrants in smaller cities outside London. Montagu's successor made no mention of the issue.

[3] *Jewish Chronicle* (20 January 1905), p. 8.

[4] Quoted in *East London Observer* (14 January 1905), p. 5.

As the campaign progressed, however, and as not only his opponent, but also the British Brothers League, weighed in against him, the Liberal candidate's attitude began to lose a good deal in clarity. His election advertisements had, from the beginning, drawn attention to the fact that he supported 'EXCLUDING THE DISEASED AND CRIMINAL ALIEN'.[1] Now, a third category was added to the list for exclusion, and that was 'the undesirable alien'. In a letter sent out with the polling cards, Strauss informed his undoubtedly delighted readers:

> The aliens question has been much discussed during the contest and, after all, on the question of excluding the undesirable, diseased and criminal, I am in agreement with my opponent and would support any measure that would provide this.[2]

Having led his constituents into the wood in this way, he then proceeded to lose them by escaping into the dense undergrowth of undesirability. For, in an interview with the *East London Observer*:

> The Liberal candidate placed the undesirable alien under three heads, thus:
>
> The Chinese indenture labourer;[3]
>
> The diseased and criminal alien; and
>
> The man who is up to no good–who is desirous of bribing and corrupting someone else for his own benefit.[4]

Official Propaganda

The last category was probably a figment of Strauss's own imagination. However, the emphasis upon Liberal willingness to exclude the diseased and criminal alien was also a characteristic of the election literature produced by the Liberal Publication Department. Most pamphlets on the subject sought to persuade

[1] In the interval between the first and second Aliens Bills, the Liberals, with the support of Vincent and Evans Gordon, had introduced a Bill to exclude the diseased and criminal alien. This was rejected by the Government, but it provided a useful election sop to more candidates than Strauss.

[2] *East London Observer* (14 January 1905), p. 5.

[3] This attempt to divert attention to undesirable Chinese labour in South Africa was a fairly common Liberal gambit in the East End. See, for example, Durham Stokes's election advert in the *East London Observer* (16 January 1906), p. 6: 'Electors of STEPNEY—*NO CHEAP CHINESE*—VOTE FOR STOKES.'

[4] *East London Observer* (14 January 1905), p. 5.

their readers that however much the Conservatives might claim that the Liberals opposed the Aliens Bill, 'This is ONLY A HALF TRUTH.'[1] They only opposed 'some parts' of it. The Government had rejected the Liberals' generous offer to exclude criminal aliens, and so: 'IF THE FOREIGN BURGLARS REMAIN IN THIS COUNTRY, THE TORY PARTY ALONE ARE RESPONSIBLE.'[2]

The Government's refusal to exclude merely those who were diseased or criminal, together with its abandonment of the first Aliens Bill, after doing nothing for so many years, also gave Liberal literature the opportunity to call it 'A SHOP-FRONT WINDOW BILL'[3] and to compare 'PROMISE AND PERFORMANCE'. As early as 1896, one leaflet referred to 'BROKEN PLEDGES' and proceeded to pour scorn and derision upon the fact that although at the election the Tories had promised to pass a Bill 'TO GIVE WORK TO ENGLISH WORKERS' and to exclude those who were taking 'the BREAD AND BUTTER out of the mouths of ENGLISH WORKING MEN', once the election was over, they had found other matters 'more pressing'—'Like the Law of Evidence Bill . . . for example!' The conclusion must be that 'it was only promised TO HELP THE TORY PARTY GET INTO POWER', and the leaflet ended with this mixture of rhetoric and searching political analysis: 'ELECTORS! THE TORIES WANTED YOUR VOTES FOR THEMSELVES BUT WHERE IS THE BREAD AND BUTTER THEY PROMISED YOU IN RETURN?'[4]

However, let us note that the propaganda message was by no means a totally pragmatic one. Although some leaflets dealt solely in the sort of terms outlined above, a high proportion

[1] *The Tory Shop-Front Aliens Bill*, Leaflet 2013 (London, Liberal Publication Department, 1904).

[2] Ibid., and *The Truth about the Aliens Bill*, Leaflet 2012 (London, Liberal Publication Department, 1904).

[3] *The Truth about the Aliens Bill*. This was probably the main burden of propaganda in the East End in 1906 as is suggested by the *East London Oberver's* interviews with Liberal agents prior to the election. Note, for example, the following exchange: [Interviewer] 'Do you think the Aliens Bill has affected the position at all?' [Mr. Legg of Whitechapel] 'I don't think it will affect us much especially when the elector comes to know the value of the Bill because the Bill is of no value at all. It isn't worth the paper it is printed on.' See *East London Observer* (19 August 1905), p. 7.

[4] *Broken Pledges*, Leaflet 1713 (London, Liberal Publication Department, 1896).

of party literature—some of which, at least, was fairly obviously aimed at 'working men'—attacked the Aliens Bill on ideological grounds—on grounds, moreover, which went beyond the popular jibe about Protectionism.[1] Thus, while placing considerable emphasis upon the workability and electioneering character of the Aliens Bill, a leaflet of 1904 also noted in heavy type that:

It was impossible so to frame the Bill as to prevent it being used to exclude political and religious refugees. . . . Liberals . . . wish to keep English harbours open *as an asylum to the persecuted.*

The same leaflet also managed to combine a crafty dig at the unworkability of the measure with an attempt to associate it with protection, and to associate protection, in turn, with anti-Semitism, by arguing that, even if worked with American vigour, the Bill would keep out only a very few even 'of Jews from Russia whom the British Protectionist chiefly hates'.[2]

In the same year another leaflet reprinted one of Winston Churchill's speeches against the Aliens Bill. Here the arguments were almost purely ideological in attempting to show that: '*The Simple Immigrant, the political refugee, the helpless and the poor—these are the folk who will be caught in the trammels of the Bill.*'

It identified the issue in the simple terms of selfishness versus unselfishness, and of tolerance versus intolerance, and thus attempted at its lowest to leave any reader who cared what others thought of him with little choice of side:

English working men are not so selfish as to be unsympathetic towards victims of circumstances or oppression. They do not respond in any marked degree to the anti-Semitism which has recently darkened Continental history, and I, for one, believe that they will disavow an attempt to shut out the stranger from our land because he is poor, and will resent a measure which besmirches those ancient traditions of freedom and hospitality for which Britain has been for so long renowned.[3]

[1] According to *Ten Years of Tory Government: A Handbook for the Use of Liberals* (London, Liberal Publication Department, 1906), p. 189, Chamberlain's intervention on protection in the debate on Second Reading in 1905 was 'the feature of the debate'.

[2] *The Truth about the Aliens Bill.*

[3] *Mr. Churchill on the Aliens Bill*, Leaflet 2006 (London, Liberal Publication Department, 1904). See also *Ten Years of Tory Government* for details of amendments 'forced' by the Liberal opposition; 'the most important' of which 'is that made in regard to the admission of political refugees' (p. 196). [*cont. opposite*]

The Message Obscured

The fact that the propaganda message being disseminated downwards was not a purely pragmatic one perhaps partly reflected and partly resulted in the fact that the information and pressure coming up from local party sources in the areas affected by immigration were by no means exclusively anti-alien in character. In the first place, by no means all the M.P.s from these areas took a line that was anti-alien or even ambiguous in character. Samuel Montagu and later Stuart Samuel, in spite of the emphasis of some of their election literature, took a line both in Parliament and outside that was, in general, staunchly and vocally against the Bill. After all, from 1906 Churchill sat for a constituency which contained most of the Manchester district's immigrant population. The rest lived in North Salford, and presumably helped return W. P. Byles, a man who was amongst the most prominent and most militant of the pro-aliens after 1906.

In the case of both Churchill and Byles it is probable that the influence of a militant Jewish vote merely intensified and stiffened an attitude and line of action which would have become apparent anyway.[1] However, there is some evidence to show that it even produced a definite change in line amongst those Liberals who felt that their majorities depended upon their giving public support to the Aliens Bill. J. Wedgwood Benn's Conservative opponent in St. George's accused him of changing his mind about the Aliens Act and pledging himself, before a meeting of Jewish electors, to press for its repeal or amendment.[2] Whatever the truth of this, certainly the Liberal candidate who had signed the memorial to the Liberal leaders asking them not to oppose the Bill, felt it worthwhile to send a special letter to each Jewish voter, praising the way in which the Liberals had administered the Act thus far:

This type of appeal was also often characteristic of the Liberal-Labour group. See, for example, *Reynolds's News* (8 January 1905), p. 7. Ben Cooper, Liberal-Labour candidate for Stepney in 1907, fought his by-election campaign in similar terms.

[1] Although Byles for whatever reason had shown no interest in the matter while M.P. for Yorkshire Shipley in 1892–5.

[2] H. H. Wells, quoted in *East London Observer* (13 January 1906), p. 2.

The Liberal Government has appointed Mr. Herbert Samuel, Under Secretary for the Home Department. He is, therefore, in charge of the administration of the Aliens Act, and the Naturalization Laws. At the next election, if the Conservative Party get in, Mr. Herbert Samuel will be dismissed, and perhaps Major Evans Gordon put in his place. Which do you prefer? If you prefer Mr. Samuel, give me your vote.[1]

Wedgwood Benn can later be discovered pressing for the establishment of receiving-houses at the Port of London,[2] and, in 1910, urging Jews to vote for him because his Conservative opponent had voted in favour of the Aliens Bill.[3]

The clarity and unanimity of the message and pressure upwards were also blurred by the fact that several of the affected Liberal politicians showed every sign of finding the dilemma between grass-roots demands and Liberal conscience a rather painful one. For, although such men as Sydney Buxton, William Pearce, and the infinitely flexible J. Wedgwood Benn never seem to have been handicapped by, or even aware of, any crisis of conscience on this matter, others obviously were. Their embarrassment found expression in a certain deviousness of line. Thus, W. R. Cremer,[4] although generally predisposed against aliens legislation, had nevertheless signed the memorial to the Liberal leadership in May 1905.[5] Yet, two months later, having apparently concluded once again that only 'a small section of the people [in this constituency] had been deluded',[6] he could be discovered claiming:

I never favoured this Bill from the first; I wanted it discussed so that we might show the hollow mockery of the whole thing.[7]

and even that:

There was not one of the candidates or Members who, in asking our Front Bench not to oppose the Second Reading expressed approval of the Bill.[8]

[1] H. H. Wells, quoted in *East London Observer* (13 January 1906), p. 8.

[2] See, for example, Hansard 5S H(11), 30 September 1909.

[3] See Percy L. Simmons's letter to the *Jewish Chronicle* (18 February 1910), p. 20. Benn's efforts to please everybody at once rather defy comparison. His sister was given to making anti-Semitic speeches from public platforms.

[4] Liberal and sometime Gladstonian Labour M.P. for Haggerston, 1885–1919 (with a break in 1892–5); and also a leading member of the Amalgamated Society of Carpenters and Joiners.

[5] His attitude, while a member of the Select Committee, was also slightly anti-alien.

[6] Hansard 4S H(149)928, 17 July 1905.

[7] Ibid., 931. Cremer rarely missed a division during the Committee and Report stages in 1905, and always voted with his party.

[8] Hansard 4S H(149)1264, 19 July 1905.

Even Henry Norman, who could be as violently rude about aliens as any Conservative, and who both spoke and voted for the Second Reading in 1904, must have totally confused his front bench by suddenly concluding after the Mile End by-election:

> The late Conservative Member had a majority of 1,160, but, this time, a Conservative only scraped in by 78. The real point in this alien question was most carefully kept in the background, namely, will the Government introduce a Bill to exclude an alien of good character on the ground of poverty alone? . . . the crux of the whole matter is whether a man, against whom nothing but poverty can be alleged, is to be excluded.[1]

Norman's behaviour is also indicative of another factor tending to obscure the anti-alien message: namely, the acute and universal embarrassment of Liberals who took such a line, in the presence of suspected anti-Semitism, and the need to divert the accusation. Norman apparently felt not only the need to avoid suspicion by frequent disavowal of 'a most deplorable and abominable prejudice';[2] he also had to disprove the charge by deed. Therefore, he sometimes seems to have felt that his most spectacular achievement, whilst serving on the Royal Commission, was to get through the entire fifteen-month period without ever once using the word 'Jew'.[3] It was also probably something rather more than mere indignation that prompted the same Member, in July 1902, firstly, to draw the attention of the House to 'the shameless and cynical manner' in which the Romanian Government was evading its responsibilities under the Treaty of Berlin by imposing upon its Jewish subjects 'the gravest and cruellest of disabilities'; and secondly, to demand to know what the Government was going to do about it.[4]

Sydney Buxton's denials of the intolerant and intolerable sin were even more frequent than Norman's. Buxton even took his brightly polished conscience to show the Stepney Liberal Association, and spent an entire speech before a public meeting of that body, satisfying a wish:

[1] Quoted in *Jewish Chronicle* (3 February 1905), p. 12. Norman took little further part in the proceedings from this point onwards.

[2] Hansard 4S H(133)1110, 25 August 1904.

[3] See ibid.

[4] Hansard 4S H(110)724, 3 July 1902.

to correct an impression that had been made by a report of his speech on the Second Reading of the Bill. It appeared as though he had said that he objected to the introduction of Polish and Russian aliens, because they were Jews. That was not his position. He had no anti-Jewish feeling in regard to the matter whatever. What he said was that he desired to exclude them on social grounds.[1]

There is some evidence (mostly from public statements, which limits its usefulness) of a severe breakdown of communication here. It suggests that just as the problem of the anti-alien East End Liberal politicians and their organizations was to prove that public opinion was anti-immigrant without being anti-Semitic, so some other Liberals at least tended to believe that if it was not anti-Semitic, then it could not possibly be anti-alien. The latter's assessment of public opinion, therefore, tended to base itself upon whether they thought public opinion was capable of such wickedness.

It need not surprise us, of course, that Samuel Montagu felt this way in 1888:

With reference to there being a prejudice against the Jews in my constituency . . . my experience over thirty years is that there is not that prejudice at all.[2]

And fourteen years later he could again say:

I have visited, I should say, every court and alley, and every little street in Whitechapel, and I have never come across prejudice against Jews or displacement, except in a very few instances. . . . I think it is a great deal artificial.[3]

It is perhaps more interesting that Winston Churchill tended to feel the same way:

English working men . . . do not respond in any marked degree to the anti-Semitism which has darkened recent continental history; and I, for one, believe that they will disavow an attempt to shut out the stranger.[4]

So, too, did Gladstone, apparently, when he told the *Pall Mall Gazette:* 'I have not the slightest fear of an agitation in England

[1] Quoted in *East London Observer* (13 May 1905), p. 5. Buxton was supporting Durham Stokes, the Liberal candidate for the constituency.

[2] S.C., Vol. I, p. 766.

[3] R.C., Vol. II, p. 619.

[4] Letter to Nathan Laski, President of the Old Hebrew congregation, in *The Times* (31 May 1904), p. 10.

against the Jews. You might as well expect one against the laws of gravity.'[1]

Finally, Atherley Jones shows this tendency in its clearest form. As far as he was concerned:

This movement in favour of the Bill does not emanate from the working-classes, but from those who think they can appeal to the prejudice, ignorance and bigotry of certain sections of the community who come closely in contact with aliens.[2]

Most of the dissident Liberals, therefore, would presumably have agreed with Henry Labouchere's lament that 'the whole issue has been prejudiced owing to the Jews being introduced into the question'.[3] Yet sometimes, even so, 'the Jewish side of the question' could be put to good use. For just as East End Liberal politicians found themselves acutely embarrassed by the charge of anti-Semitism, so they, in turn, apparently felt able to rely on a sufficiently similar grass-roots reaction (at least in its public manifestation) to use that charge to excuse and explain the Liberal leadership's opposition to the Aliens Bill. Durham Stokes provides us with the classic example of this manoeuvre during a speech at the Annual General Meeting of the Stepney Liberal Association. Whilst very definitely realizing the need for:

some sort of legislation upon that subject . . . he deprecated in the strongest terms bringing in, as had been brought in by the Government's Bill, a spirit of inflammatory and racial prejudice. . . . He pledged himself to them that he would do all he could to support a sober and solid Bill of real service to the crying needs of the people of East London.[4]

The Leadership

Although adopting an attitude throughout the period that was generally hostile towards the possibility of aliens legislation, the Liberal Parliamentary leadership at no time exactly defined their attitude until the Second Reading of the first Aliens

[1] Quoted in *Jewish Chronicle* (14 February 1890), p. 8.

[2] Hansard 4S H(145)789, 2 May 1905. Dilke's and Trevelyan's charges, quoted earlier, also fall within this category, for, as we have seen, the charge was as much reaction as political manoeuvre. See also Bradlaugh's remarks to the Anglo-Jewish Association quoted at the head of Chapter V.

[3] Hansard 4S H(8)1220, 11 February 1893.

[4] *East London Observer* (21 January 1905), p. 3.

Bill in 1904. Up until that time, they maintained an attitude which, if hostile, was also flexible, giving an official appearance of 'keeping an open mind upon it'.[1] As early as February 1893, although officially opposing a motion in favour of aliens legislation both by speech[2] and vote, the Liberal Government's official reason for so doing was the need for further information:[3] 'with respect to aliens who are really destitute . . . that is a question which we recognize as a perfectly fair subject for investigation'.[4] Thereafter, although the party's chief whip in the Commons made it perfectly clear to Salisbury that his Bill of July 1894 would be thoroughly squashed the moment it descended from the Lords, the Liberal Government officially still refused to define its attitude towards legislation.[5]

In 1904, the party vigorously opposed the first Aliens Bill with both Asquith and Bryce making long and principled speeches from the front bench. Vigorous opposition continued until the Bill was finally talked out in Committee stage. Moreover, even as late as December 1904, Campbell-Bannerman could be discovered telling an East End audience in Limehouse that 'the Liberal attitude towards the Government's Aliens Bill needs no defence or apology'.[6]

A very different situation, however, was apparent in regard to the second Bill. Now, with the memorial from the East End M.P.s and candidates to back up the pressure exerted from within by Sydney Buxton,[7] a close associate of Asquith, the leadership chose to abstain on Second Reading, or, as Balfour

[1] James Bryce, Hansard 4S H(118)960, 26 February 1903.

[2] Both Gladstone and Mundella spoke against it; Mundella was especially hostile.

[3] Mundella sent a two-man team to the United States to investigate the laws there.

[4] Gladstone, Hansard 4S H(8)1180, 11 February 1893.

[5] For example, see Mundella in Hansard 4S H(12)1358, 19 May 1893: 'It is not possible yet to make any statement as to legislation.'

Rosebery had officially opposed the Bill in the Lords; but, true to his position as Liberalism's lone wolf, he had done so merely on the grounds that the case was exaggerated. He was 'not one of those who take the high line that in no circumstances shall there be any restriction on alien immigration into this country'. See Hansard 4S H(27)119, 17 July 1894. By 1904, Rosebery was in favour of aliens legislation.

[6] Quoted in *Jewish Chronicle* (23 December 1904).

[7] Buxton had entered Parliament with Asquith in 1886 and had worked with Asquith from that time on. He was Under-Secretary for the Colonies in 1892 and Postmaster-General from 1906.

would have it, 'avoided expressing the feelings doubtless boiling in their breasts at a time when, according to the practice of this House, it is most appropriate to show them'.[1] They did so on the grounds that it was 'a different Bill'; in other words, many of the most objectionable clauses had been removed, and those which remained could be tackled in Committee.

This was really no more than a return to the older pattern of hostility without formal opposition, for one of 'the very objectionable' features still represented the basis of the Bill: namely, exclusion on grounds of poverty. This was a clause 'which we shall do our very best to remove'.[2] Even so, the practical result was that the opposition to the Bill could only muster some 59 members,[3] including ten Nationalists, one Jewish Liberal Unionist,[4] and five members of the Labour Representation Committee.

This was only a temporary (though fairly crucial) lapse, however. The Liberal Whip was restored in Committee stage, and Government majorities were reduced to as little as 24 and rarely rose above 70 thereafter. Finally, in spite of the continuing rebellion of Sydney Buxton and several others, Campbell-Bannerman led some 103 M.P.s into the Opposition lobby against the Third Reading of the Bill on 9 July 1905.

The Pro-aliens

Even so, apart from applying the Whips and lending the moral support of its presence in the division lobbies, the conventional Liberal leadership took little active part in opposing the Bill in its Committee and Report stages. As a survey of the list of proposers and supporters reveals, the great burden of the pressure for amendment was carried by an identifiable group of militant pro-aliens. In fact, here, as indeed throughout most of the period up to 1905 (and even, perhaps, afterwards) the Liberals, with varying degrees of willingness, were being led from behind on this issue.

A somewhat motley collection performed this leadership

[1] Hansard 4S H(149)1279, 19 July 1905.

[2] Asquith, Hansard 4S H(145)744, 2 May 1905. During his speech on Second Reading, Campbell-Bannerman gave a similar indication at Aldershot on 19 May 1905.

[3] Plus Charles Dilke and C. P. Trevelyan, the tellers.

[4] Walter de Rothschild.

function. However, by far the largest and most prominent group were Radicals, mostly of the school which demanded a wider sphere of state action, though including some of the older militant *laissez-faire* school (like J. M. Robertson[1] at the end of our period, and Bradlaugh[2] himself at the beginning). Radicals, in the first place, provided pro-alienism with a high proportion of its leadership. Charles Dilke, himself the acknowledged leader of the Radicals, began leading militant opposition to aliens legislation almost from the moment he re-entered Parliament in 1892. Similarly Charles Trevelyan, eventually to become a Labour Minister, seconded Dilke's motions against Second Reading in both 1904 and 1905. George Harwood was extremely active in the Committee stages in the same years, and, in company with W. P. Byles, was, from 1906, amongst the most prominent and militant of those pressing for amendment or repeal of the Act.[3]

Radicals were also conspicuous in the division lobbies of the pro-aliens. Of the forty-five Liberals[4] who voted against the Second Reading of the Aliens Bill in 1905, at least ten can be positively identified as Radicals: Charles Dilke (Forest of Dean), C. Trevelyan (Yorkshire Elland), J. E. Ellis (Nottinghamshire Rushcliffe), Sir W. Lawson (Cornwall), A. Priestly (Grantham), H. R. Mansfield (Spalding), J. A. Channing (East Northamptonshire), C. Grant (Rugby), M. Levy (Loughborough), Leif Jones (Appleby), and probably also S. T. Evans (Mid Glamorgan).

Meanwhile, the forces of Lib-Labbery further reinforced the connection, within Liberalism, between political radicalism and militant pro-alienism. On the division list examined above,

[1] Leader writer for *The National Reformer* and M.P. for Tyneside, 1906–18.

[2] Bradlaugh was amongst the first to show hostility to the anti-alien movement. He served on the Select Committee; and, apart from Samuel Montagu and Lord Rothschild, was the only member prepared, during the drafting of the Report, to vote against any hostile reference to the aliens. See R.S.C., Vol. II, pp. 284 ff.

[3] Harwood was also President of the Jewish Protest Committee. Also prominent amongst those pressing for amendment were Radicals Leif Jones (Westmorland Appleby), C. V. Wedgwood (Newcastle-under-Lyme), Sir Wilfred Lawson (Cumberland Cockermouth). Once he had decided whose side he was on, Thomas Lough (Islington) was also prominent.

[4] Including the tellers, 61 entered the division lobby, but amongst these were 10 Nationalists, 1 Liberal Unionist, and 5 members of the L.R.C. These are eliminated. Of the 45 who are left, 6 are not identifiable in *Who Was Who*, so the figure is really 39.

a further four votes come from Liberal-Labour members: Thomas Burt (Morpeth), William Abraham (Rhondda), William Parrot (Normanton), and T. C. Ashton (Luton). Several others—among them John Wilson (Mid Durham) and Charles Fenwick (Northumberland Wansbeck)—missed this particular division; however, they missed few others. Liberal-Labour members were also verbally prominent. John Burns made a long and passionate speech against Second Reading in 1904, whilst Fred Maddison, M.P. for Burnley, believing that the Aliens Act was 'one of the most fraudulent pieces of legislation which even the late Government produced' was one of those who after 1906:

> would endeavour to eliminate from the Act, everything which was against the honour, not only of this country, but of humanity, so that no one would be kept out unless he was suffering from infectious disease, or was a criminal.[1]

However, the Radicals and their associates, although prominent almost to the point of domination, were neither entirely united on the issue, nor were they, by any means, the only militants. To begin with, neither Radicalism nor Lib-Labbery was any guarantee of pro-alienism. J. Havelock Wilson[2]—though he changed his mind later—seconded James Lowther's amendment to the address of 1893. Moreover, such men—even when sitting for immigrant constituencies—tended eventually to move towards pro-alienism.[3] Henry Labouchere, under mild pressure from the Northampton bootmakers, remained an unrepentant anti-alien to the very end. Luke White, Radical M.P. for the Buckrose division of Yorkshire—and with no other reason for so doing than his own beliefs—moved with characteristic silence into the Government lobbies for the Second Reading in 1904.

Secondly, by no means all the pro-aliens were classifiable as Radicals in any sense of the term. Indeed, two of the most prominent leaders of the militants, i.e. Winston Churchill and J. E. B. Seely, were scarcely classifiable at all. (Seely refused to

[1] Hansard 4S H(153)134, 5 March 1906.

[2] Leader of the Seaman's Union, he was chiefly worried about foreign lascar seamen on British ships—although he also used some of the conventional anti-alien arguments.

[3] For instance, Thomas Lough (Islington), W. R. Cremer (Haggerston), and also Havelock Wilson.

keep out diseased aliens, as well as paupers.) Several of those who played an important part during the Committee and Report stages in both 1904 and 1905 were identifiable only as conventional Liberals—if such beings existed at all.[1]

Occupationally, the militant group seems to have been most conspicuously composed of lawyers and businessmen. Of the 45 Liberals who voted against the Second Reading in 1905, the occupations of 32 have been identified, showing twelve lawyers and nine members engaged in business, trade, or commerce.[2] Moreover, several of the pro-alien M.P.s involved in business, whilst actively opposed both to the Bill and later to the Act, did not vote in this particular division.[3] Presumably this business group were particularly susceptible to arguments about the wickedness of labour protection, and to the Smilesean imagery with which the immigrant could be associated.

Geographically, the pro-aliens do not really deserve the jibe of William Evans Gordon, with which we opened this chapter. A high proportion sat for constituencies in urban and industrial areas,[4] and several, like Stuart Samuel, W. P. Byles, and Winston Churchill, had constituencies within immigrant areas.[5] One interesting fact about the group is just how many of them were closely associated by constituency, birth, occupation, or some mixture of all three, with the industrial areas of the North,[6] especially the North-West—a connection, again,

[1] There was little that was conspicuously extreme in men like Alfred Emmot of Oldham, D. Dalziel of Kirkaldy, Reginald McKenna of North Monmouth, Lord Edmund Fitzmaurice of Cricklade, W. Runciman of Dewsbury, or Atherley Jones, M.P. for North-West Durham.

[2] There were five manufacturers, two bankers, one tea trader, and one newspaper proprietor. The next largest group were trade unionists.

[3] See especially James Joicey (Chester-le-Street, Durham), owner of the Joicey and Lambton Collieries, the two largest collieries in the county; George Harwood, Chairman of Harwood and Son, Cotton Spinners; J. T. Brunner (Northwich); D. Dalziel, proprietor of *Reynolds's Illustrated News* and Chairman and Managing Director of United Newspapers (including the *Daily Chronicle*).

[4] Even the Forest of Dean (Dilke's constituency) contained a large number of miners.

[5] See also Ben Cooper, Liberal-Labour candidate for Stepney, who made no secret of his pro-alien views. After some preliminary ambiguity, W. R. Cremer and Thomas Lough, eventually took a vigorous part in opposing aliens legislation in 1904–5.

[6] Namely, J. T. Brunner (M.P. for Cheshire Northwich, and proprietor of an alkali company); W. Runciman (Dewsbury, and Durham shipowner); George Harwood (Bolton, and cotton spinner); A. Emmot (Oldham); W. Churchill

which may partly originate with the Smilesean imagery of the self-made man. It also fits in with the impression we gained in Chapter IV: namely, that the Manchester area was the most active centre of opposition to the Aliens Bill.

(Oldham and later North-West Manchester); James Joicey (Chester-le-Street, and Durham mine-owner); George Toulmin (Bury, and Lancashire newspaper proprietor); J. F. Cheetham (M.P. for various Lancashire constituencies from 1852 and finally for Stalybridge, 1905–9, and Lancashire banker); N. W. Helme (M.P. for Lancaster and President of Lancashire Chamber of Commerce); Sir J. Leigh (Stockport, 1892–5 and 1900–6, and first Chairman of Manchester Ship Canal). Also later, W. P. Byles (Salford North); F. Maddison (M.P. for Burnley, 1906–10, and member of Hull Trades Council).

PART IV

ALIEN IMMIGRATION AND THE NEW LEFT

IX

Trade Unionism and the Immigrant

Yes, you are our brothers and we will do our duty by you. But we wish you had not come.

BEN TILLETT[1]

Trade union reaction to Jewish immigration lay along two parallel lines. In the first place, hostility found expression in demands for the exclusion or restriction of the immigrants—a line of action which reached its peak with the passing of anti-alien resolutions by the Trades Union Congress in 1892, 1894, and 1895. Secondly, English trade unionists attempted to organize the Jewish worker. Such attempts continued throughout our period, and achieved dominance after 1895, not because the problems or hostility associated with immigration had lessened, nor even because of any conspicuous success, but because the dilemma between brotherhood and grass-roots had first blurred and then, for most trade unionists, paralysed the first line of action.

'We wish you had not come'

The Causes of Hostility

Sweating

Through a mixture of reasons connected with their previous occupations, personal predilections, lack of skill and opportunities, and the location of immigrant quarters, the great majority of the aliens entered trades (e.g. bootmaking, tailoring, cabinet-making, and so on) which were undergoing the classic transition from domestic workshop to factory production —a sort of long-delayed and long-continuing industrial revolution, transforming a system whereby a skilled workman made an article in its entirety to one in which he made only a small part of it and required less skill to do so. The 'immigrant

[1] To a group of newly-arrived immigrants at the London docks; quoted in C. Russell and H. S. Lewis, p. 13.

trades', or, more correctly, the parts of each trade with which the immigrant was associated, represented a sort of compromise between the two systems of production. In the first place, the manufacture of an article was actually divided between factory and workshop, between machine and hand production, with the immigrants taking the latter part of the process. Secondly, within the workshop, there was an extensive and often minute division of labour, a machine style of production without the machine. These characteristics, together with a good deal of dirt, overcrowding, underpay, and overwork, presided over by what Gartner calls a small 'craftsman entrepreneur', were generally associated with the sweating 'system'.

With some exceptions, English trade unionists in these industries were agreed that the immigrants were 'largely the cause of sweating'[1] or, at least, that the increase in sweating was due to 'the increase in foreign labour'.[2] Some even came near to putting it at the level of malignant intention, believing that Jewish workers 'exhibited an unmistakable ambition to become sweaters'.[3]

According to many observers, the ambition originated from the fact that the Jewish worker was now, and always would be, above all things an individualist, a man undeterred either by social consequences or personal sentiment from making whatever sacrifice was necessary in order to become an entrepreneur, 'a sweating master'. The same supposed characteristics that placed him so near to the hearts of many Liberals were 'incorrigible' faults to some trade unionists, causing them to see the immigrant as somebody with 'no manhood', to whom 'it was impossible to appeal . . . through his heart'.[4] The aliens were accused before the Trades Union Congress of being willing to work fifteen hours a day:

> . . . on cold coffee and bread and cheese, and though they did not seem to earn any wages, they often in a short time, were able to set up in business for themselves. [Laughter.][5]

[1] George Keir, General Secretary, Amalgamated Society of Tailors, in S.C., Vol. IV, S.P. 1889, XIV, p. 332.

[2] James Quinn, President, Manchester Central Branch, Amalgamated Society of Tailors, in S.C., Vol. IV, p. 320.

[3] Charles Freake, President of the National Boot and Shoe Workers Union, to members of the Jewish branch; quoted in *Jewish Chronicle* (7 June 1907), p. 33.

[4] Charles Freake, quoted in Trades Union Congress, *Report*, 1895, p. 45.

[5] Knight, Fur Skin Dressers Union, quoted in Trades Union Congress, *Report*, 1894.

The causal connection thus made between Jewish immigrant and the sweating system was not, in fact, without a certain amount of validity. It is understandable, at least, that the connection should have been made. Immigrant trades were generally also sweated trades. Moreover, although the bestial conditions associated with subdivided outwork were more a reflection of the immigrant's economic weakness than of any natural docility or ruthless ambition, when given the choice of factory or workshop, he usually seems to have preferred the latter. Placed in a factory, he tended to trickle back to the workshop, and he generally vacated trades that were being taken over by the factory system. Thus, the presence of the alien in certain trades, to some extent at least, helped delay the introduction of this system. As one friendly observer noted: 'The grave objection to this alien labour is that it takes the place of machinery.'[1]

However, let us note that immigration did not cause the sweating system, though it may have contributed to its prolongation. In the first place, the sweating system existed in areas and in industries that were not affected by immigration. The House of Lords Sweating Committee elicited a large amount of information about sweated conditions in chain-making, nail-making, and cutlery-making industries which had scarcely even heard of the alien influx. Nor were aliens, by any means, the only sweaters within the industries affected by their presence. Tailors and bootmakers trade unions complained of sweating in areas where aliens were absent.[2] Moreover, as an inquiry of the Scottish National Operative Tailors Society into sweating in Glasgow concluded: 'From cases studied in detail, it would appear that the Scottish sweaters are quite as numerous as the foreigners, and [of] quite as low a type.'[3]

Finally, in spite of his 'taste for entrepreneurship',[4] there was no necessary connection between the immigrant and a minute subdivision of labour. In Leeds, although the Jewish immigrant was still blamed for sweating, and although he kept out of the factories and largely monopolized the city's fifty-one

[1] David Schloss, quoted in *Jewish Chronicle* (11 April 1890), p. 5.

[2] See, for example, Thomas Gall, Secretary, Sheffield Branch, Amalgamated Society of Tailors, in S.C., Vol. IV, p. 236.

[3] S.C., Vol. V, *Appendix and Proceedings*, S.P. 1890, XVII, p. 1023.

[4] Gartner's phrase; see Gartner, p. 88.

clothing workshops, these workshops were smaller in number and far larger in size than those existing in East London or Manchester. This was due not to any special quality of Leeds Jewry, but to the fact that while the London workshops took outwork from small merchant clothiers, in Leeds the workshop received its orders in quantity from the excess backlogs of clothing factories.[1]

Sweating also predated immigration. E. P. Thompson has noted that as early as the 1840s, there was a clear distinction between the 'honourable' and 'dishonourable' parts of some trades, between those making quality goods involving a high degree of craftsmanship, and those making 'cheap and nasty'. This division was 'notorious' in trades like cabinet-making, carpentry and joinery, boot-making and tailoring, and Thompson's description of conditions within the 'mushrooming' dishonourable section of cabinet-making is typical of all of them:

> . . . middlemen had set up 'slaughter houses' or great furniture warehouses, and poor 'garret masters' in Bethnal Green and Spitalfields employed their own families, and 'apprentices' in making chairs and shoddy furniture for sale to the warehouses at knock-down prices.[2]

These were also the conditions that Charles Kingsley graphically depicted both under his own name and as 'Parson Lot'. Indeed it was probably he, in his novel *Alton Locke*, who first thought of the term 'sweating'.[3]

In fact, a good deal of the resentment against the alien Jewish worker was no more than a continuation and extension of the old hostility for the common urban labourer felt by the skilled artisan—the man who believed himself to be part of the aristocracy of the working class. This hostility was intense because it involved questions of threatened status and independence. E. P. Thompson has noted that 'where a skill was involved, the artisan was as much concerned with maintaining his status against the unskilled man as he was in bringing pressure upon the employers'.[4] (It is, perhaps, ironic that the 'independence' which the skilled workers most feared losing was

[1] See Gartner, pp. 88–90, for a fuller discussion of the conditions existing in Leeds.

[2] E. P. Thompson, *The Making of the English Working Class* (London, Gollancz, 1964), p. 251.

[3] Charles Kingsley, *Alton Lock: Tailor and Poet* (London, Everyman's Library, 1928).

[4] Thompson, p. 244.

the quality most prized by the Jewish worker who were in many ways the embodiment of much that they held dear.)

As one 'Journeyman Tailor' told the Sweating Committee, unless foreign labour was checked, skilled workers would gradually be driven from the large towns and replaced by the unskilled.[1] Similarly, several trade unionists demanded that an Aliens Bill comprise 'a simple test of efficiency'.[2]

Again, although the Jewish immigrant sometimes found himself an unwitting obstacle in the way of a Gentile union campaigning for the wholesale introduction of the factory system, the resentment against him and the contempt for his work reflected in part the fears of the skilled worker whose ideal was to make the whole article as against subdivision of labour in principle—whether through sweating or mechanization. The alien not merely 'took the place' of the machine, he was also a more tangible object of resentment than the machine. There was an atmosphere of pure nostalgia in Northampton, where for instance:

Thirty years ago, boot-making was a home handicraft. Now, from half to two thirds of the workers are employed on machines. The men who can make a boot are very few. The young men and women know only one process. The artist has given place to the machine tender![3]

In Leeds, however, a trade unionist could be discovered complaining that 'subdivision of labour is peculiar to aliens. English workmen are only considered proficient if they can make a garment from start to finish.'[4]

It is also clear that Owen Conellan, Secretary of the Leeds Trades Council, was talking as much about the principle of subdivision as about the ill effects associated with it, when he admitted under pressure that the aliens had not caused the phenomenon. It increased with the increase in machinery and:

You can find plenty of large factories in Leeds in the clothing and boot- and shoe-making trades where there are no Jews employed and where the same subdivision goes on.[5]

[1] Mr. Goodman, past executive member of the Liverpool Operative Tailors Society, in S.C., Vol. IV, p. 182.

[2] J. Murfin, Sheffield Amalgamated Tailors, in R.C., Vol. II, p. 512.

[3] R. B. Suthers, 'Boots! The Distress in Northampton', *Clarion* (7 December 1901), p. 1.

[4] William Marston, Leeds Branch, Amalgamated Society of Tailors, R.C., Vol. II, p. 503.

[5] Ibid., p. 523.

It was still a sin; the focus of blame had merely shifted.

Competition and Blacklegging

Connected both with the sweating system and with the supposed characteristics of alien workers was the less specific charge that they competed unfairly with their English counterparts. Such complaints took a number of lines. Bakers alleged that their Jewish rivals' practice of baking on Sundays was not at all the reflection of differing beliefs about the location of the Sabbath, but was done with:

> the great object . . . that they should supply Christians with bread. . . . It is well known that the Jew supplies five times as much bread to the Christian than [*sic*] his coreligionist.[1]

Quite apart from the fact that this practice forced other bakers in the district to follow suit in order 'to protect themselves', the Jew cheated, it was claimed, by opening on Saturdays as well. English costermongers made the same allegation and complained, in addition, that immigrant costers stole their pitches and caused them to lose money because Jews preferred to buy from Jews.

A charge more generally made was that the alien's 'lower standard of life', his lower social morality, and his willingness to work for long hours enabled him also to work for lower wages than his English counterpart, who was consequently either driven on to the streets or (less frequently since he was a good trade unionist) forced to take the same rates of pay, destroying the fruits of years of patient union negotiation and weakening the negotiating position for the future.[2] Even if the alien was not himself a pauper, he forced others into pauperism.

These same supposed qualities also put the alien in a particularly sensitive position when strikes were in progress. They made him, in the eyes of many English trade unions, a

[1] John Jenkins, Secretary of the Amalgamated Union of Operative Bakers and Confectioners to a Brixton audience; quoted in *Jewish Chronicle* (16 July 1897), p. 26. This union was a staunch opponent of the mooted legislation to enable Jews to bake on Sundays and during the course of 1897 took out a long series of summonses against those who did so.

[2] '. . . they simply stultify what we do.' A. Inskip, National Union of Boot and Shoe Operatives, in letter to Henry Labouchere, quoted in Hansard 4S H(8)1220, 11 February 1893.

potential and actual blackleg *par excellence*, and a considerable part of the hostility towards the immigrant was identical with that older hostility reserved for blacklegging in any form. It is not surprising, therefore, that the Trades Union Congress resolutions of 1894 and 1895 should have identified alien immigration as a 'wholesale importation'; nor that the London Secretary of the Bootmakers Union should have complained to the Royal Commission about 'these poor wretches they bring over'.[1]

The result of such competition, together with what some saw as unfair price competition,[2] was that the Englishmen were being, or had already been, driven from certain parts of some trades altogether, the aliens having 'simply taken [those parts] to themselves'.[3] This displacement normally took place in the 'middle or commoner class of work' and complaints about it were often accompanied by the allegation that the immigrants had thus broken down the system of apprenticeship. They had taken away 'the work that our people learn on, and there is practically nothing to teach the lads on'.[4] In addition, they were making a 'lot of cheap and nasty stuff that destroys the market and injures us',[5] the sort of work that 'is getting London, and will get England a bad name'.[6]

Finally, the consequences of alien competition were felt, it was claimed, in areas and in industries outside those directly affected by their presence. Several witnesses suggested that in damaging the bootmaking trade of London, the immigrants also harmed that of Northampton, Leicester, and elsewhere via price competition.[7] Meanwhile Ben Tillett believed that the bad conditions and intense competition in the docks, and the deprofessionalization of dock workers, were produced in

[1] Thomas O'Grady, R.C., Vol. II, p. 470. Others talked of the 'indiscriminate introduction of alien labour'.

[2] See, for example, William Marston, Leeds Branch, Amalgamated Society of Tailors, quoted ibid., p. 503: 'the main grievance'.

[3] Charles Freake, R.S.C., Vol. I, p. 29.

[4] Ibid., S.C., Vol. I, p. 336. The same allegation was also made by the cabinet-makers; see R.C., Vol. II, p. 511.

[5] Ibid., R.S.C., Vol. I, p. 29.

[6] Thomas O'Grady, in R.C., Vol. II, p. 470. It was sometimes also alleged that the decline in English wages was due to the English workmen having to spend time on making alterations to work imperfectly done. See Gartner, p. 92.

[7] See, for example, S.C., Vol. I, p. 106.

large measure by the influx of men 'ousted from their own trades by the foreigners'.[1]

The real situation was, however, rather more complex than some English trade unionists imagined. In the first place, the immigrants did not cause the low wages in the trades which they entered, although their weak economic position and lack of skill did render them almost helpless against the imposition of such wages. What they did was to contribute to flooding still further a labour market that was already seriously overstocked because of the influx of women and agricultural workers and because of the high rate of unemployment endemic to trades that were seasonal in character[2] and undergoing the transition from hand to factory production.

The nature of the competition between alien and host—in so far as there was competition—depended, to a considerable extent, upon the trade concerned. It perhaps came nearest to the trade union stereotype in the bootmaking trade. Here, the immigrants were competing with the English in the lower, 'dishonourable' class of ready-made outwork. It was here, also, that hostility seems to have been most intense. The Trades Union Congress resolutions appear to have been passed mainly under pressure from the Bootmakers Union, while the anti-alien resolutions before the London Trades Council were proposed and seconded by members of this union.[3]

It is worth noting, however, that the numbers of immigrants scarcely justified, to say the least, the volume of complaint levelled against them. In an industry which employed, nationally, 202,648 males and 46,141 females in 1891[4]—a figure which rose from census to census through the rest of our period—the number of Jewish employees (irrespective of country of origin) never reached 10,000. Their influence upon the trade must, therefore, have been very slight. Secondly, if there was displacement, from at least 1890 it was more a matter of the

[1] See Ben Tillett's evidence in S.C., Vol. II, pp. 111 ff.

[2] Just how closely the tailors' wages and conditions depended upon the season may be judged from Beatrice Potter's observation on machinists and pressers: 'In the busy season, they swear at the employers; in the slack season, the employers swear at them.' See S.C., Vol. I, p. 327.

[3] A great deal of hostility originated from the union campaign to force all boot workers into factories. Jewish workers tended to drift back to the workshops.

[4] Census of 1891, quoted in Gartner, p. 75.

English displacing aliens than vice versa. For here, the Jew was allied to a declining and contracting system of production. Technological changes originating in America and spreading to London via Northampton, Leicester, and Norwich were rapidly making ready-made outwork an increasingly unnecessary and uneconomic proposition, thus leading to the triumph of the factory over the workshop,[1] and to the steady reduction of the Jewish share of the trade. This process was accelerated by the determined and successful campaign of the powerful National Union of Boot and Shoe Operatives[2] aimed at forcing all boot and shoe workers into factories.[3] As a consequence of these pressures, an industry which in 1889 had attracted 'the largest number of [foreign] "greeners" '[4] began rapidly to close its doors to them, and between 1891 and 1911, the number of immigrant workers it employed barely remained stationary.[5] Thus, in 1902, when the bootmakers complained before the Royal Commission (and before the Trades Union Congress in 1894) about the immigrants displacing them, they were complaining about a situation which, if it had ever existed, had by that time passed away. Meanwhile, if English workers were 'left with nothing to teach the lads on', it was at least as much due to the actions of their own union, as to the effects of any alien flood.

A very different situation existed in the tailoring trade where the great bulk of Jewish immigrants were employed and where they 'were becoming the symbol of a new era'.[6] Here, they and their system of production were intimately associated with the development of the cheap, mass-produced, ready-made

[1] For an analysis of these changes and their effect, see Gartner, pp. 76 ff.

[2] With a membership composed of factory and workshop employees.

[3] The high point of this campaign was a highly successful strike against some 400 employers who were giving outwork. This gave rise to an arbitration agreement which required the manufacturers to bring their outworkers indoors 'as soon as possible'. Although Jewish workers tended to drift back to the sweat shops, this was really the beginning of the end for their system of production. By 1911, except for top quality work and slipper-making, the factory had virtually taken over completely.

[4] See Gartner, p. 80.

[5] According to the 1891 Census, there were 1,560 'Prussian and Polish' males and 31 females earning their living in the trade in East London and Hackney; in 1911, 1,936 males and 74 females were so employed.

[6] Gartner, p. 81.

clothing trade. Some of this was 'slop' or 'cheap and nasty', but mainly it had arisen to satisfy the needs of:

> . . . a huge and constantly increasing class . . . who have . . . wide wants and narrow means. Luxury has soaked downwards and a raised standard of living among people with small incomes has created an enormous demand for cheap elegancies . . . cheap clothes and cheap furniture.[1]

Ready-made clothing eventually rose to dominate the clothing market, much against the wishes of the traditional English tailor who continued to believe that morality and the principle of 'one man one garment' were inextricably connected. Their complaints about displacement were unjustified since they had never shown any interest in this part of the trade. The Jewish tailor did not pauperize the Christian, nor deprive him of work;[2] for, as Beatrice Potter pointed out, the Jewish and Gentile tailoring trade were in 'watertight compartments':[3]

> You have practically the English mechanic doing the best hand-sewn goods; then the Jewish contractor taking all the overcoats; and then you have the Gentile women doing the lower branches; viz., the vests and trousers.[4]

Although this analysis was made in 1888, it remained essentially accurate until 1914. In so far as competition took place, it did not lie between individuals doing similar work, but was:

> a form of indirect competition which works by changing the taste of the consumer, and giving rise to the substitution of one class of goods for another, and it is impossible to determine the effect of such competition upon the workers affected by the change of trade with any accuracy.[5]

Jews as Trade Unionists

At least until the last few years of our period, the immigrants were, for a variety of economic, social, and cultural reasons,

[1] Arthur A. Baumann, M.P., 'Possible Remedies for the Sweating System', *National Review* (XII, November 1888), quoted in Gartner, p. 82.

[2] The membership of the National Union remained almost stationary (14,352 in 1875 and 12,143 in 1910). These figures also show how little English workers adapted themselves to the expanding section of the tailoring trade.

[3] S.C., Vol. I, p. 327.

[4] Ibid., p. 333.

[5] Evidence of H. Llewellyn Smith of the Board of Trade, as summarized in R.C., Vol. I, p. 20. Even this analysis is somewhat dubious in the light of the fact that the clientele of English tailors were generally fairly wealthy and unlikely to be tempted by cheap, ready-made clothing.

generally organized in separate trade unions, and the third and final area of hostility centred around the actual and imagined characteristics of those organizations. Many English labour leaders believed that Jews, almost by definition, made bad trade unionists: the unions of 'these self-assertive and individualistic' people possessed 'but the faintest idea of the principles of unionism'[1] and were almost necessarily characterized by impermanence and infirmity of purpose, indiscipline and internal strife, aloofness and bad leadership.

For once, the stereotype possessed a good deal of accuracy, but the causal connection with racial or immigrant characteristics is obviously rather more dubious. Gartner, however, is probably going too far in dismissing such factors out of hand. He tells us that as trade unionists 'the Jews were not inherently better or poorer than other workers' and ascribes the strength and weakness almost entirely to 'the nature of their trades'.[2] It is true that blacklegging, the tendency to filter back to work during strikes, and the failure to maintain union agreements were phenomena by no means confined to Jewish immigrants. They were far more easily explicable in terms of overwhelming economic need and the seasonal nature of the trades concerned, than in terms of any inherent Jewish individualism. The 'Children of the Ghetto' were no more susceptible than other sections of the working population to situations in which 'the brotherly love of employees breaks down under the strain of supporting families'.[3]

There is also nothing inherent about the impermanence of Jewish unions. Admittedly, with a few exceptions,[4] they never really flourished in London where a myriad of small workshops, constantly opening, closing, or disappearing altogether, provided an infertile soil for permanent unionization. This was particularly tragic since the reputation of Jewish unions stood or fell by what happened in the capital. Yet, amongst the larger

[1] John Burns's *People's Press* (21 June 1890), p. 11. This is an example of how even normally friendly quarters could become decidedly irritated when the characteristics of Jews as trade unionists were at issue.

[2] Gartner, p. 119.

[3] Zangwill, p. 249.

[4] For example, the Mantle Makers Union which, after 17 years, was still going strong in 1904. It was also one of the few Jewish unions to be permanently represented on the London Trades Council.

and stabler units of production in Leeds, such organizations achieved a high degree of continuity and effectiveness. Thus, for example, the Amalgamated Jewish Tailors, Machinists and Pressers Union of Leeds had an income of £615, an expenditure of £533, and a reserve fund of £664. Its membership of 950 in 1909 grew to 4,000 by 1913 under the stimulus of the Trades Boards Act of 1910.[1] From 1895, it was affiliated to the Leeds Trades Council, and (almost uniquely for a Jewish union) never failed to send a delegate to the Trades Union Congress.

English trade unionists also complained about the tendency of Jewish organizations to recruit by public meeting rather than by the slower but more effective methods of unionization at the shop-floor level. Yet this, too, was a natural consequence of the nature of Jewish trades. It was virtually impossible to utilize English methods in workshops that irregularly employed perhaps a dozen people, and whose very existence was subject to the vicissitudes of a seasonal trade.

Finally, some of the conflict between Jewish and Gentile trade unions can be directly related (as indeed can the very existence of separate Jewish unions) to differing economic interests caused by an attachment to differing methods of production. Thus, for instance, in 1892, we discover a letter from the Secretary of the International Outworking Tailors Federation complaining about the campaign of the English Amalgamated Society to prevent the master tailors from giving outwork. According to the Jewish official, this was 'the last straw to break [the Jew's] back . . . a ruinous and tyrannical proposition in this land of liberty'. He advocated the urgent organization of all Jews into a single union to agitate 'to protect their interests'.[2] A milder form of the same type of conflict can be seen in 1899, when a meeting of the various London Jewish tailors unions in Whitechapel decided against amalgamation with the Amalgamated Society of Tailors 'because the rules of that society do not apply to conditions prevailing amongst East End Jewish tailors'.[3] Even so, eleven

[1] Gartner, p. 138. Contrast this with the London Jewish Branch of the Amalgamated Society of Tailors which struck in 1906 with £3. 12*s*. 9*d*. in the till and a very small membership.

[2] Letter to *Jewish Chronicle* (30 September 1892), p. 9.

[3] *Jewish Chronicle* (15 December 1899), p. 23.

months later, the English union was reported to be 'determined upon gaining a foothold amongst Jewish employees . . . notwithstanding repeated rebuffs'.[1]

On one occasion, such differing methods of production seem to have given rise to conflict over methods of pay. In 1895, the Alliance Cabinet Makers were merged into the Amalgamated Furnishing Trades Union, but a large section of the Jewish workmen broke away to form the Independent Jewish Cabinet Makers Association because of the Amalgamated Union's campaign on behalf of day work against piecework. The Jewish workers complained that this would prevent them from getting their full wages, and even from obtaining employment at all. Eventually, in 1905, a compromise was arranged with the formation of a temporary Jewish union which was to admit only pieceworkers, on the pledge that when they obtained day work, members should transfer to the English union.[2]

Having said all this, however, let us note that several of the more irritating characteristics of Jewish unions (from the point of view of English labour leaders) were, at least in part, connected with the nature of Jewish society in general and immigrant society in particular. In the first place, the bad leadership and impermanence, even some of the divisiveness of Jewish unions, could, in considerable part, be ascribed to the consequences of life in a society that was essentially transient in nature, to the chronic inexperience endemic to a situation where 'almost every Jewish artisan is more or less "*en route*" '.[3] Given the absence of a tradition of organization, the existence of Jewish societies was more than usually dependent upon their founders. The constant movement of Jewish labour leaders to America rendered consistent leadership and, therefore, permanent organization near impossibilities. Consequently also, the tendency to strike without adequate preparation or funds was only one of many mistakes 'repeated with clock-like regularity'.[4] For, as even Jewish observers noted:

[1] *Jewish Chronicle* (5 November 1900), p. 22.

[2] Ibid. (28 April 1905), p. 37.

[3] Labour Correspondent, *Jewish Chronicle* (28 July 1905), p. 29. There was also the fact that few Jewish unions possessed sufficient funds to employ paid officials.

[4] Ibid. (27 March 1908), p. 25.

the one permanent feature of Jewish trade societies was that . . . the actual men at the helm were utterly oblivious of the period immediately preceding them. The benefits derived from accumulated experience are nill [*sic*]. . . . Even at this period, there prevails a general ignorance of the immediate past.[1]

An example of the practical effect of such factors can be seen in 1905. Early in that year, David Policoff, secretary of the Manchester Jewish Tailors Society, emigrated to America. For the first time in ten years, his union was not represented at the Trades Union Congress, and, although it had earned itself a reputation as one of the stabler Jewish unions, collapsed soon afterwards. Contrariwise, the stability of the Leeds Jewish Tailors and their continuing and almost unique interest in the activities of the Trades Union Congress must, in part, be ascribed to the consistent presence of their general secretary, Sam Freedman.[2] The continuity of the Mantle Makers Union is similarly associated with the continuity of its leadership in the person of General Secretary, Joseph Finn, a man who was perhaps the ablest of Jewish trade union leaders at this time.

A further source of hostility arose from the cultural baggage which some of the immigrants brought with them. The use of the public meeting was not merely a matter of necessity, it was also a characteristic of East European methods of unionization. Moreover, although continental socialism had little permanent influence over Jewish trade unions, its noisy manifestation provided some of the immediate occasions of conflict with native organizations, influenced as they were by 'pure and simple' unionism, or, at most, by empirical socialism. It explains, in the first place, why the proceedings of Jewish unions tended 'throughout' to be 'exciting and disorderly',[3] but with little practical effect, and, in part, why these proceed-

[1] Labour Correspondent, *Jewish Chronicle* (7 September 1906), p. 26.

[2] With the disappearance of the Manchester Jewish Tailors, Freedman was the sole Jewish representative at the Trades Union Congress for a number of years, although Jewish unions were entitled to at least six representatives. This further enhanced their reputation for aloofness.

It is also interesting that in 1902, a group of Jewish unions applied to Jewish labour circles in America to send over a leader to help them achieve stability. See *Jewish Chronicle* (10 January 1902), p. 23.

[3] Report of a meeting of the Mantle Makers in *Jewish Chronicle* (25 September 1896), p. 11.

ings were continually riven by internal strife between socialist and socialist, or between socialist and those who eschewed all political action.[1] As the *Jewish Chronicle*'s Labour Correspondent observed disparagingly: 'Each man's particular shibboleth is declared to be as important as if the whole world depended upon it.'[2] English sources, even those normally friendly to the immigrants, were even less charitable, and were apt to observe that:

> quarrelling is a much more amusing way of passing the time than the dry details of organization, and so beneficial agitation is hampered more from within than without.[3]

Such an impression can only have been confirmed in October 1899, when the Amalgamated Society of Tailors held a meeting to form a Jewish branch. The meeting which had 'cost several pounds to convene' broke up in disorder after a disturbance created by members of the international union, with expressions of 'disgust' from the English officials.[4]

The influence of continental socialism also explains the impatience of some of the immigrants with the slow methods of English trade unionism and why, for instance, the Jewish Upper Machinists severed their connection with the National Operatives Boot and Shoe Union, complaining that 'the National Union devotes too much attention to immediate necessities'.[5] Some of the indifference to the activities of the Trades Union Congress, and such similar bodies as the trade councils, may also be explained in these terms; for, 'It is not unusual for some Jewish labour men to consider English labour conferences as of no importance unless they happen to approach continental methods.'[6] For several years after the Russian Revolution of 1905, Jewish trade unionism was strongly influenced by syndicalism and the propaganda of the

[1] In many ways Jewish trade unionism was a microcosm of its English counterpart, but the battleground was smaller and the effects, therefore, far more devastating.

[2] 'Labour News', *Jewish Chronicle* (27 March 1908), p. 28.

[3] *People's Press* (21 June 1890), p. 11.

[4] *Jewish Chronicle* (6 October 1899), p. 18. The International Union had seven members. The meeting was reconvened the following week, with stringent safeguards against a recurrence of such trouble.

[5] Quoted in *Jewish Chronicle* (8 February 1907), p. 38.

[6] Labour Correspondent, ibid.

'universal strike', much to the disgust of many English trade unionists who looked upon the leaders of such activities as men 'who were not even capable of leading babies'.[1]

Paradoxically, another factor exacerbating the hostility between Jewish and Gentile trade unions lay in the reality behind the Smilesean symbolism discussed in previous pages. For although Liberal enthusiasm made the Jewish immigrant into something more than he really was, there is little doubt that he placed a very high value upon 'independence'. This may well help to explain the acute discomfort experienced by Jewish branches in acclimatizing themselves to the high degree of centralization of Gentile unions. By the beginning of 1906, for instance, most of the London Jewish tailors had been organized into branches of the Amalgamated Society of Tailors. In June, a general strike was undertaken without sanction from the central headquarters and carried on in defiance of its advice. Organizers of the central group complained about 'the propaganda of disloyalty',[2] and in November, an Independent Tailors Union was reported to be in existence, its members having broken away from the Amalgamated Society because of 'the rules making a branch submit details of a dispute to headquarters for sanction before striking'.[3] All in all, in this dispute there seems to have been a failure to understand and an inability to adjust, on both sides. As the scrupulously fair Labour Correspondent of the *Jewish Chronicle* was later to complain:

> The quick temperament of the Jewish workers, accustomed to independent action, might have been recognized by the Executive of the Amalgamated Society. A few concessions and slight encouragement would have been sufficient to maintain enthusiasm. . . . Instead of this, a rigorous discipline was aggravated by a certain measure of haughty disregard for the claims and demands of Jewish branches at headquarters.[4]

However, more important than any preference for independent action was the fact that the Jewish immigrant did not

[1] J. Daly, Organizing Secretary of the Amalgamated Tailors, to a meeting of the Mantle Makers, quoted in *Jewish Chronicle* (31 August 1906), p. 30. There had been a general strike and lock-out in the East End in June 1906, leading to 'complete disorganization' for the tailors.

[2] D. Rollaston, a member of the District Organizing Committee, quoted ibid.

[3] *Jewish Chronicle* (2 November 1906), p. 12.

[4] Ibid. (11 October 1907), p. 25.

regard himself as one endowed with a fixed station in life—an impression which can only have been confirmed by some of the characteristics of the Jewish 'community',[1] and by the structure of the trades Jews entered. Here, the continual and much desired movement from journeyman to small master (and vice versa) led to a situation where each could see himself in the other's position. It made the immigrant unsusceptible to much of the class-consciousness stirring English workers. It led to an intimacy between master and man which hampered the cohesiveness of Jewish workers during strikes and, on other frequent occasions, was expressed in joint action and 'Joint Committees' 'to co-operate in the abolition of sweating'.[2] This latter phenomenon, although perhaps a sensible answer to the sweating system, was one which English unions at first vigorously opposed[3] and, even to the end, never entirely understood.

'Yes, you are our brothers'

The Dilemma

However, when this hostility came to be expressed in the form of concrete demands for the exclusion or restriction of aliens, it turned out to be a rather damp squib. The Trades Union Congress, as we have seen, passed resolutions against the landing of 'pauper aliens' in 1892, 1894, and 1895. Various trade councils (like those of Blackburn in 1892, Liverpool in 1893,

[1] An interesting example of the sort of attitude this engendered even amongst socialists was the action of Lewis Lyons who led a deputation of Jewish unemployed to the Chief Rabbi 'to persuade him to organize the Jewish workers into a compact phalanx', to change the behaviour of the sweaters by having their names read out in synagogues, and to allow the preaching of 'labour sermons'. See *Jewish Chronicle* (18 November 1892), p. 13.

However, the community was often more of a help than a hindrance. Witness the *Jewish Chronicle*'s 'Labour News' column, and the Jewish Dispersion Committee's insistence that those dispersed take the trade union rate of wages.

[2] *Jewish Chronicle* (27 December 1901), p. 30.

[3] For instance, the International Tailors, Pressers and Machinists Union was expelled from the London Trades Council for forming a Board of Conciliation with the masters after the union's strike against Messrs. Bousfield Ltd. (this strike was supported by the International Union).

Although by 1907 the Amalgamated Tailors Society favoured 'any practical scheme of that sort', the issue formed one of the immediate grounds for a dispute with the Jewish Garment Workers Union—although the underlying cause was an attempt by the latter to steal the former's members. It was also a cause of friction within and between Jewish unions.

and Leeds in 1894) did the same. Yet from 1895 onwards, although the remarks and demands of certain trade unionists before the Royal Commission showed that hostility had not decreased, institutionalized protest seems to have ceased almost completely.[1] The Trades Union Congress never revoked itself, but when in 1898 it decided to submit 'the resolutions of this and former Congresses' to Cabinet Ministers in the form of a questionnaire, the aliens resolution was not included.[2] After 1895, moreover, no resolutions of this sort were even submitted to that body for consideration.

In part, this was due to the weakness of the trade union anti-aliens. The resolution of 1895 was passed by a margin of only 20,000 in a total vote of 512,000, and it would have been defeated altogether but for the abstention of the Miners, who had been insulted by James MacDonald's jibe that many delegates were wearing the results of sweated labour. Moreover, the anti-aliens were never sufficiently strong to convert the London Trades Council which, presumably under the influence of George Shipton,[3] Secretary, and Ben Cooper,[4] President, twice resoundingly rejected restrictionist motions, and in 1895, condemned the one passed by the Trades Union Congress,[5] an action in which it was joined 'almost unanimously' by its counterpart in Glasgow.[6] Meanwhile, the Manchester Trades Council seems not to have considered the question until June 1904, when, in company with the Jewish Tailors Union, it planned a public meeting of protest against the Aliens Bill in Heaton Park.[7] Finally, although most of the hostility to the alien came from unions and union branches

[1] That is, apart from an anti-alien resolution by the Stockton Trades Council in 1905.

[2] See *Labour Leader* (24 December 1898), p. 6.

[3] Secretary of the Amalgamated Society of House Decorators and one of the leading members of the Trades Union Congress after the break-up of the 'Junta' which had dominated English trade unionism in the 1870s.

[4] Secretary of the Cigar Makers Union, whose membership was half Jewish (mainly those of Dutch extraction).

[5] See evidence of Joseph Finn, in R.C., Vol. II, p. 732. In December 1891, it had set aside a resolution of its own investigating committee calling for the exclusion of those not in possession of £3; and in August 1894, it defeated a resolution by 53 to 17.

[6] *Labour Leader* (21 December 1895), p. 9.

[7] *Jewish Chronicle* (10 June 1904), p. 30. The meeting never took place owing to the abandonment of the Bill by the Government.

whose trades were (or were claimed to be) affected by his presence,[1] these sources were by no means united. J. H. Wilson's remark that only the trade unions from unaffected trades were against restriction is rather less than true.

This disunity in turn (as well as the 'silence of the Trades Union Congress and the pro-alienism of the London Trades Council')[2] was partly due to the increasing influence of socialism. Where a union or branch even in an affected trade was strongly influenced by socialists, it generally tended to come down on the side of the alien.[3] Thus William Parnell, Secretary of the West End Branch of the Alliance Cabinet Makers and Independent Labour party candidate for Fulham in 1895, argued before the Sweating Committee that 'the competition from the enormous number of foreigners in the trade [was] not more keen than English competition'.[4] The Cabinet Makers as a whole spoke and voted for the Trades Union Congress resolution in 1894, but opposed it in 1895. The West London District of the Amalgamated Tailors acted similarly, and James MacDonald[5] made the main speech against the 1895 resolution. Similarly, the Dock Labourers National Union, under the leadership of men like James Sexton (I.L.P.),[6] argued consistently and loudly against aliens legislation throughout our period even to the extent of submitting an undiscussed resolution against the Aliens Bill to the Trades Union Congress in 1904.

However, perhaps the main factor behind the silence of the Trades Union Congress and other bodies after 1895 was paralysing embarrassment. For a policy of restriction or exclusion—even without the influence of socialism—ran into direct

[1] This was not always so; for example, the resolution of 1892 was seconded by the Railway Servants. This action, together with the number of votes mustered by the anti-aliens in 1894 and 1895, must have been the reflection of horse trading.

[2] Reported to be in favour of collective ownership, 1894.

[3] There are again exceptions here: Ben Tillett, for example, Secretary of the Dockers and General Labourers Union; and James O'Grady, Organizing Secretary of the National Amalgamated Furnishing Trades Association. See R.C., Vol. II, p. 492.

[4] S.C., Vol. I, p. 289.

[5] Independent Labour party candidate for Dundee, 1895; Secretary, Central Glasgow Branch, I.L.P.; and Tailors' delegate to the London Trades Council and, from 1896, Secretary of that body.

[6] Labour Representation Committee candidate for Hull Central, 1904, President of the Trades Union Congress, 1905; and Labour M.P. for St. Helens, 1918–31.

conflict with trade union notions of international brotherhood, labour mobility, and free trade, and their strong attachment to the tradition of political asylum.

In the first place, trade unionists were at least as anxious as other sections of English society to avoid the suspicion that either they, or their members, were motivated by anti-Semitism. Time and again, for example, they sought 'to make it plain that, as Englishmen, we have no objection to a Jew because he is a Jew';[1] that given the right conditions of work, 'we welcome them. It is not racial feeling or creed';[2] and that 'if it was, I would not come here to give evidence'.[3] Although Ben Tillett only just managed to save himself from a fate worse than death in complaining that the English were being driven from some trades 'as the Jews, or at least the foreigners, get to monopolize them',[4] in general, the proprieties were maintained. Indeed, the word 'Jew' was so rarely used in trade union circles that Lewis Lyons,[5] almost in exasperation, sought to remind the Royal Commission of what the issue was really about:

> . . . most of them are Jews; and we may as well speak of them as Jews, because it is known all over the country that this is a Jewish question, and we might as well say that they are Jews who are working here.[6]

This sort of reticence may well help to account, for instance, for the silence of the Leeds Trade Council after its anti-alien resolution of 1894; for, as Sam Freedman of the Leeds Jewish Tailors noted nine years later, the resolution was passed 'just before our affiliation with that body and I am certain that the same council would not endorse such a resolution at the present time'.[7]

Moreover, for most trade unionists, apart perhaps from Ben Tillett, it was a matter of equal embarrassment that the immigrants, besides being Jews, were also foreigners (and poor foreigners at that). As such, they were compulsory objects of trade union sympathy. It was difficult enough having to argue

[1] Joseph Murfin, Sheffield Amalgamated Tailors, R.C., Vol. II, p. 514.

[2] William Marston, Leeds Amalgamated Tailors, ibid., p. 503.

[3] T. W. Whatley, London Clothiers and Cutters Trades Union, ibid., p. 473.

[4] S.C., Vol. II, p. 134.

[5] At the time, General Secretary of the United Garment Workers of Great Britain.

[6] R.C., Vol. II, p. 494.

[7] Ibid., p. 738.

for the exclusion of 'these poor wretches',[1] of 'the very poorest and miserablest class of men in the world'.[2] When one also had to persuade one's listeners that 'there is no feeling against foreigners as foreigners . . . as foreigners we are not opposed to them',[3] one's statements began to lose a little lucidity.

When all of this was combined with the recognition of the sacredness of the doctrine of political asylum, the result was near-paralysis and woolliness of expression, even for those unions who felt that they had good reason for hostility towards the alien. George Shipton, although a pro-alien, noted that:

> some of our people in the building and house decorating trades are strongly opposed to [alien immigration] and would go to almost any length to stop it. But, at the conference, we did not come to any conclusion.[4]

The same was true a year later when Shipton told the Sweating Committee:

> We have discussed [checking immigration] among the trades and we find a very great difficulty in coming to any definite opinion upon the matter. We are rather afraid that it would limit a man's choice of living . . . and that [such a law] might be worked to prevent a man, perhaps oppressed in his country, obtaining a livelihood in another country. . . . At the same time, if it was proved that there was simply a pauper class shelved [*sic*] on to English shores to live by charity. . . . I think the state would have a right to interfere.[5]

George Shipton, as we have noted, seems to have been largely pro-alien in predisposition, and the members of his union can rarely have been affected by the immigrants. However, the same fuzzing of hostility is observable amongst spokesmen for unions which came into much closer contact with the aliens. Thus the members of the Sweating Committee must have been utterly mystified as to just what the Amalgamated Society of Tailors really wanted, when the President of that union told them:

[1] Thomas O'Grady, Secretary, London Branch of the Boot and Shoe Operatives, R.C., Vol. II, p. 470.

[2] Charles Freake, S.C., Vol. I, p. 336.

[3] Charles Freake, R.S.C., Vol. I, p. 130.

[4] Quoted in *Jewish Chronicle* (3 February 1888), p. 14. Shipton, on this occasion, was a member of the Compton Committee on the Condition of the Working Class to Lord Salisbury.

[5] S.C., Vol. IV, p. 517.

I hardly know that it would be wise to stop immigration; that would be an unnatural, and hardly fair way of doing the thing, but I think it ought to be regulated in some way, and that the poorest, and most miserable, and the most unskilled perhaps of foreign labour ought not to be thrown upon the market of England. . . . I do not think it would be wise, and I do not know that we could advocate, and I am sure any intelligent man would not advocate altogether, the complete prohibiton of foreign labour, but, at the same time, I think there must be . . . some means devised whereby skilled labour should contend against skilled labour. . . .[1]

Of all the unions, the National Union of Boot and Shoe Operatives displayed, by far, the most consistent and savage hostility towards the alien. Yet, its official policy statement was a mild and elusive beast indeed, for it observed in part:

it is inadvisable to increase the ranks of unskilled workers, alien or native. . . . Legislate to keep out some of this vast horde of unskilled, but let the legislation be flexible enough as not to be guilty of injustice, or not to be in opposition to those principles of religious and political liberty which are still adhered to by some of the best men in England. On the [one] hand, we must avoid that early-nineteenth century individualism which talked too much of 'liberty' without understanding it; and, on the other, that narrow and selfish spirit which finds its expression in protection.[2]

Even hostile trade unionists, in fact, wanted the best of both worlds. If the Government ultimately produced a vague and partially unworkable piece of legislation, in a sense it was doing no more than reflecting what trade unions wanted. Liberal action after 1906 also reflected their wishes: for, deterring a man from coming at all was far less painful and embarrassing than turning him away at the gate.

'We will do our duty by you'

Brotherhood in Action

The third theme in the trade union reaction to the immigrant took the form of an attempt to unionize him. Here, whatever stereotypes of Jewish workers some of them may have held, English trade unionists—with the possible exception of the

[1] S.C., Vol. IV, p. 329.

[2] Report prepared by Solomon Van Amstell (of the London Metropolitan Branch and a Dutch Jew) and later adopted by the Executive Committee of the Union as its official policy statement. Printed R.C., Vol. II, p. 415.

bootmakers—revealed a good deal of patience, perseverance, and insight into the special conditions of Jewish labour.

Socialists played a major part in this process. Thus, the persistence and flexibility of the unionizing activities of the Amalgamated Society of Tailors owed a good deal to the attitude of the man who, by 1896, had become its General Secretary, James MacDonald. The influence of socialism also seems to have accounted for the interest taken by men whose unions were unaffected or, at most, marginally affected by immigration. Jewish trade unions in Leeds received strong support from Ben Turner,[1] Secretary of the Weavers and Textile Workers Union. Similarly, representatives of the National Union of Dock Labourers gave considerable assistance to Jewish workers in London. Finally, the man who took 'by far the keenest interest in Jewish trades union affairs' all over the country, who almost, in fact, made them his life's work, was Herbert Burrows, the son of a tailor and a leading member of the Social Democratic Federation:

> Few Englishmen have mixed so intimately with Jews as I have done during the past thirty years. I have shared their sorrows, and sympathised with the darker side of their lives, and this from the international as well as from the English standpoint, but I have not really got near to their inner personalities. I have always felt . . . that, to the Jews, the Western Gentile is but the baby of humanity.[2]

The main burden of these activities lay necessarily in lending support to separate Jewish unions. As Ben Cooper pointed out, separate unions were often 'unavoidable because customs, habits and modes of work and, unfortunately, often language, stood in the way'.[3] Leaders of both English unions and local trade councils'[4] appeared regularly on the platforms of organizing and recruiting meetings of Jewish workers.[5] They

[1] I.L.P. Batley and Labour candidate for Dewsbury, 1906.

[2] *Jewish Chronicle* (23 April 1909), p. 14.

[3] Cooper was advocating the formation of a separate Jewish Trades Council in co-operation with the London Trades Council. See *Jewish Chronicle* (28 June 1901).

[4] In 1902, for example, a recruiting meeting of the Manchester Jewish Tailors was chaired by J. Harker, Vice-President of Manchester and Salford Trades Council, and supported by George Tabbron, President of that body. See R.C., Vol. II, p. 784.

[5] Sometimes individual trade unionists even started Jewish unions themselves, for example, James Sweeny, Secretary of the Leeds Jewish Tailors Trade Society. See S.C., Vol. IV, p. 351.

attempted, rather uneasily, to settle inter-union disputes, encouraged Jewish unions to amalgamate, and, with rather more success, mediated disputes between masters and men.[1] They lent moral and, where union rules allowed, also financial support to Jewish strikes.

For the most part, English trade unionists took a merely persuasive role. Occasionally, however, they attempted shock tactics. Thus, James MacDonald refused to take part in a meeting of Jewish tailors on the grounds that:

> The conduct of the Jews in return for our assistance to them has proved to be far from what we expected or desired. In every dispute that has occurred of late years in our trade, the masters had in the Jewish workers, with a few honourable exceptions, a ready and willing lever to help to defeat the workmen. . . . When you show us something done in this direction, you will be proving that you are trades unionists in reality as well as by profession. We, therefore, decline to be represented at this meeting.[2]

Into the same category comes the Trade Union Congress resolution of 1907, condemning small unions as unnecessary. On these grounds, the Leeds Trades Council refused affiliation to the bizarre mixture of trades called the Jewish Riveters, Slipper-Makers, Furnishers and Upper Machinists Trades Union.[3]

For their part, meanwhile, Jewish trade unions attempted to counteract their reputation for aloofness by lending their support in the trials of their English counterparts. Jewish unions gave financial support to the dockers strike of 1889 'though their own position was not good',[4] and a Jewish Workers Committee sent £34 to the general relief fund of the miners strike in October 1893.[5] All the London Jewish unions subscribed to the engineering strike of 1897, sold 'penny tickets printed in Yiddish', and organized a procession through the East End, while the Cigarette Makers levied 3*d.* on every member, 'even

[1] Thus, for instance, the Leeds Trades Council was 'instrumental' in opening negotiations between Jewish employees and employers in the tailors strike of 1908. See *Jewish Chronicle* (7 February 1908), p. 8.

[2] Letter to J. Finn, Secretary of the Mantle Makers, quoted in *Jewish Chronicle* (24 July 1903), p. 26.

[3] *Jewish Chronicle* (21 February 1908), p. 10.

[4] Cited *Jewish Chronicle* (7 January 1898), p. 25.

[5] *Jewish Chronicle* (27 October 1893), p. 12.

the girls'.[1] In times of disaster, moreover, Jewish workers sometimes received official sanction from the community at large in their efforts to prove that they were not aloof. The *Jewish Chronicle* in 1893, for example, opened its columns to an appeal by the Reverend D. Wasserzug to raise funds for the relief of sufferers in a disastrous colliery explosion at Pontypridd so as to mark Jewish sympathy 'and thereby give the people at large an illustration of the catholicity and unsectarianism of their charities'.[2]

Towards the end of our period, there are also signs of a general move to persuade Jewish workers to organize themselves into branches of general unions. In 1901, the Jewish Tin Plate Workers became a branch of the Tin Plate Workers Society, and, at its conference in 1902, the English union unanimously agreed that efforts should be made by its various London branches to maintain the Jewish branch.[3] More important, in 1906 there were reported to be two Jewish branches of the Amalgamated Society of Tailors who, from some unspecified time, 'have increased their membership by ten'.[4] In spite of a suicidal strike later in 1906, which resulted in the formation of the Independent Tailors Union, by January 1907, there were apparently eleven Jewish branches in existence.[5] By 1910, they were being instructed on how to play their part in the Trades Boards Act.

The success of such efforts up to 1914, as indeed of Jewish trade unionism as a whole, was rather limited. However, even when confronted by Jewish workers determined to go their own sweet way, English trade unions could sometimes display a remarkable degree of flexibility and patience. We can see an example of this at an earlier period. In 1893, the Hebrew Cabinet Makers became a branch of the Cabinet Makers Alliance. Within two years, however, an independent society had reappeared, formed by the Jewish workers who objected to the higher fees of the Gentile union. Even so, the latter continued to assist both organizations, giving, for instance, £554 in strike pay and £161 in picketing expenses to the independent society.[6]

[1] *Jewish Chronicle* (7 January 1898), p. 25. [2] Ibid. (21 April 1893), p. 13.
[3] Ibid. (30 May 1902), p. 25. [4] Ibid. (20 April 1906), p. 28.
[5] Ibid. (6 February 1907), p. 37. [6] Ibid. (11 October 1901), p. 19.

Meanwhile, from at least 1902, this process of unionization was backed up by what seems to have been a changing sphere of trade union activity away from anti-alienism towards a more constructive approach to the immigrant problem. There was increasing pressure, particularly from the Amalgamated Society of Tailors via the Trades Union Congress, for anti-sweating legislation—an agitation which bore fruit in the Trades Boards Act of 1909. The society also agitated for a 'thorough revision of the present system of factory and workshop inspection' and for 'the compulsory provision of workshops by firms, for those who are in their employ'.[1] It instituted a trade union label in 1909 and began pressing for a national minimum wage.

Secondly, from 1902 onwards, the Trades Union Congress annually and unanimously began passing resolutions for the abolition or reduction of the naturalization fee and the simplification of the naturalization procedure. Such resolutions were generally moved by Jewish trade unions, and supported by English organizations, 'to show that this is not a purely Jewish question, but affects all aliens'.[2] In some ways, this campaign took the place of anti-alien activity since it attempted to make it possible for 'every workman who had been a member of a trades union for a period of five years, and with the approval of such a trades union, [to] apply for naturalization'.[3]

[1] Resolution to I.L.P. Conference, 1908; quoted in *Jewish Chronicle* (13 March 1908), p. 19. This type of pressure was not new, but the intensity with which it was applied was; previously, resolutions of this kind had only demanded 'an extension' of the Factory Act and more power for factory inspectors. See Trades Union Congress, *Report*, 1894, p. 49.

[2] Ben Cooper, quoted in *Jewish Chronicle* (8 September 1902), p. 21. Such support was also essential since there was, from 1902, rarely more than one Jewish union represented.

[3] Trades Union Congress, *Report*, 1902, p. 108. On this first occasion, the motion was moved by the Amalgamated Tailors and seconded by the engine men. Later the clause about trade union membership disappeared. In 1910, the London Society of Compositors moved a resolution to allow naturalized aliens to receive old age pensions.

X

The Socialist Attitude

If a community of goods were established in one country, would not a million or more needy people from foreign parts crowd into that country within one year?[1]

It ought to be an admirable test for Socialists who are constantly proclaiming the internationalism of Labour.

AN ISOCRAT.[2]

The Socialist Stand

With a few notable exceptions, and with a greater or lesser degree of enthusiasm and interest, spokesmen for all the main socialist movements in Britain condemned aliens legislation as reactionary, unbrotherly, inhuman, undemanded, and unnecessary. During the short period of its existence, the Socialist League under the leadership of William Morris maintained a close and friendly contact with the immigrants in the East End,[3] and denounced the agitation against 'THE BLARSTED FURRINERS' as early as April 1888.[4] By February 1903, the Social Democratic Federation, though less friendly to the immigrants in general, and to Jews in particular, was somewhat sheepishly expressing suitable disgust about 'all restrictive legislation against alien immigration' at meetings in East London'.[5] The Fabians, though largely ignoring the issue, had dismissed immigration as a cause of sweating in a pamphlet of 1895.[6] Keir Hardie's paper, the *Labour Leader*, denounced the

[1] Advertisement requesting correspondence on the subject of alien immigration for inclusion in the *Labour Annual*, 1897, in *Clarion* (19 September 1896), p. 4. For responses, see *Labour Annual*, 1897 (Manchester, Labour Press Society, 1897), p. 215.

[2] Letter to *Labour Leader* (6 January 1905), p. 474.

[3] When Morris died, a meeting of 1,000 Jewish tailors voted to send a letter of condolence to his family. *Jewish Chronicle* (9 October 1896), p. 15.

[4] *The Commonweal* (28 April 1888), p. 130.

[5] *Jewish Chronicle* (13 February 1903), p. 31.

[6] H. W. Macrosty, *Sweating: Its Cause and Remedy*, Fabian Tract No. 50 (London, The Fabian Society, 1896).

Trades Union Congress resolution of 1895[1] and featured a series of articles against aliens legislation from April 1904 onwards. Meanwhile, the movement for which it was the mouthpiece, the Independent Labour party, heavily defeated an anti-alien resolution at its conference in 1903.

It was sometimes suggested that leading socialists took a principled attitude 'because, in the first place, their trade has not been attacked, and secondly [and mainly], because . . . of the assistance they hoped to get from the Liberals at the next election'.[2] The first of these claims is only partially grounded in fact. Although Ben Tillett and James O'Grady[3] occasionally advocated restriction, they never did so with much consistency, and James MacDonald, William Parnell, and other trade unionists from affected trades dismissed the suggestion as a 'mere palliative'.[4] The second suggestion does not seem to be true at all. 'Labour' M.P.s went far beyond official Liberalism on this issue. Keir Hardie, both inside and outside of Parliament, regretted that the Liberals 'had run away from the Aliens Bill',[5] and all four members of the Labour Representation Committee voted in the unwhipped division on the Second Reading of the Aliens Bill in 1905.[6] After 1906, the Labour party officially placed itself in the van of the pro-aliens agitating for amendment or repeal.[7]

Basically, leading socialists took this attitude because it was what they were 'temperamentally inclined to do'.[8] As a foreigner, as a Jew, as a refugee, and as a poor fellow worker, the newcomer was a compulsory object of socialist sympathy. As with the Liberals, to attack the alien was to attack the basis

[1] 'Our London Letter', *Labour Leader* (17 August 1895), p. 3.

[2] T. Hunt in letter to *Clarion* (28 July 1905), p. 7.

[3] Secretary, National Amalgamated Furnishing Trades Union. O'Grady later seems to have associated himself with the demands for repeal, although rather gingerly. See *Jewish Chronicle* (13 April 1906), p. 11.

[4] Trades Union Congress, *Report*, 1895, p. 45.

[5] 'Our Own Outlook', *Labour Leader* (5 May 1905), p. 58.

[6] Keir Hardie (Merthyr Tydfil); D. J. Shackleton (Clitheroe); Will Crooks (Woolwich); Arthur Henderson (Barnard Castle).

[7] Apart from the above, the most active were James Ramsay MacDonald (Leicester); Will Thorne (South West Ham); and outside Parliament, George Lansbury, the Labour candidate for Bow and Bromley in 1900 and 1910, and M.P. from December 1910.

[8] J. Bruce Glazier, 'Socialism and the Anti-alien Sentiment', in *Labour Leader* (30 April 1904), p. 40.

of party philosophy. In fact, the dilemma between the dictates of ideology and suspected grass-roots opinion was more acute for the socialists because socialism at this time (even without its Christian overtones) was what Liberalism once had been in its Gladstonian heyday: a religion and a way of life. Thus, arguments tended to be less about facts than about ideology, and for a man to remain a socialist, there were really only two choices: to embrace the alien or to hold his peace. As we shall see later, the one action complemented the other.

Ideology and the Immigrant

Anti-alienism, of course, first and foremost, directly affronted socialist notions of international brotherhood and solidarity. Socialists attached 'only a conventional meaning to the word "foreigner"' and recognized 'our working comrades of other lands as members of the Army of Labour whose emancipation is fast approaching'.[1] Thus, there was 'no alien question in a national sense . . . only a parochial alien question'.[2] The very word itself was taboo, for socialists were 'entirely opposed to the workers of any country being regarded as alien'.[3] Exclusion was just another means of creating an artificial division amongst the international working class, and those trade unionists who preached it were doing the capitalist's work for him, 'acting out the old, old policy—"Divide and Conquer"'.[4]

It also achieved two other things. In the first place, exclusion and restriction were 'but a step away' from the 're-erection of toll-gates which fined people for locomotion from one place to another'.[5] Secondly, it offended the socialist ideal of the isocratic commonwealth. Once one excluded the foreigner, one placed him in an inferior position to oneself, and, after all:

> was it not contrary to 'good socialism' to assert that any one human being has rights superior to those of another human being. Would not a privileged country stand on the same unsound basis as a privileged class?[6]

[1] *The Commonweal* (21 June 1890), p. 194.

[2] H. Snell, 'England and the Dirty Foreigner', *Labour Leader* (23 April 1904), p. 33.

[3] J. F. Green of the Peace Association, at a Social Democratic Federation meeting against the Aliens Bill; quoted in *Jewish Chronicle* (13 April 1906), p. 11.

[4] Mrs. J. Fyvie-Mayo, 'That Aliens Question—A Reply', *Clarion* (9 November 1895), p. 360.

[5] *The Commonweal* (21 June 1890).

[6] Fyvie-Mayo.

For these reasons, even if the immigrants were not religious refugees, 'we should none the less open our doors and welcome them in to share our freedom and toil.'[1]

Aliens legislation was also 'unscientific',[2] a crowning sin in the eyes of many socialists: it attempted to deal with the symptoms rather than the causes of social *malaise*. It was bogus and, like imperialism, a manifestation of the old capitalist trick of diverting the workers' eyes away from the true sources of their distress, a trick typical of 'this time of shams, hypocrites and petty crusades'.[3] Even the *Clarion*, a paper, as we shall see, not distinguished for its sympathy towards the immigrant, cried 'herrings' when it set the Aliens Bill against the Conservative policy of importing Chinese labour into South Africa.[4] To others, it was 'an almost laughable proposition to suggest that a system which is based upon competition should be protected in some particular instance from competition'.[5] For such suggestions, indeed, socialists produced some of their choicest sarcasm. Thus, as *The Commonweal* pointed out, once an Aliens Act was in operation:

> we may safely assume that poverty in the British Isles will soon be a thing of the past! . . . How easy and how well-to-do the East End workmen and workwomen would then become, all of a sudden. How all of their troubles would cease. . . .
>
> For observe, that the British workmen never compete with each other, and therefore reduce their wages. . . . To Ireland, the poor foreign Jews have, as yet, not penetrated . . . and hence the standard of the Irish peasants and wage workers is an almost ideal one.[6]

Meanwhile, socialists were as deeply attached as Liberals to the doctrine of political and religious asylum. To Hyndman, in another context, 'the Right of Asylum [was] worth defending

[1] Editorial, *Labour Leader* (6 July 1906), p. 104.

[2] Aveling's term; see *Labour Leader* (10 September 1895), p. 20.

[3] E. Kitz, 'The Blarsted Furriners', Part II, *The Commonweal* (5 May 1888), p. 138.

[4] *Clarion* (10 January 1903), p. 4. The Conservatives became doubly inconsistent in socialist eyes when they refused Keir Hardie's amendment to exclude 'imported blacklegs' and later, in 1906, defeated a Bill to that effect via the Lords.

[5] Kitz, p. 138.

[6] 'Neo Jingoism', an editorial by Andreas Scheu, in *The Commonweal* (19 May 1888), p. 123.

at any cost'.[1] Ramsay MacDonald was certain that 'the working classes were prepared to maintain the incurables . . . even at their own expense rather than close the doors of this country to refugees'.[2] The vision of England as a refuge for the oppressed tempted one socialist into ringing, if rather bad, poetry:

> England! for myriad ages past
> The hospice of the World,
> Upon whose White Cliffs in the Breeze
> Freedom's flag unfurled
> Beckoning from every land
> The outcast and oppressed
> In a thousand thankful tongues
> Has thy name been blessed. . .[3]

The suggestion that many of the immigrants were refugees caused Keir Hardie to reverse his position before the Commons Select Committee in 1889,[4] and, at a later date, to ask whether:

> these poor creatures who have been shot down in the streets of Warsaw and other parts of Russia, those poor, poverty-stricken human beings who have been hunted down as beasts of prey are to be condemned by this Bill to remain in a country that does not know how to treat them.[5]

In a sense, the socialists had more reason than the Liberals to regard the doctrine as sacred, for many of the people who were fleeing at this time were not the Liberals of '48 to whom Palmerston extended the hand of friendship, but revolutionary socialists. The cry against Russian oppression often emanated 'from the Socialist Jews who have found refuge on our shores', and whose brothers, as the *Labour Leader* 'reverently acknowledged', showed 'faithfulness, even unto death, for the Socialist cause'.[6] It was no accident, therefore, that after 1906 many of the Labour party's protests against the operation of the Aliens

[1] H. M. Hyndman, *Further Reminiscences* (London, Macmillan, 1912), p. 401. Hyndman was referring to his advocacy of a large navy and citizen army for defence against Germany.

[2] Hansard 4S H(153)148, 5 March 1906.

[3] Harry Lazenby, *Labour Leader* (13 January 1905), p. 487. There are five verses.

[4] R.S.C., Vol. II, pp. 63 ff. See especially questions 1430–5 and 1577–9. Hardie was, at this time, Secretary of the Scottish Miners and of the Scottish I.L.P. Shortly thereafter, he became firmly pro-alien.

[5] Hansard 4S H(145)780, 2 May 1905.

[6] Editorial, *Labour Leader* (6 July 1906), p. 104.

Act centred around specific cases of foreign socialists who were excluded on grounds of want of means.

The Smilesean Symbol

In fact, here we begin to see where Liberal and socialist parted company, not only on this issue but, by implication, on a host of others. Although men like Lansbury sometimes spoke of the doctrine of asylum 'making England what she was', they were far less prone than the Liberals to hold up the Huguenot as proof that the Jew would make good. The very qualities that so endeared the immigrant to the Liberal—his industry, sobriety, thrift, and self-help—appalled and even infuriated most socialists.[1] John Burns, nominally a Liberal, but arguing the case against restriction from a socialist standpoint, could find but one fault in the alien—a fault that, admittedly, 'disarmed all the arguments against him', but which nevertheless led to his having:

> none of the vices of the free man. He yielded to authority with ox-like submission. He was patient, thrifty, sober and industrious to an extent which made his gorge rise.[2]

Keir Hardie, attending a Jewish trade union meeting, noticed that:

> The crowd . . . was sober and indulgent, and, in many respects, indicated wherein the Jew is superior as a sweater's victim to the British Gentile. For twelve and fourteen hours a day, these patient creatures will work in a room in which there is barely space to turn, and in a temperature which is killing, and yet, they never complain except when work cannot be had. This problem of the foreign worker is not the least perplexing of the many-sided Labour question.[3]

It is very significant in this regard that the *Clarion* which normally managed to ignore the Jewish immigrants with an adroitness that would have earned it the admiration of Nelson, should have suddenly discovered their existence when, in 1898,

[1] Very occasionally, one finds examples of the Liberal view on socialist lips. George Lansbury felt that 'the Christian working men . . . . would do well to imitate the Jewish aliens' example of industry, sobriety and thrift, qualities which made them a welcome element in the population'. See *Jewish Chronicle* (10 March 1905), p. 12.

[2] Hansard 4S H(133)1157, 25 April 1904.

[3] *Labour Leader* (28 April 1894), p. 2.

the head of the Parochial Mission to the Jews advised English workers to copy the industry, sobriety, and thrift of these otherwise misguided people. In his 'By the Way' column, 'Dangle'[1] commented:

> How like a reverend secretary of a mission to the Jews. How ready his ingenious proposal to lower the standard of the English workers' existence. How unctuously patronizing his cool suggestion that, rather than cause any unpleasantness to his Jewish rival, John Smith should unresistingly abandon all the advantages his father's and forefathers' privations and struggles have won for him in the past. . . . Should we push back the English worker because a handful of Jewish aliens refuse to advance? No sir, we shan't do it that way—a thousand times, sir, no.[2]

A month earlier, Robert Blatchford himself had written his eighth 'Letter to Working Men' and neatly reversed the Liberals' secret image of the Jewish immigrant as a living tribute to self-help, by asking his readers:

> . . . do you not know very well that the 'Greeners'—the foreign Jews who came to England for work and shelter—are very sober and industrious and that they are about the worst paid workers in this country?[3]

The difficulty was that many socialists suspected that the unfair exercise of these qualities did bring its reward. They were what made the immigrant 'such a terrible competitor . . . the ideal "economic man", the fittest person to survive in trade competition'.[4] Harry Quelch, Editor of *Justice*, complained that so many Jewish workers were 'always dreaming of becoming master men',[5] and the *Clarion* was convinced that 'they breed their own capitalists'.[6]

Socialists and Anti-Semitism

In fact, whatever Blatchford might have believed, there was a danger that the poor Jew might become a rich Jew, against whom, as far as many socialists were concerned, no holds were

[1] A. M. Thompson.

[2] *Clarion* (7 May 1898), p. 145.

[3] Ibid. (2 April 1898), p. 112. The next notice taken of the alien was in 'High Rents and the Alien', *Clarion* (26 December 1902), p. 4—another attack upon Smilesean symbolism.

[4] J. A. Hobson, *Problems of Poverty* (London, Methuen, 1891), pp. 59–60.

[5] At a meeting of Jewish Journeymen Bakers; quoted in *Jewish Chronicle* (18 December 1903), p. 31.

[6] Editorial by R. B. Suthers, *Clarion* (8 April 1904), p. 5.

barred. Many of them do not seem to have regarded rich-Jew anti-Semitism as coming within the forbidden category of racialism at all.

In the first place, this type of radical anti-Semitism, and the Jewish conspiracy theory of history that went with it, possessed a history that was both long and honourable, in the sense that it was respectable. In 1806, for example, William Cobbett observed that:

> Till lately, the richest Jews amongst us affected poverty for fear of envy, and ate their unleavened cakes and courted their usurers in secret. And now, they are the companions of our feasts, the pride of our assemblies, the arbiters of our amusements. . . . The treatment of the Jews has always been milder in proportion to the commercial advancement of the states in which they lived.[1]

Chartist newspapers, whilst decrying anti-Jewish excesses abroad, also contained references to the evil power of Jewish finance, to England's being delivered into the 'thraldom of Jews and Jobbers',[2] to 'the false, cunning and remorseless Jews',[3] to Christian usurers who 'like Jews and vermin . . . flourish amid impurity and disease'.[4]

Secondly, the expression of hostility against rich Jews in particular, and even all Jews in general, was a favourite pastime for some sections of continental socialism at the turn of the century. Bakunin regarded Jews as '*par excellence* exploiters of others' labour';[5] whilst Edmond Picard, the Belgian socialist, saw them as 'an inferior race [who] suck and corrode' Europe, and against whom the only remedy was 'L'anti-sémitisme scientifique et humanitaire'.[6] A resolution of the International Socialist Labour League of 1891 condemned 'both anti-Semitic and philo-Semitic agitation', after amendment by a French

[1] *Political Register* (6 September 1806), quoted in Modder, p. 99.

[2] Thomas Attwood, 1832, quoted in Edmund Silberner, 'British Socialism and the Jews', *Historia Judaica* (Vol. XIV, 1952), p. 33. This article is handicapped by too much emphasis upon the Social Democrats and a determination to find an anti-Semite under every stone.

[3] Samuel Kydd, *The Labourer* (1847), quoted in Silberner.

[4] Anonymous, *Poor Man's Guardian* (16 March 1833), quoted ibid.

[5] Quoted in Silberner, 'Modern Anti-Semitism', *Historia Judaica* (Vol. XV, 1953), p. 96.

[6] Quoted ibid., pp. 108 ff.

delegate who complained about Jewish financiers and Jewish bankers being 'great oppressors of labour'.[1]

Amongst English socialists at the turn of the century, a pre-existing radical tradition was reinforced by the intense anti-capitalism of 'the gilded age'. *Justice*, the mouthpiece of the Social Democratic Federation, showed this hostility in its most vigorous form. It believed that 'the Jewish financier is a living type of international capitalist',[2] and sometimes went to the point of arguing almost wistfully:

> We have no feeling against Jews as Jews, but as nefarious capitalists and poisoners of the wells of public information, we denounce them. It would be easy enough to get up a capitalist Jew-bait here in London, if we wish to do so, and the proletarian Jews would gladly help us.[3]

However, hatred of Jewish capitalists was not confined to the pages of *Justice*. *New Age* complained that 'the materialism of the age [is] promoted by Jewish financiers, who rarely assist in any humanitarian movement, but usually oppose it';[4] while Ben Tillett, in the *Labour Leader*, mused:

> If 'getting on' is the most desirable thing in this earth, then the Jew, as the most consistent and determined money-getter we know is worthy of the greatest respect. That his money-grubbing is not universally respected only proves that the bulk of civilized nations, even now, do not believe in the commercialistic ideal of clean hands and blood-stained money.[5]

Rich Jew anti-Semitism was intensified also by the events in South Africa. In *Justice* Hyndman editorialized at length about 'the Jews' War on the Transvaal',[6] and, thirteen years later, reminisced about 'the abominable war on behalf of German–Jew mineowners and other international interlopers'.[7] Similarly, in 1900 the *Clarion* referred sarcastically to 'the suffering Uitlanders of Jewhannesburg'[8] and in 1904, regaled its readers with 'a list of "British" Randlords who are prepared to sing

[1] Quoted in *Jewish Chronicle* (21 August 1891), p. 38.

[2] *Justice* (28 January 1893), p. 2, quoted in Silberner, 'British Socialism and the Jews', p. 43.

[3] *Justice* (21 January 1893), p. 1, quoted ibid.

[4] Quoted in *Jewish Chronicle* (6 May 1910), p. 17.

[5] *Labour Leader* (29 December 1894), p. 2.

[6] *Justice* (7 October 1899), p. 4.

[7] Hyndman, p. 150.

[8] Editorial by A. M. Thompson, *Clarion* (29 September 1900), p. 312.

"Rule Britannia! Britannia Rulth the Wavth, ma tears!" on the least encouragement'.[1]

The English version of rich Jew anti-Semitism, however, only rarely spilled over into a more general form of racialism. It does not seem to have produced hostility towards the immigrants. In fact, it led the new left to argue still more fervently against the exclusion of Jews on grounds of inequality of treatment. Thus, John Burns was again arguing from a socialist standpoint when he told the House of Commons that, rather than excluding poor Jews flying from persecution, they should be passing:

> an Aliens Bill for the rich Jews of Bayswater, Fitzjohn's Avenue, Hampstead . . . but the Government dare not include these people in the schedule of the Bill. The political power and financial influence of these rich Jews were so great that they could pull the Government from Dan to Beersheba. . . . They should not persecute a man simply because he was a poor Jew.[2]

Time and again, we find this indignation being expressed in socialist arguments against legislation. *The Commonweal* sarcastically demanded to know why the anti-aliens did not bring legislation 'within the range of practical politics by proclaiming a crusade against *poor* Jews (not the moneylenders who are all honourable men)'.[3] Will Crooks told his constituents at Woolwich that Labour men 'wanted an Act which would keep out the gang of foreigners who polluted Park Lane . . . an Act which would apply as much to Park Lane as to Petticoat Lane'.[4] Pete Curran informed the Labour Representation Conference that:

> It was the West End Aliens who were most needing to be deported . . . [those who] exploited white men in their own country and then went to South Africa and exploited yellow men against white men.[5]

[1] 'Echoes of the Week', *Clarion* (1 April 1904), p. 5. There followed a list of about 40 Jewish names. The 'Echo' was headed 'British Thwelp Me'.

[2] Hansard 4S H(133)1149, 25 April 1904. *Reynolds's News* (2 July 1905) argued against 'the Anti-Jew Bill' in a similar fashion, complaining about the Jewish M.P.s who had voted for the Aliens Bill—an indication that 'the ingratitude of rich Jews to the Liberals is monumental. . . . The rich Jews are becoming a menace to the British community.' On 23 April 1905, the paper even argued that the rich Jews would have been excluded also, but for the Government's 'depending for its existence upon Jewish financiers'.

[3] *The Commonweal* (19 May 1888), p. 156.

[4] Quoted in *Jewish Chronicle* (6 January 1906), p. 32.

[5] See report of preliminary Conference on the unemployed in *Labour Leader* (27 January 1905), p. 16.

Even the gentle George Lansbury 'did not favour exclusion of any kind, but, if he had his choice, he would make a start with the non-productive alien millionaires of Park Lane, rather than with the workers who come to East London'.[1]

Moreover, although it was possible to say rude things about rich Jews without apology,[2] once this type of hostility was identified as anti-Semitism by others, socialists reacted in the normal way. Accused of talking about 'the Jewish gang of vampires who had arranged the South African war', Philip Snowden went out of his way to deny ever having used the phrase, and called it 'a gross insult to charge him with anti-Semitism as he [was] an Internationalist and consequently a friend of everybody. . . . [It was] an electioneering dodge.'[3] A writer in the *Clarion*, accused of making similar remarks in 1899, was careful to identify himself on the side of the angels by pointing out: 'I do not despise, and have never despised either a Jew or a Gentile for being such.'[4] Finally, after a long series of attacks upon rich Jews, *Justice* apparently found the protests of its readers becoming a little too pointed, and, on the grounds that 'the subject has been well ventilated on both sides',[5] declared that further discussion must cease. Thereafter its columns were completely free of anti-Semitic material.

Hostility towards poor Jews, meanwhile, was identified quite positively as being anti-Semitic and, therefore, for the most part, taboo. When A. M. Thompson expressed concern in the *Clarion* about the influx of 'poor unshorn and unsavoury children of the Ghetto', he was assailed by a storm of protest from socialist bodies and other organs of the socialist Press. The *Labour Leader* sent a strong letter of protest, and *Justice* (significantly, in the light of its previous record of rich Jew hostility) published letters against this 'most revoltingly unsocialist and anti-Semitic attack upon the Jewish workers'.[6] Thompson's

[1] Quoted in *Jewish Chronicle* (10 March 1905), p. 12.

[2] Even so, as the references to 'aliens' in the previous quotations perhaps show, some were careful even here.

[3] Quoted in *Jewish Chronicle* (7 January 1910).

[4] 'Mont Blong' (H. Blatchford), *Clarion* (21 October 1899), p. 411. Thereafter, he referred to 'the Jew and Gentile financiers of Capetown'.

[5] *Justice* (11 November 1899), p. 3, quoted in Silberner, 'British Socialism and the Jews', p. 49. See also pp. 46–9 for a discussion of the way the matter developed.

[6] Ibid. (7 July 1906), p. 6, quoted in Silberner, 'British Socialism and the Jews', p. 41.

reaction to the 'blunder-headed rabble who have been assailing me with frantic abuse . . . and foaming futilities' was equally significant. He told them how a 'lifelong intimacy with Jewish friends and close observation of the Russian refugees have brought the problem [of the Jews] very near to my personal interest'.[1]

A similar impression of the reaction of many socialists towards the expression of anti-Semitism is to be gained from reading between the lines of Glazier's article in the *Labour Leader*. Although generally pro-alien, Glazier attempted to persuade his fellow socialists that they should 'not treat anti-alien sentiment as necessarily inhumane or anti-social'. They would not kill it by mere denunciation:

> By showing . . . that we rightly comprehend the ground and the sense of the grievance which alien immigration usually inspires, we can speak with greater earnestness and courage to the public.[2]

Some sections of the new left—particularly those influenced by Social Darwinism—had not entirely formulated their attitude towards all the various forms of racial hostility: they were not always sure whether or not it was 'a still useful protective instinct' or 'a no longer beneficial prejudice', and did not know 'to what extent, and under what conditions, the intermixing, or even the cooperation, of different races is good or bad for the physical health or social progress of nations'.[3]

[1] Editorial, *Clarion* (13 July 1906), p. 6. To prove Thompson's claim to innocence, the *Clarion* (28 August 1906) then gave some space for a two-and-a-half-column article on the case for the International Trade Organization by M. D. Eder. This was the first time the paper had taken notice of the broader Jewish problem.

[2] *Labour Leader* (30 April 1904), p. 40.

[3] Ibid. *Clarion* also published a long series of articles for and against the South African treatment of Negroes, including one comparing the latter with the ape and basing its argument on the *Origin of the Species*. See Mr. Puff, *Clarion* (26 October 1906), p. 2.

The *Labour Leader*, however, identified itself in recognizably twentieth-century terms by publishing frequent and unqualified attacks upon discrimination against 'our coloured brothers and sisters' in Africa and in the Southern states of America and spoke of the 'horrible cruelty of it'. Socialist branches sometimes invited American Negroes to lecture them on the problem of the South, for example, the Bradford Labour Church organization, as reported in *Labour Leader* (7 July 1894), p. 4. On 5 November 1898, the *Labour Leader* also attacked the *Daily News* for emphasizing a coloured composer's African descent as 'lending itself to the upholding of colour prejudice'.

Nevertheless, racial prejudice was already becoming a sensitive issue. Most socialists believed that it *was* wrong, and all agreed that it was something incomprehensible, menacing, and somehow uncontrollable—something, in fact, very much like black magic. An advertisement inserted in the *Labour Leader* described the race question as 'probably the most interesting and vital question Socialism has to deal with'.[1] Lynchings in the Southern states of America stimulated A. M. Thompson into an almost cosmic description:

> The phenomenon of race prejudice stands out still—portentous, black, colossal, a ghastly revelation of racial difficulties and hatred before whose atavistic force, the restraints of civilization are as powerful as are a child's sand castles to resist the Atlantic tide.[2]

Viewing the situation nearer home, J. Bruce Glazier observed that anti-alienism was 'derived partly from that most mysterious of human emotions—race aversion—accentuated by numerous strangenesses and impediments of language, religion, tradition and economic conflict'.[3] Meanwhile, a reviewer in the *Labour Leader*, writing in the first person plural, was 'afraid that the question of alien immigration is one which most Englishmen have settled in their own minds solely from prejudice'.[4] Five months later, his paper expressed heartfelt thanks that, due to the 'towering ineptitude' of the Tories during the Mile End by-election, the cry 'Down with the Alien' was almost spent. Without such blunders, there would have been 'an ugly sting in [the cry] and, if used with discretion, it might have been hurled with alarming effect from half a thousand platforms in the country'.[5]

The suspicion that public opinion, and particularly working-class opinion, was, to say the least, not entirely on the pro-alien side, made the dictates of socialist ideology a rather difficult burden to bear. While most leading socialists resolved the dilemma in favour of the immigrant, many of them did so

[1] *Labour Leader* (13 July 1906), p. 119.

[2] A. M. Thompson, 'Black versus White', *Clarion* (26 October 1906), p. 2. The language of cataclysma, of course, is not always confined to the political left. Witness Enoch Powell's reference to the 'Tiber foaming with much blood'.

[3] Glazier.

[4] *Labour Leader* (5 August 1904), p. 207.

[5] Ibid., 'The Anti-alien Crusade' (13 January 1905), p. 483.

rather unwillingly, and only when forced to take up a position by the onrush of events. Some did not do so at all.

Anti-alienism

A few Socialists took up an anti-alien position. Delegates from Hyde and Nottingham argued in favour of restriction at the Independent Labour Party Congress of 1903. From 1902 onwards, the *Clarion* was subject to what can best be described as anti-alien spasms. Although recognizing that using immigration as a unicausal explanation of unemployment savoured 'too much of the red-herring policy', and although recognizing the technical difficulties in the way of legislation, the paper felt, nevertheless, that 'something of course ought to be done'.[1] The great objection to the immigrants was not that they were aliens, nor that they were poor; rather, it was 'their ability to make a living at our expense'.[2] Although they would have been 'a source of health and wealth to Russia', to the East End of London, 'these ignorantly fanatical sweaters' slaves, [these] marred and maddened spoils of barbarism [were] economically and socially a menace'.[3] While England was 'sending out [her] finer specimens of humanity' she was receiving in exchange men who could only be considered 'as so much poison injected into the national veins'.[4]

Clarion also occasionally published articles hostile to the alien. In 1895, Leonard Hall, President of the Manchester and Salford Independent Labour party, argued in favour of a poll-tax on all immigrants except political refugees, on the grounds that immigration, although not 'a primary cause, or even a greatly important factor, of poverty and misery', did contribute to 'the lowering of our already debased standard of living'. Moreover:

> . . . wherever a colony of Jews has established itself, the direct result has been to render more difficult any attempt to alleviate abuses, and to intensify

[1] *Clarion* (16 January 1903), p. 4.

[2] Ibid. (8 April 1904), p. 3.

[3] Ibid. (13 July 1906), p. 6.

[4] Ibid. (22 June 1906), p. 4. A. M. Thompson seemed to feel he was softening the blow in explaining later (13 July 1906) that the word 'poison' was 'being used in its right sense', i.e. meaning 'any substance injuring the health of the body into which it is absorbed'.

competition amongst employers tenfold by the facilities which their cheaper labour affords.[1]

Yet, although these were remarkably pragmatic sentiments, they were, in a sense, still dominated by socialist ideology. The very violence of language is significant: for to take this line, one had, deliberately and quite self-consciously, to throw socialism out of the window. Thus, according to Leonard Hall, this was a matter of 'legitimate self-preservation . . . not a subject for cheap sentiment or mock heroics, but of ordinary and hard necessity'.[2] Several weeks later, when his article had been attacked as being 'contrary to good socialism',[3] Hall replied by characterizing his opponents' arguments as 'inspired by a somewhat too sanguine estimate of the quality of fraternity . . . sheerest Utopian impracticableness . . . a squint-eyed patriotism and a spurious humanitarianism'.[4]

The basis of Leonard Hall's socialism lay, moreover, well outside, or, perhaps, well 'in advance' of the mainstream of English socialist thought at this time. He believed that socialism would only come 'by appealing to the selfish instincts of the mob', and that 'a swinishly selfish people can only be gotten enthusiastic over a reform that is going to benefit them right here and right now'.[5] He felt, too, that people would 'not be moved to action by exhortations to brotherliness, love or self-sacrifice'.[6]

To such a bloody-minded empirical approach to the question there was but one alternative: to find some justification for exclusion in the socialist bible. It is significant that the only other anti-alien arguments discoverable within the socialist

[1] *Clarion* (12 October 1895), p. 322. Hall was also the Independent Labour party candidate for Salford South in 1892. The seat was retained by Mr. Howorth (C.), one of the early anti-aliens.

[2] Leonard Hall, *Clarion* (12 October 1895).

[3] Fyvie-Mayo.

[4] *Clarion* (7 December 1895), p. 391. See also 'Clarion Postbag' (28 July 1905), p. 7, for a letter from T. Hunt: 'Can you wonder that I am not prepared to beslaver the alien blackleg with a lot of sickly and canting sentiment about his being "a man and a brother"?'

[5] Ibid. (8 February 1896), p. 46.

[6] Ibid. (2 May 1896), p. 141. Hall also wanted an appeal to the lower-middle class to take socialism out of its 'manual-labourers groove'; see *Clarion* (8 February 1896), p. 40.

sphere, were contained in an article by Alfred Russell Wallace.[1] This was an article almost totally devoid of factual material and the writer first called down 'our great philosopher Herbert Spencer' for:

the important principle that, when a state of society is fundamentally unsound, there is as regards many social problems, no *right* course, but only a choice between greater or lesser degrees of wrong-doing.

On this principle, Wallace argued that although 'we all feel it to be wrong to refuse admission to any foreigner able and willing to work', when one's own people were scarcely able 'to keep body and soul together', it was 'a great wrong' to admit people who could but transform 'a miserable insufficiency into a gulf of absolute starvation'.

However, thought Wallace, there was 'another and more general reason for this view', and it was a remarkably ingenious, indeed self-contradictory, one. Immigration was a bad thing because in the host country:

it blinds people to the real causes of unemployment and starvation in the midst of superfluous wealth, while, in the country from which the emigration takes place, it, to some extent, relieves the pressure of competition and enables the Government and people to shut their eyes to the real causes of the evil.[2]

Embarrassment and Deafening Silence

However, with or without ideological chapter and verse, pragmatism was a luxury few socialists felt able to afford. Even the *Clarion* was never consistently anti-alien. It denounced those who pointed to the immigrant as *the* cause of unemployment. It sometimes quoted arguments and statistics favourable to the alien.[3] It expressed sympathy for the Jews in Russia, and announced that 'we would give of our treasure and our blood to force their bloody oppressors' hands from their throats'.[4] Finally, in May 1905, A. M. Thompson sawed right through the branch upon which *Clarion* was sitting, by expressing disgust at the:

[1] Wallace was a naturalist and explorer of some note who had collaborated with Darwin in producing the *Origin of Species* in 1858.

[2] Wallace, 'The Immigration of Aliens', *Clarion* (3 June 1904), p. 8.

[3] See 'Our Observatory', *Clarion* (30 June 1905).

[4] 'Socialists and Russia', *Clarion* (6 July 1906), p. 7.

poor Lenten fare that is offered. There is an Aliens Bill that will exclude none of the cunning exploiters who are the bane of the East End, nor any of the bawds and panders that swell the vice of the West, but only the most pitiful of the victims of Russian oppression in Poland. . . . England will not shut out the sweater. It proposes only to abdicate its proud position as the refuge of the oppressed.[1]

Meanwhile, in its spasms of anti-alienism, the *Clarion* and its contributors had revealed something else besides the half-spoken sentiment of 'let ideology be damned'; it had revealed a quite remarkable ignorance of the facts. Thus, for example, the paper had quoted what it regarded as 'the pertinent remarks' of the Recorder of London to the effect that:

we have the riff raff of the whole world pitchforked into this country, and we spend days and days at the Court every session trying these disreputable foreigners.[2]

This was no more than a rather weary anti-alien cliché, but Leonard Hall, in 1895, had gone beyond even this. Even Arnold White at his most frenzied had never claimed what Hall apparently believed: namely, that 'there is scarcely a town of any dimensions in the country in which the foreign element has not menaced and injured the position of local workmen'.[3]

It was, therefore, with some justice that the *Jewish Chronicle*, after one such attack in June 1906, asked: 'Where was the *Clarion* all these years . . . ?'[4]

A clue to the answer to this inquiry had been given at the head of Leonard Hall's article of October 1895. Holding the issue at arm's length and examining it gingerly, the *Clarion*'s sub-editor had pronounced it to be 'That Aliens Question'. The title was symptomatic of an almost paralysing embarrassment, and the most significant feature of the *Clarion*'s treatment of the question was the way in which the paper contrived, at least up until the beginning of 1903, to ignore it totally. The

[1] A. M. Thompson, 'By the Way', *Clarion* (5 May 1905), p. 4.

[2] Ibid. (16 January 1903), p. 4. This was the *Clarion*'s first revelation of editorial feeling on the issue. Alien crime rates were very low.

[3] Ibid. (12 October 1895), p. 322. Also read between the lines of 'An Isocrat's' letter to the *Labour Leader* (6 January 1905), p. 474: 'See to it that your speakers are well grounded in the facts and politics of the subject before they speak.'

[4] *Jewish Chronicle* (20 July 1906), p. 39, referring to A. M. Thompson's article 'Exchange is sometimes Robbery', *Clarion* (22 June 1906), p. 4.

Trades Union Congress resolution of 1894 had escaped unnoticed. The similar resolution of 1895 produced three articles, but failed to darken the editorial columns. During the next seven years, as far as both editors and contributors were concerned, the alien might have disappeared from the face of the earth. The only inkling given to the *Clarion*'s readers of the immigrant's existence took the form of a description of 'A Pleasant Saturday Afternoon'[1] spent in the East End in 1896 which told them very little, and a review of Zangwill's *Children of the Ghetto* which told them everything. For, it noted: 'We socialists are perhaps accustomed only to regard the Jew as a perplexing problem of alien immigration.'[2]

In January 1903, the editors emerged from under the blanket, but only to cry 'herrings'.[3] In fact, it was not until April 1904, with the introduction of the first Aliens Bill, that the *Clarion* really seized its pragmatism in both hands, and finally decided that 'it was high time that legislation dealing with the alien should be considered'.[4]

The paralysis that gripped Robert Blatchford's periodical seems to have held its correspondents similarly pen-tied. The three articles of 1895 produced not a single letter in the 'Clarion Postbag'. Indeed, as far as the present writer has been able to ascertain, the latter remained empty of correspondence on the subject until July 1905.[5]

The rule that silence is golden extended far beyond the pages of the *Clarion*.[6] In January 1905, a letter appeared in the *Labour Leader* asking that 'more vigour' be put into the championship:

> of our brother man from abroad. There is, it seems to me, something half-hearted in the way the subject of the anti-alien campaign is being met by Socialist branches and speakers of all sections in this country. . . . I hope the question will figure more frequently in your lecture lists.[7]

[1] *Clarion* (22 August 1896), pp. 268–9. See Chapter IV.

[2] H. P. Holmes, ibid. (4 June 1898), p. 178. During this period there were several articles and letters about the race problem in America and Africa.

[3] Ibid. (16 January 1903), p. 4.

[4] Ibid. (8 April 1904), p. 5.

[5] See anti-alien letter of T. Hunt, in *Clarion* (28 July 1905), p. 7, which produced one letter in reply—see *Clarion* (1 September 1905), p. 7.

[6] *Justice*'s treatment of the issue seems to be similar to *Clarion*'s. See Silberner, 'British Socialism and the Jews'.

[7] 'An Isocrat', *Labour Leader* (6 January 1905), p. 474. There were no replies to this letter.

A perusal of the lecture lists and reports of meetings published in the *Clarion* and *Labour Leader* by the branches of the Independent Labour party, the Social Democratic Federation, and the Christian Social Union, shows that this criticism was understated. Between 1894 and 1906,[1] as far as the present writer has been able to discover, branches of these organizations held a grand total of eighteen meetings[2] on the subject of alien immigration. Of these, nine were held by branches of the Independent Labour party (three in Manchester, one in West Salford, three in the Leeds area, one in Keighley, and one in Clapham), four were held by the Social Democratic Federation (three of which were protest meetings held by the East London Jewish branch),[3] four by the Labour Church Movement (two in Birmingham, two in Hyde), and, finally, one by the Birkenhead Socialist Society. The location of these meetings suggests that, although a high proportion took place in cities (especially provincial cities) containing a large number of immigrants, few occurred in the areas of those cities directly affected by immigration[4]—unless, like the East London Social Democratic Federation, they were held by Jewish branches. The titles of the lectures,[5] the names of the lecturers,[6] and the fact that a few were protest meetings, suggest that most of them were pro-alien in tone. However, the fact that, with the one exception of the Ashton Meeting of the Social Democratic Federation (10 June 1899), all the meetings occurred in the periods 1895–6 and 1903–6, seems to point to the conclusion that notice was only taken of the problem in the last resort.

For the most part, in fact, socialist branches turned a blind eye to the immigrant. If large sections of public opinion were hostile towards the alien—as some leading socialists seem to have suspected—this hostility was never transmitted by the branches to the leaders. Confronted by the dilemma we have

[1] In 1894, an average of 30 to 50 branches were regularly advertising in the *Clarion* and *Labour Leader*. By 1906, this figure had risen to well over 100.

[2] See Appendix II for full summary.

[3] The fourth was held in Ashton in June 1899. See *Clarion* (10 June 1899).

[4] Thus the Independent Labour party held meetings in South-West, East, and Central Manchester and West Salford, but never in North-West Manchester or North Salford, both of which possessed active branches.

[5] 'Alien Immigration and the Brotherhood of Man', for instance.

[6] I. Loewy, of North-West Manchester by-election fame, gave two lectures; J. Dyche, another Jewish pro-alien, gave three; and J. Bruce Glazier gave four.

been describing, together with the possibility, indeed the probability, of being suspected of racial prejudice, the former preferred to remain silent. From 1895, as we have seen, the Trades Union Congress was similarly quiescent. Thus, with pro-alien pressure coming from Jewish socialists[1] and from a few idealistic Gentiles, socialist leaders could either ignore public opinion or interpret it according to their own predilections:

> the working classes were prepared to maintain the incurables . . . even at their own expense rather than close the doors of this country to refugees.[2]

Either way, they could indulge their ideology.

[1] See editor's note about *Clarion*'s editorial of 22 June 1906 on the Jews in *Labour Leader* (6 July 1906), p. 105: 'We have received many resolutions and letters of protest from Jewish socialist organizations and correspondents' on this subject.

[2] Ramsay MacDonald, Hansard 4S H(153)148, 5 March 1906.

XI

Conclusion: The Immigrant Situation

This has been an historical study of English, and particularly left-wing, reactions to Jewish immigration around the turn of the century. However, it will, I hope, have become evident that the Jewish immigrants elicited a set of English reactions conspicuously similar to those aroused by the more recent influx of newcomers from the Commonwealth. These similarities are sufficiently close to suggest a number of rather surprising generalizations about the English reaction to immigration, at least as it has been manifested over the past seventy-five years.

In both cases, we discover the political left wing challenged at what seems to be its weakest point—the point where ideology, or its logical extension, and the wishes and assumed interests of at least a section of the grass-roots run into direct conflict. In both cases, the left wing finds itself defending the *status quo* against a Conservative party willing and able to pose as the champion of the ordinary British voter.

In each case also, the immigrant, because of his racial background, is believed to be the object of a hostility that is qualitatively and quantitatively different from resentment against any other foreigner, against any other minority group. What this study has suggested, in the first place, is that it is not the hostility itself which strongly influences and perhaps rules the situation, but the reactions and beliefs about that hostility.

Towards anti-immigrant feeling, the left wing seems to have two possible reactions. The resentment may be seen as being so wicked that one cannot possibly give way to it—and it would be dangerous to do so—and, for some, that public opinion cannot possibly be guilty of it. Alternatively, it may be regarded as being so dangerous, so potentially catastrophic in effect, and so electorally damaging that one must give way in order to neutralize it. The two attitudes may coexist within the same party. The treatment given to the immigration issue by Liberal candidates and organizations in the East End was very different from that accorded it by the bulk of the party within Parliament. One attitude may also rapidly succeed the other. The Labour party vigorously opposed the Commonwealth Immigration Bill up until the Third Reading in February 1962, when, quite suddenly, it almost completely reversed its position. The Liberal leadership strongly opposed legislative restriction of alien immigration throughout 1904, withdrew formal opposition to the Aliens Bill of 1905, only to reapply it on Third Reading.

Underlying and partially explaining the adoption of these attitudes and the rapid shift from one to another, is an assessment of public opinion that seems to be based less on empirical observation (which is difficult anyway because of the essential ambiguity and embarrassment of public opinion in expressing something that might be construed as racial prejudice), than on differing and changing beliefs about what the masses are capable of. The result is either extreme optimism or extreme pessimism, and the latter, perhaps, finds its origin in the age-old fear of 'King Mob'.

On the surface, the left wing seems to be in a very weak position on the immigration issue. Short of throwing ideology out of the window, it cannot take the lead in agitating for exclusion. It must either welcome the immigrant, or undertake a rather shamefaced withdrawal under the ragged banner of 'me-tooism'. Whatever course it chooses, it seems bound to be the loser.

However, this impression is rather less than accurate. Public opinion is essentially ambiguous. There is a greater degree of hesitancy about expressing grievances about immigration than about any other problem. In fact, what a cursory study of the present situation has suggested, a detailed examination of that existing seventy-five years ago seems to have confirmed, namely, that the right wing has at least as difficult a task as that which confronts the left. For the anti-immigrant agitators must convince those for whom, and those to whom, they speak (and perhaps also convince themselves) that the grievances that they are giving expression to, do not interfere with social and official norms of tolerance, generosity, and so on;[1] that

[1] In a sense, this study has resolved itself into a sort of private argument with Seymour Martin Lipset, who has suggested that the lower class is subject to a

they are not to be subsumed under the disreputable category of racial prejudice. Thus, we discover the agitators, in each case, becoming almost neurotic in their declamations of innocence, avoiding the words 'Jew' and 'coloured' as if they were the plague, and the anti-aliens making determined attempts to secure the public support of prominent members of the Jewish community. Similarly, we see even Sir Oswald Mosley forming a coloured branch of the Union Movement.[1] The role of the agitators, in fact, is to legitimize hostility, to give private grievance public legitimacy.

In the English political situation, the amount or extent of racial prejudice is really irrelevant, except in so far as overt racialism serves to embarrass and handicap the agitators. What matters is the suspicion of its existence; and the suspected presence of racial prejudice serves to muffle, rather than increase, hostility. As the anti-aliens themselves admitted more than once: 'nothing can harm the question more' than 'going into the religions of these people'.

Because of this factor, the left wing is in a stronger position than at first seems likely. It can exploit the public notoriety of prejudice. Its role, as well as its natural reaction, is to convince its listeners that exclusion, or restriction, does interfere with traditional norms, blurring the line—so painstakingly drawn by the agitators—between grievance and intolerance. Even if, as has been suggested, 'the lower strata' are predisposed 'to view politics as black and white, good and evil',[2] the left wing can, and naturally tends to, paint the issue in those terms: as a battle between selfishness and generosity, between tolerance and intolerance.

In general, at the turn of the century, the Liberals and socialists reacted, and continued to react, to the anti-immigrant agitation in a way that was consistent with the dictates of party ideology. In the mid-twentieth century, the Labour party (in

variety of tensions 'which tend to produce deep-rooted hostilities expressed by ethnic prejudice, political authoritarianism. . . .' From these 'underlying personal values', it may sometimes be diverted in countries where 'norms of tolerance' and commitments to democratic procedures are 'well developed'. See *Political Man* (London, Heinemann, 1960), pp. 120 and 100. My own study has tended to emphasize the attachment to those norms, both in regard to the working class, and as they affect the over-all political situation.

[1] *Guardian* (9 April 1965).

[2] Lipset, p. 100.

regard to the issue of immigration control)[1] has not done so, at least not since February 1962. In assessing the factors behind these differing reactions, let us note, firstly, that nearly all the historical circumstances that in Chapter II we selected as likely to make the aliens' case conspicuously different from the present situation, in fact redounded to the advantage of the left wing, or at least tended to push it into pro-alienism. The underlying belief in *laissez-faire*, in so far as it affected the situation at all, constituted a private reason for the welcome given to the immigrant by the Liberals. Except perhaps as trade unionists, the immigrants were a highly assimilable group who, unlike the present newcomers,[2] possessed in Anglo-Jewry not only a conspicuous example of the possibility and desirability of assimilation, but also a source of material and moral encouragement to the achievement of that ideal. Anglo-Jewry also constituted a source of embarrassment to the agitators, and, as we saw in Chapter VII, from 1906, a highly effective and powerful means of neutralizing the effects of their activities. The equivalent of Smethwick was not Mile End in 1905, but North-West Manchester in 1908. It is true that the conspicuous wealth and power of the Anglo-Jews aroused the special and long-standing prejudices of the new left, but even this provided the latter with a powerful motive for opposing the exclusion of the former's poor co-religionists.

The widespread unemployment and poverty of the times may also have tended to the advantage of the left wing in this matter. For, while it may have driven some in the East End to seek out the most obvious scapegoat, poverty in the midst of plenty drove many more, including the left itself, to seek elsewhere for the causes of their discontent. If the agitation is seen as a device for diverting attention from the real sources of discontent, then it was perhaps less easy to create that diversion in an atmosphere of conspicuous deprivation than it is amid the more complex problems of the mid-twentieth century. 'Red herrings' were much easier to spot.

[1] This, of course, leaves out of consideration anti-discriminatory legislation. Here, the dictates of ideology are rather easier to obey, since opposition to such legislation is, almost by definition, impossible to separate from the defence of disreputable emotion.

[2] Coloured sportsmen, however, are as popularly acceptable as was, for instance, the Jewish boxer in Golding's *Magnolia Street*. See p. 14.

We suggested in Chapter II that the intellectual framework of Social Darwinism seemed likely to create a greater respectability for the expression of racial prejudice. However, as we also saw, it was perfectly possible to argue, bearing in mind the examples of the Huguenots and the Anglo-Jews, that the newcomer would prove himself to be 'a regenerating force and a most useful acquisition to our citizenship'. Social Darwinism could be turned savagely against the foreigner, but, in this case, it was difficult to forget that the foreigner was also a Jew; and what is interesting about Social Darwinism is not how much respectability it gave to racial prejudice, but how little. This was, perhaps, because the intellectual framework was largely irrelevant to the discussion of racialism. Then, as now, the reaction to prejudice was as much an essentially emotional reaction as was prejudice itself—particularly when the Jews were being subjected to hideous cruelties in Russia, and to lesser persecution in the rest of mainland Europe.

The Liberals, as we observed in Chapter VII, were also extremely fortunate in the circumstances which existed when they came to administer the Aliens Act—a good fortune not shared by the Labour party fifty-eight years later. The anti-alien strength within Parliament had been almost completely denuded by the 1906 election, and the group was to be still further weakened by the death and retirement of its two most prominent members, Howard Vincent and Evans Gordon. The immigration figures were no more than steady, and at no time had the immigrants affected as many areas as has the present influx. Overcrowding in the East End, one of the two main problems associated with the influx, was largely solving itself. The influence of *laissez-faire* did not prevent sweating, the other problem, from being subject to determined Liberal attack in the Trades Boards Act of 1910.

Most important of all, perhaps, was the fact that the years 1905–6 witnessed a series of Russian pogroms, savage even by East European standards. This made it virtually impossible to oppose the Liberal administration of the Act without seeming to be uncharitable. This factor of the immigrant being a religious refugee was, in fact, quite crucial to the whole situation. Unlike his Commonwealth successor, the alien Jew was not merely the object of what was felt to be a special prejudice in his country of adoption: he was also demonstrably fleeing from the manifestation of that prejudice in his country of origin. Unlike the present immigrant, the Jew had not merely come to better his economic position, he was not just 'out for himself'. Moreover, it was not possible to argue that exclusion could be accompanied by a programme of overseas development. It was persecution that ultimately made it impossible to demonstrate that exclusion did not interfere with traditional norms, to separate grievance from intolerance. Although restrictive resolutions, disguised as curbs upon 'importation', rose (as they have not in the present case) to the level of the Trades Union Congress in 1892, 1894, and 1895, thereafter the threat to religious and political asylum, at all levels, thoroughly muffled the sharpness and clarity of the hostility that lay behind them. The constant lip-service to this doctrine also suggests that it had penetrated the national consciousness to an extent that the Commonwealth ideal has not. Every Englishman was 'something of a Liberal at heart'. All of this left the Liberals after 1906 with considerably more room to manoeuvre than the Labour party after 1964.

In assessing the reasons behind the differing reactions of the left wing in the two situations, let us finally note that the alien had a total impact upon party ideology and past policy that is, perhaps, not entirely possessed by his Commonwealth successor. Not only did the former raise in an acute form all those issues around which Liberalism rallied, even at its moments of greatest internal strife, but he also went to the very heart of Liberalism by symbolizing its half-secret economic and social ideal. Although the coloured immigrants put Labour's Commonwealth ideal to the ultimate test, and raise its egalitarian creed in an acute form, they do not raise other questions of past and present policy in so all-embracing, and in quite so specific, form as the Jewish aliens raised questions of, for instance, free trade and religious asylum, or even temperance reform.[1] Moreover, Labour's basic belief in the principle of 'to each according to his means' can be partially satisfied by a policy of overseas development.

We can see a more important difference if we compare the position of socialism at the turn of the century, with Labour's

[1] Via Samuel Smiles, of course.

position now. For what we have said in the previous paragraph might, on the surface, also be applied to early socialism. However, the latter had, at this time, all the attributes of a religion. Every issue raised had to be examined from the ideological standpoint. It almost goes without saying that Labour now is far more pragmatic, far more national in orientation. While the belief in equality may still lie at the base of party policy at home in practice, and abroad in theory, it is now rather easier to shrug off the theory. Meanwhile notions of the international brotherhood of labour receive little more than token salutations from all except the left wing.

In spite of all this, however, the dilemma raised for the Labour party has been acute enough. Moreover, although the General Council of the Trades Union Congress has from time to time made reference to the issue, the Congress itself has never discussed immigration control. Even if the Commonwealth ideal has not penetrated the national consciousness to the same extent as did political and religious asylum half a century ago, the suspicion of racial prejudice has embarrassed agitators, the Conservative front bench, and public opinion in a very similar way to that in which anti-Semitism affected them at the turn of the century. Viewing the over-all political situation, one is left with the distinct impression that both sets of immigrants would have been easier to exclude, if only they had not been, respectively, Jews and coloured men.

APPENDICES

APPENDICES

APPENDIX I:

Estimating Immigration

We should note that those Jewish immigrants who settled here did so in considerably smaller numbers than their present-day counterparts. Lloyd P. Gartner has estimated the figure at 120,000.[1] Although methods of enumeration at the turn of the century were, as we shall see, extremely haphazard, even allowing for a fair degree of approximation, this figure is still considerably below the estimated one million Commonwealth citizens[2] who have settled in England since 1948.

This apparent contrast, however, particularly from the point of view of English reactions to the immigrants, is weakened by a number of factors. The Jewish immigrants achieved an even greater geographical concentration than have their successors. As early as 1891, 21,951 aliens were living in a two-square-mile area of the East End;[3] and, in 1901, aliens represented some 31·8 per cent of the total population of Whitechapel.[4]

More importantly, England was also a major stopping-off place for aliens *en route* to the United States. While only 120,000 immigrants may have settled in England, many times that number stopped here long enough either to change ships or to earn sufficient money to pay for a transatlantic passage. From the point of view of English reactions, transmigrants were as important as settlers—for even those who remained but a few hours added to the general impression of 'invasion' and were worth a bout of rhetoric; while those here for a few months needed employment and accommodation, and were therefore as suspect as those whose stay was permanent.

In fact, as a measure of English reactions, the actual figures of immigration were an irrelevancy, except perhaps as a guide to comparative volume, for, as both the Select Committee, near the beginning of our period, and the Royal Commission, near the end, noted, figures simply did not exist. The main source of governmental information about the newcomers was an Act of 1836—brought out of moth-balls in May 1890—requiring the

[1] 'In 1911, 106,082 "Russians and Poles" were enumerated in England and Wales, and it is reasonable to raise this to 120,000 by adding Jewry in Scotland and including East European Jews from Germany, Austria and Rumania.' See Gartner, p. 49.

Using a different method of calculation, D. Lipman estimated that 100,000–150,000 Jewish immigrants settled in England between 1881 and 1914 (see p. 81).

[2] *The Times* (18 January 1965). This figure included Cypriots. The total number of coloured immigrants was estimated at 820,000.

[3] Lipman, p. 85.

[4] R.C., Vol. II, p. 150.

master of every ship arriving in England from abroad to submit to the Board of Trade a list of aliens on board together with details of their trades or occupations. These, when supplemented by lists of steerage passengers voluntarily supplied to the same body by the shipping companies, reappeared as the monthly and annual aliens lists. Some attempt was made to distinguish between those *en route* to places outside the United Kingdom and those 'not stated to be "en route"'. The usefulness of this division was, however, almost completely vitiated by the fact that the only criterion for being *en route* was not the intentions of the migrant, but the possession of a transatlantic ticket.[1] Thousands of immigrants did not purchase such tickets until they reached England. As a result of all this, the monthly and annual returns provided succulent fare for anyone wishing to exaggerate the volume of immigration.[2]

If, with good reason, one mistrusted the reliability of this system, and if one wanted to find out how many aliens, in fact, left for America, one could try comparing the total movement of passengers to and from England. Although the Board of Trade obtained what Gartner calls 'moderately satisfactory results' using this method in 1894—and with the help of private information not now available—it was normally subject to several crippling handicaps. It was complex. It took no account of the nationality of immigrants or emigrants beyond noting whether or not they were foreign. There was difficulty in separating the comings and goings of alien seamen. Finally, in utilizing these figures, one had to assume that the number of Englishmen who crossed over to the Continent equalled the number returning—a rather dubious assumption particularly in view of the fact that a small but unspecified number of English emigrants left from continental ports.

Perhaps the most accurate of the official statistical sources were the decennial censuses which enumerated aliens by their nationalities. However, the accuracy is only comparative and the amount of potential information limited. The count was short in 1871 and 1881 and high in 1891, and, in the latter years, the enumerators were handicapped by the immigrants' tendency to associate the census with the practices of Russian autocracy, and by their consequent attempts to avoid taking part. Apart from these deficiencies (which make inter-census comparison a rather dubious process anyway), the figures could only show the total increases from decade to decade. While historians can roughly estimate the average annual net

[1] A deficiency which the 1905 Aliens Act did nothing to remedy. Most of the material for the rest of this chapter is drawn from Lloyd P. Gartner's 'Notes on the Statistics of Jewish Immigration to England, 1870–1914', *Jewish Social Studies* (Vol. XXI), pp. 97–102; other references used were Lipman, and Julius Gould and Shaul Esh, *Jewish Life in Modern Britain* (London, Routledge and Kegan Paul, 1964).

[2] See, for example, the treatment given to the Board of Trade Return for 1904 which stated that there were '95,724 aliens not described in the aliens lists as "en route"'. In the *Daily Mail* this received the headline '95,000 more Aliens'; and in the *Express*, '95,000 not "en route" to places outside the United Kingdom'. See *Jewish Chronicle* (13 January 1905).

gain by immigration, by dividing the figures by ten and subtracting a hypothetical number of deaths, the emigration of resident aliens to America and elsewhere, and naturalization, such calculations were of only limited value to contemporaries—for censuses came only once in ten years. Thus, the census of 1901 was of little real use to anyone arguing about the Aliens Bill of 1905, since the figures were then four years old and can scarcely have taken into account the results of the period of mass immigration which began in 1900. The only really accurate picture came from the census of 1911, by which time the agitation had died away.

While both Jewish and non-Jewish sources were generally agreed that the overwhelming majority of what were technically described as alien immigrants[1] were Jews,[2] none of the governmental statistics made any attempt to classify by religion. This was perhaps the only deficiency remedied by the non-governmental and mainly Jewish sources of information. In general, the very ingeniousness of the latter's methods of calculation revealed as much about the lack of direct information as it did about the numbers of the immigrants.

Thus, the three Jewish bodies concerned with giving material help to the immigrants—the Jewish Board of Guardians, the Poor Jews Temporary Shelter, and the Russo-Jewish Committee—kept details of the numbers, origins, and destinations of those passing through their hands. From these very limited figures, various observers have attempted to adduce the over-all immigrant-transmigrant figures by taking, for example, the ratio of those going on to America to those remaining behind, that is shown by the records of the Jewish Temporary Shelter.[3]

Other methods of computation have been even more indirect. Joseph Jacobs in 1894[4] and the *Jewish Chronicle* throughout our period attempted to relate the United Synagogue's yearly figures for Jewish burials to the over-all British death-rate, and so to produce some guide to the increase in the Jewish population resulting from immigration. However, one cannot rely on the Jewish death-rate being identical with that of the over-all population, partly because of the high proportion of young people[5] and the high birth-rate amongst the immigrants, and partly because of economic and various other differences in the conditions of life of the two races. Equally indirect, but perhaps a little more reliable, because open to fewer objections, was the method used by H. Llewellyn Smith,[6] who took the absences from

[1] Russians, Russian-Poles, or Romanians, plus some Austrians and Germans. Even in the last two cases, a sizeable proportion were Jews.

[2] For instance, the figure of 23,569 given to the Royal Commission of 1903 elicited hardly any information about immigrants who were not Jews.

[3] See Lipman, pp. 87–90. As Gartner points out, the results are not very satisfactory. Another method has been to take the yearly figures of the co-joint Committee of the Jewish Board of Guardians and to work out estimates based on ratios suggested by American ratios.

[4] Gartner, 'Notes on the Statistics of Jewish Immigration to England'.

[5] According to the figures of the Jewish Temporary Shelter, 26 per cent of immigrant males passing through their charge were under 20, 63 per cent between 21 and 40, 10 per cent between 41 and 60, and 0·5 per cent over 60.

[6] See 'The Influx of Population' in Booth (ed.), Vol. III, Ch. II.

general schools at Yom Kippur, compared them with the total population, and then transposed the resulting ratio on to the general population, hopefully arriving eventually at the total number of Jews.

We can see from the foregoing that, as Gartner points out, 'almost all statistical attempts [to estimate the number of Jews who settled in England in this period] have proved fruitless'.[1] If this is so now, then life was even more difficult for the immigrants' English contemporaries. Most of the statistics then available, moreover, tended to give an exaggerated rather than an underestimated picture of the real situation. Their only real value was as a guide to the comparative volume of immigration. Otherwise, they merely intensified the tendency observable in the present case—whereby it was easier to exaggerate and to alarm than to show the real situation, whereby the statistical arguments against the aliens were very simple and the refutations necessarily complex. Moreover, while one might, by such means, destroy the figures of the anti-aliens, one had few of one's own with which to replace them.

[1] Gartner, 'Notes on the Statistics of Jewish Immigration to England', p. 97.

APPENDIX II:

Socialist Meetings on Alien Immigration

Independent Labour Party	Social Democratic Federation	Labour Church Movement
Leeds J. Dyche on 'Alien Immigration', 14 July 1895.		
South-West Manchester I. Loewy on 'Alien Immigration and the Brotherhood of Man', 3 November 1895.		
East Manchester I. Loewy.		
Leeds Central (Literary and Debating Class) A. R. Orage on 'Alien Immigration', 28 January 1896.		
Rothwell J. Dyche, 29 January 1896.		
	Ashton A. Lewis on 'Alien Immigration and the Poverty Problem', 10 June 1899.	
London (Clapham) Mr. Charrington on 'Alien Immigration', 20 April 1903.	*East London* (Jewish) Protest Meeting, 13 February 1903.	*Hyde* Mr. Charrington on 'Alien Immigration', 6 February 1903.
Manchester Central Messrs. Lewis and Schoor (of Jewish Tailors) on 'The	*East London* (Jewish) 'Socialism and the Alien Question', 1 April 1904.	*Birmingham* Mr. Charrington, 21 March 1903.

Manchester Central (cont.)
Aliens Bill'. Protest Resolution, 27 May 1904.

West Salford
Protest Meeting, 17 June 1904.

East London (Jewish)
Protest Meeting, 19 May 1905.

Hyde
J. Bruce Glazier, on 'The Empire and the Alien', 24 June 1904.

Keighley
J. Bruce Glazier on 'The Empire and the Alien', 8 July 1904.

Birmingham
J. Bruce Glazier, 2 September 1904.

Also:

Birkenhead Socialist Society
A. E. Killip on 'Alien Immigration', 9 December 1904.

Leeds Labour Hall
J. Dyche on 'Alien Immigration', 30 January 1896.

Select Bibliography

CONTEMPORARY MATERIAL

Documentary Sources:

Board of Trade (alien immigration), *Reports on the volume and effects of the recent immigration from Eastern Europe into the United Kingdom, 1894*, C. 7406, 1894 (S.P. 1894, LXVIII, p. 341).

This is the only statistical source which approaches accuracy; of little direct use for English reactions to the immigrants. Available British Museum.

House of Commons Select Committee on Alien Immigration, *Report and minutes of evidence*, Vol. I, 27 July 1888; Vol. II, 8 August 1889 (S.P. 1888, IX, p. 419; 1889, X, p. 265).

Like the other reports in this period, this contains rather more unsubstantiated opinion than factual material. It is therefore invaluable for a study of English attitudes to the immigrants, but of considerably less use for analysing the immigrants themselves, or their real effect. Available British Museum.

House of Lords Select Committee on the Sweating System, *Report and minutes of evidence*, Vol. I, 11 August 1888; Vol. II, 20 December 1888; Vol. III, 24 May 1889; Vol. IV, 17 August 1889; Vol. V, *Appendix and Proceedings*, 1890 (S.P. 1888, XX, XXI; 1889, XIII, XIV; 1890, XVII, p. 257).

Particularly useful for the examination of the trade unions' attitude, especially the extent to which immigration and sweating were connected, and the validity of that connection. Chaotic. Available Central Reference Library, Manchester.

Royal Commission on Alien Immigration, Vol. I, *Report*, Cd. 1742, 1903; Vol. II, *Minutes of evidence*, Cd. 1742, 1903; Vol. III, *Appendix*, Cd. 1741, 1903; Vol. IV, *Index and analysis to minutes of evidence*, Cd. 1743, 1904 (S.P. 1903, IX).

Useful for trade union and popular reactions to the immigrants. Considerable information as to their real effect. Available Central Reference Library, Manchester.

Royal Commission on Labour, 1891–1894, 11 vols., C. 6708, 6795, 7063, 7421. Worth a glance down the index for the extent to which trade unionists, at least in the early 1890s, ascribed their troubles to alien immigration when not under pressure to do so. Available Central Reference Library, Manchester.

Reports of H.M. Inspector, with statement as to expulsion of aliens, 1907–1914. Useful for the working of the Aliens Act. Available British Museum.

Liberal Publication Department's pamphlets and leaflets.

For Liberal treatment of the aliens issue. Available in collected form in the Library of the London School of Economics.

Trades Union Congress, *Reports*, 1892, 1894, 1895 (debates on the anti-alien resolutions); 1902–1910 (naturalization and anti-sweating resolutions; also James Sexton's presidential address of 1905, containing a scathing reference to the Aliens Act).

Available British Museum.

For other material relating purely to the immigrants themselves, see bibliography in Lloyd P. Gartner, *The Jewish immigrant in England 1870–1914*, pp. 285–8.

Books and Periodical Material Published Prior to 1914:

Anderson, Robert. 'The problem of the criminal alien'. *The Nineteenth Century and After*, Vol. LXIX, No. 408, February 1911.

Written in the aftermath of the Siege of Sydney Street.

Barham, C. N. 'The persecution of the Jews in Russia'. *Westminster Review*, Vol. CXXXI, 1891, pp. 138–47.

Baumann, Arthur A., M.P. 'The Lords Committee on the sweating system'. *National Review*, Vol. XII, No. 68, October 1888, pp. 145–59. Mild Toryism.

—— 'Possible remedies for the sweating system'. *National Review*, Vol. XII, No. 69, November 1888, pp. 289–307.

Besant, Walter. *East London*. London, Chatto & Windus, 1899.

Probably a somewhat idyllic picture in so far as it concerns Jewish-Gentile relations.

Booth, Charles (ed.). *Life and labour of the people of London*, 9 vols., London, Macmillan, 1892–7.

Much useful material on the problems associated with immigration.

Cadbury, Edward, and Shann, George. *Sweating*. London, 1907. (Social Service Handbooks, No. 5.)

Campbell-Bannerman, Henry. 'Speeches'—1899–1908. *The Times*, 1908.

Cunningham, W. *Alien immigration to England.* London, 1897.

A rare attempt to cast light on alien Jewish immigration by an objective examination of the real value of past immigrations.

Drage, Geoffrey. 'Alien immigration'. *Fortnightly Review*, N.S. LVII, No. 337, 1 January 1895, pp. 37–46.

Dunraven, 4th Earl of. 'The invasion of destitute aliens'. *Nineteenth Century*, Vol. XXXI, No. 184, June 1892, pp. 985–1000.

Dunraven was the chairman of the Sweating Committee and one of the early leaders of the anti-immigrant agitation.

Dyche, J. A. 'The Jewish workman'. *Contemporary Review*, Vol. LXXIII, January 1898, pp. 35–50.

Dyche was an alien Jewish workman and a Liberal, and his article is an extreme example of Smilesean symbolism and the unfavourable comparisons with English workers which it inspired. See Arnold White's article which followed that of Dyche, in *Contemporary Review*, February 1898.
—— 'The Jewish immigrant'. *Contemporary Review*, Vol. LXXV, March 1899, pp. 379–99.

Evans-Gordon, W. *The alien immigrant*. London, 1903.

Evans-Gordon was the main figure in the British Brothers League.
—— 'The stranger within our gates'. *The Nineteenth Century and After*, Vol. LXIX, No. 408, February 1911, pp. 210–16.

Finn, J. 'A voice from the aliens'. London, n.d.

About the anti-alien resolution of the Cardiff Trades Union Congress, 1895. Quoted at length in the *Jewish Chronicle* (6 December 1895), p. 12. See also R.C., Vol. II, p. 732.
—— 'Foreign undesirables'. *Blackwood's Magazine*, Vol. CLXIX, February 1901, pp. 279–89.

Fox, Stephen N. 'The invasion of pauper foreigners'. *Contemporary Review*, Vol. LII, June 1888, pp. 855–67.

Fyfe, H. Hamilton. 'The Alien and the Empire'. *The Nineteenth Century and After*, Vol. LIV, No. 319, September 1903, pp. 414–19.

Hobson, J. A. *Problems of poverty*. London, Methuen, 1891.

Kingsley, Charles. *Alton Locke: tailor and poet*. London, Everyman's Library, 1928.
—— ('Parson Lot', pseud.). 'Cheap clothes and nasty'. *Works*, Vol. II. London and New York, 1899.

Landa, M. J. *The alien problem and its remedies*. London, 1911.

Leppington, C. H. d'E. 'Side lights of the Sweating Commission'. *Westminster Review*, Vol. CXXXVI, Part 3, March 1891, pp. 273–88; Part 5, May 1891, pp. 504–16.

Diluted Manchester Liberalism.

MacDonald, J. Ramsay. 'Sweating; its cause and cure'. *Independent Review*, Vol. II, No. 1, February 1904, pp. 72–85.

MacDonald, James. 'Government sweating in the clothing contracts'. *New Review*, Vol. XI, No. 5, November 1894, pp. 471–4.

Macrosty, H. W. *Sweating: its cause and remedy*. London, 1896. (Fabian Tract No. 50.)

One of the best short analyses of the 'system'.

Mayhew, Henry. *London labour and the London poor*, 4 vols. London, 1861.

See especially the section on 'Street Jews'.

Manson, E. 'The admission of aliens'. *Journal of the Society of Comparative Legislation*, N.S. IV, December 1902, pp. 114–27.

Potter, Beatrice. 'East London labour'. *Nineteenth Century*, Vol. XXIV, No. 138, August 1888, pp. 161–84.
—— 'Pages from a work-girl's diary'. *Nineteenth Century*, Vol. XXIV, No. 139, September 1888, pp. 301–14.
—— 'The Lords and the sweating system'. *Nineteenth Century*, Vol. XXVII, No. 160, June 1890, pp. 885–905.
—— *How to do away with the sweating system*. Manchester, 1892. (Co-operative Union Pamphlet.)

See also Sydney and Beatrice Webb.

Russell, C., and Lewis, H. S. *The Jew in London*. London, 1900.

Excellent if rather optimistic about relations with the host population.

Schloss, David F. 'The sweating system'. *Fortnightly Review*, N.S. XLVII, No. 280, 1 April 1890, pp. 532–51.
—— 'The Jew as a workman'. *Nineteenth Century*, Vol. XXIX, No. 167, January 1891, pp. 96–109.

Sherard, Robert H. *The child slaves of Britain*. London, 1905.

Sherard was a philanthropist and one of the more rabid of the anti-aliens: see also his series of articles in the *Standard* beginning 5 January 1905.
—— *The white slaves of England*, 2nd edn. London, 1898.

Smiles, Samuel. *Self help*. London, 1859; centenary edn., 1959.
—— *Thrift*. London, 1875.
—— *Duty*. London, 1881; popular edn., 1905.

Tawney, R. H. *The establishment of minimum rates in the tailoring industry under the Trades Boards Act of 1909*. London, 1915. (Studies in the Minimum Wage, No. 11.)

Webb, Sydney and Beatrice. *History of trades unionism*, rev. edn. London, 1920.
—— *Industrial democracy*, 2 vols. London, 1907.

See especially pp. 698n. and 744n. See interview in *Jewish Chronicle* (9 July 1909), p. 18. See also section on material published since 1914.

Whelpey, James D. *The problem of the immigrant*. London, 1905.

White, Arnold. *The modern Jew*. London, 1899.

Like Sherard, a mixture of philanthropist and anti-alien. This book is indicative of much of the ambiguity that characterized English anti-Semitism.
—— *Problems of a great city*. London, 1886 and 1895.
—— 'The invasion of pauper foreigners'. *Nineteenth Century*, Vol. XXIII, No. 133, March 1888, pp. 414–22.
—— 'Alien immigration, a rejoinder'. *Fortnightly Review*, N.S. LVII, No. 339, 1 March 1895, pp. 501–7.
—— 'A typical alien immigrant'. *Contemporary Review*, Vol. LXXIII, February 1898, pp. 241–50.

White's reply to John Dyche (see *ante*).

—— (ed.). *The destitute alien in Great Britain*. London, 1892.
—— *English democracy: its promises and perils*. London, 1894.

Wilkins, W. H. *The alien invasion*. London, 1892. (Social Questions of To-day, No. 6.)

Newspapers:

Clarion: Interesting for the way in which it ignores the issue; but the search for negative evidence is a somewhat trying one. Difficult to obtain complete collections. The British Museum must be supplemented by the London School of Economics Library.

The Commonweal: William Morris's paper and voice of the Socialist League. Available British Museum Newspaper Library.

East London Advertiser: Anti-alien. Available British Museum Newspaper Library.

East London Observer: Generally Conservative, but not on the immigration issue. A useful source for activities in the East End, especially those of the political parties and the agitators; also useful for election addresses. Available British Museum Newspaper Library.

Jewish Chronicle: Because of the paper's sensitivity to anything relating favourably or unfavourably to the Jewish community, this is by far the most useful source for material on the immigrants and the English reactions to them. Besides giving the views of Anglo-Jewry, it also contains reprints or reviews of most of the articles on the aliens, reports of anti-Semitic behaviour, interviews with the agitators and their opponents, and much useful material on Jewish trade unionism, the working of the Aliens Act, and events in the East End. It also contains the most effective and closely argued case against aliens legislation that I have found anywhere: see *Jewish Chronicle* (11 October 1907), p. 14, and three weeks that follow. Rather difficult to use as a source because of the absence of an index. Microfilm copies. Available Central Reference Library, Manchester.

Labour Elector: 'An organ of practical socialism', and, from June 1893, 'the organ of the Independent Labour Party'. Anti-alien. See 11 February 1893, p. 6, and 18 February 1893, p. 7. Available British Museum Newspaper Library.

Labour Leader: Keir Hardie's paper and the mouthpiece of the Independent Labour party. Useful also, in conjunction with the *Clarion*, for advertisements and reports of the activities of the socialist branches. Available British Museum Newspaper Library and London School of Economics Library.

Labour Record: Pro-alien, although it largely ignores the issue till 1905. Available British Museum Newspaper Library.

Justice: Mouthpiece of the Social Democratic Federation. Contains some extreme examples of the socialist version of anti-Semitism. Ignores the issue wherever possible. Available British Museum Newspaper Library.

People's Press: The paper of John Burns and the 'New Unionism'. Available British Museum Newspaper Library.

Reynolds's News: Interesting as the unofficial mouthpiece of Liberal Labourism. At first, anti-alien (see 21 July 1895), but, by 1904, against aliens legislation. Some nice pieces of rich Jew anti-Semitism, including cartoon (16 July 1905).

I have also made use of the *Daily News*, the *Daily Chronicle*, but most of my material from these newspapers has been obtained via the *Jewish Chronicle*.

BOOKS AND ARTICLES PUBLISHED SINCE 1914

On Jewish Immigrants:

Elman, Peter. 'The beginnings of the Jewish trades union movement'. *Transactions of the Jewish Historical Society of England*, Vol. XVII, 1951–2, pp. 53–62.

Gartner, Lloyd P. *The Jewish immigrant in England 1870–1914*. London, Allen & Unwin, 1960.

—— 'Statistics of Jewish immigration to England'. *Jewish Social Studies*, Vol. XXI.

George, M. D. *London life in the eighteenth century*, 2nd edn. London, Routledge & Kegan Paul, 1930.

Halevy, E. *Imperialism and the rise of labour*. London, Ernest Benn, 1951.

Krausz, Ernest. *Leeds Jewry*. Cambridge, W. Heffer & Sons, for the Jewish Historical Society of England, 1964.

Lansbury, George. *Looking backwards—and forwards*. London, Blackie & Son, 1935.

Levy, Arnold. *History of the Sunderland Jewish community*. London, McDonald, 1956.

Lipman, V. D. *Social history of the Jews in England, 1850–1950*. London, Watts & Co., 1954.

—— (ed.). *Three centuries of Anglo-Jewish history*. Cambridge, W. Heffer & Sons, for the Jewish Historical Society of England, 1961.

Modder, H. F. *The Jew in the literature of England*. Philadelphia, Jewish Publication Society of America, 1944.

Maccoby, H. *English radicalism 1886–1914*. London, Allen & Unwin, 1955.

Rabinowicz, Oscar, K. *Winston Churchill on Jewish problems*. London, Thomas Yosseloff, for the Popular Jewish Library, 1956.

Robb, W. H. *Working class anti-Semite*. London, Tavistock, 1954.

Silberner, E. 'British socialism and the Jews'. *Historia Judaica*, Vol. XIV, No. 1, April 1952, pp. 26–52.

—— 'Modern anti-Semitism'. *Historia Judaica*, Vol. XIV, 1952, pp. 96–120.

Thompson, E. P. *The making of the English working class*. London, Gollancz, 1963, Ch. 8.

On Commonwealth Immigrants and Others:

Banton, Michael. *The coloured quarter*. London, Cape, 1955.

—— *White and coloured: the behaviour of British people towards coloured immigrants*. London, Cape, 1959.

Clapham, N. *Irish immigration into Great Britain in the nineteenth century*. (Bulletin of the International Committee of the Historical Sciences, V.)

Davison, R. B. *Commonwealth immigrants*. London, Oxford University Press, for Institute of Race Relations, 1964.

Deakin, N. (ed.). *Colour and the British electorate 1964*. London, Pall Mall Press, 1965.

Desai, R. *Indian immigrants in Britain*. London, Oxford University Press, for Institute of Race Relations, 1963.

Foot, Paul. *Immigration and race in British politics*. Harmondsworth, Penguin Books, 1965.

Glass, Ruth. *The newcomers: the West Indian in London*. London, Allen & Unwin, for Centre for Urban Studies, 1960.

Griffith, Henderson, Usborne, and Wood. *Coloured immigrants in Britain*. London, Oxford University Press, 1960.

Jackson, J. A. *The Irish in Britain*. London, Routledge & Kegan Paul, 1963.
—— 'The Irish in Britain'. Paper read before the British Association for the Advancement of Science, 1961.
—— 'The Irish immigrant in England'. Paper read before the British Sociological Association, 1958.
Patterson, Sheila. *Dark strangers*. London, Tavistock, 1963.
Patterson, Sheila. 'The Polish exile community in Britain'. Annual Proceedings of the British Association for the Advancement of Science, held in Norwich, 1961.
Redford, Arthur. *Labour migration*. Manchester, Manchester University Press, 1926.
Richmond, A. H. *Colour prejudice in Britain: a study of West Indian workers in Liverpool*. London, Routledge, 1954.
—— *The colour problem*. Harmondsworth, Penguin Books, 1961.
Salvidge, S. *Salvidge of Liverpool*. London, Hodder & Stoughton, 1934.
Shinwell, Emanuel. *Conflict without malice*. London, Odhams Press, 1955.
Tannahill, J. A. *European volunteer workers in Britain*. Manchester, Manchester University Press, 1958.
Thornberry, Cedric. *The stranger at the gate*. London, 1964. (Fabian Research Series 243.)
—— 'Race prejudice and the law'. *Socialist Commentary*, November 1964.
Strauss, E. *Irish nationalism and British democracy*. London, Methuen, 1955, ch. XIV.
Wickenden, James. *Colour in Britain*. London, Oxford University Press, for Institute of Race Relations, 1958.
See also E. P. Thompson, previously cited, pp. 429–40 (on the Irish).

FICTION

Golding, Louis. *Magnolia street*. London, Gollancz, 1932.
Tressell, Robert. *Ragged trousered philanthropists*. London, Lawrence & Wishart, 1955.

Scattered references, mainly interesting because its subject is the building and house decorating trade. Note the remarks of George Shipton on p. 177.

Zangwill, Israel. *Children of the ghetto*. London, Heinemann, 1909; Philadelphia, 1938.

Index